POWER PLAYS

POWER PLAYS

*How to Deal
like a Lawyer
in Person-to-Person
Confrontations
and Get Your Rights*

John M. Striker
& Andrew O. Shapiro

Rawson, Wade Publishers, Inc.
New York

Library of Congress Cataloging in Publication Data

Striker, John M
  Power plays.

  Includes index.
    1. Law—United States—Popular works.
  2. Consumer protection—Law and legislation—
  United States—Popular works.   3.   Sex discrimination
  against women—Law and legislation—United States—
  Popular works.   4.   Landlord and tenant—United
  States—Popular works.   5.   Assertiveness
  (Psychology)   I.   Shapiro, Andrew O., joint
  author.   II.   Title.
  KF387.S8   1979   340'.0973   78–64811
  ISBN 0–89256–094–0

Published simultaneously in Canada by McClelland
and Stewart, Ltd.
Composition by American–Stratford Graphic Services, Inc.,
Brattleboro, Vermont
Printed and bound by Fairfield Graphics, Fairfield, Pennsylvania

Designed by Gene Siegel
First Edition

Acknowledgments

Ken Rawson urged us to undertake this writing project shortly after he had published our last book. It was his conviction that many Americans are in need of basic legal information about their rights in such troublesome areas as getting credit, holding on to a job, and buying a new house or car; and these same consumers need a practical method for asserting their rights, without necessarily having to incur huge legal fees. With Ken's encouragement and editorial input, we developed a system of legal self-help, which we hope will have broad utility for our readers.

Don Congdon, our literary agent, gave us strong support from the inception of this book; as in the past, he guided us with sound judgment and loyalty through the world of New York publishing.

Wide-ranging legal research was essential to document the principles explained in this book. In this effort we were ably assisted by Diane Ungar, a bright law student at Fordham University School of Law.

For the sixth time since our graduation from New

York University School of Law in 1968, we wish to thank the staff of the school's law library. We are especially grateful to Margaret Aycock, Gerome Leone, Julius Marke, Michael Matthew, and Diana Vincent-Daviss for satisfying our every research need promptly and thoughtfully.

For typing our manuscript quickly, clearly, and accurately, Bernice Blohm and Jessica Lottman deserve great credit.

Finally, we thank the National Center for State Courts for allowing us to draw upon data in their 1978 report, *Small Claims Court: A National Examination,* as a basis for our Appendix A.

A Word of Caution

Just what America needs now: another power manual—as if there weren't enough self-help, assertiveness-training guides to last for the rest of the century. Let us confess at the outset that we offer no panaceas or pep talks; we do not reveal the true way to bliss; there are no mantras in this book. We are just a couple of hard-nosed lawyers—not psychologists, seers, or gurus of any stripe.

The power we write about is not something you must journey toward in ritualistic stages. In fact, it is yours already. And while it won't lift you to a heightened level of consciousness, it may get you a cash refund on that defective stereo you bought. The source of power we're concerned with is: *your legal rights.*

We use the term "power plays" to designate personal confrontations where you seek to enforce your rights against an adversary who has wronged you. In the course of a power play, you will use as leverage knowledge of your legal rights as well as techniques of persuasion that lawyers use daily. That's what we mean by the phrase dealing like a lawyer in person-to-person confrontations.

This book is not a substitute for professional legal assistance. If you decide, after reading *Power Plays,* that you have a substantial legal problem—either in terms of money or principle—you should consult a lawyer, rather than deal like one on your own. Only by retaining counsel can you receive the kind of personalized attention to your individual needs that no book can possibly provide. In those situations, however, where hiring a lawyer will cost more than your claim is worth, and you're determined to vindicate your rights instead of letting yourself be victimized again, it will behoove you to confront your adversary directly and deal with him like a lawyer.

We have done much painstaking research and careful writing in order to explain your legal rights in an accurate and straightforward manner. Extensive appendixes document our explanations with specific legal citations. Still, the law is not always black and white; lawyers, as well as judges, may differ in their interpretations of what the law is. And while it is unlikely that the key statutes and court cases reported in this book will undergo major revision, it is possible that some of the legal principles recited may, from time to time, grow outmoded.

Therefore, we cannot predict results, nor guarantee a favorable outcome, to readers who use this book. We can only express our belief that whether you win or lose a power play, you will gain something valuable from the experience: namely, the satisfaction of having stood up for yourself where, formerly, you might have swallowed your pride and let yourself be taken.

J.M.S.
A.O.S.

New York City
February, 1979

Contents

POWER
PLAYS

I

The Strategy of the Power Play

Turning the Tables

Have you ever slinked away from a nasty confrontation wishing you'd been clever enough to talk the other guy down? "Why did I let him get away with that?" you bemoan. "I know I must have *some* rights in this mess. How beautiful it would have felt if I could have looked that bastard dead in the eyes and said something to stop him cold!"

For example, when your cagey landlord claimed all sorts of trumped-up deductions from your security deposit, you could have replied with icy assurance: "Your little game happens to be a violation of the state security-deposit law. I'm going to give you seventy-two hours in which to come up with an itemized accounting of your deductions or a complete refund. If you're one minute late, I will sue you for everything the law allows—that's treble damages plus my attorney's fees!"

When that snooty bank officer refused to issue a credit card in your maiden name because you're married, you could have calmly said, smiling: "I am surprised to meet a pin-striped banker who flirts with financial disaster the way you do. What you're doing now is an open-and-shut violation of the Equal Credit Opportunity Act. Either you issue this card in my maiden name or you'll wind up in federal court paying me ten thousand dollars in punitive damages —not to mention my attorney's fees."

When the boss said he was thinking of replacing you with a younger man, you could have given him second thoughts by responding: "Forcing out an older employee happens to violate the federal Age Discrimination Law. If you try that on me, I'll get a court order for full reinstatement—not to mention back pay. Personally, I'd love to see you argue your case before a jury of retired employees!"

If you could talk back like that, you would be making strategic use of *codewords*—intimidating phrases like *treble damages, attorney's fees, Equal Credit Opportunity Act, ten thousand dollars in punitive damages,* and *back pay.* Codewords are the warning signals that you flash when getting tough with an unruly adversary. They trigger an alarm in his head: "I'm heading for trouble," the alarm cautions; "this person clearly knows his rights. I'd better not jerk him around, or it may wind up costing me more than it's worth."

Codewords are part of a new system for asserting yourself and getting what is rightfully yours. We call it the *power play* system, and you can use it in person-to-person confrontations whenever your adversary is violating your legal rights. Before we take a closer look at how this system works, let's pause to consider a more extended example of a power play in action.

The Power Play in Action

To gauge the full impact of a power play, let's take a typical consumer hassle and examine two possible responses to it—

first the outburst of a frustrated consumer, then the power play of a savvy consumer. By comparing these two responses we can see what *not* to say and do in a confrontation, as well as what really works.

Our situation is simple enough, and perhaps painfully familiar. It's the ill-fated purchase of a product that turns out to be a lemon. The product in this case is an air conditioner. Two consumers—Mike Keller and Susan Phelps, we'll name them—each purchase the same model Arctic Blast room air conditioner from Fast Eddy's World of Appliances, paying the full cash price of $419.95.

From the moment the air conditioners are installed, they create almost identical headaches for Mike and Susan. One thing after another goes wrong. First the air-conditioner fans don't blow out any air; then the air that is blown out proves to be lukewarm; next, the cooling systems cycle on and off too abruptly; eventually strange whistling and rattling noises develop; finally, moisture drips into the room, even though the units are properly tilted toward the outside.

Because of these defects, the air conditioners spend more time in Fast Eddy's shop than in Mike's or Susan's bedroom window. Even when the units are installed and running, Fast Eddy's repairmen are constantly having to visit Mike and Susan to tighten screws, replace switches, lubricate shafts, and stand there, hands on their hips, saying "Sounds good to me" while the Arctic Blast whistles and rattles up a storm.

Enough is enough! Our two lemon owners decide to return to Fast Eddy's and confront the owner, Eddy Eckert. Let's eavesdrop on these confrontations, first to see how Mike flails about helplessly and then to watch Susan pull off a successful power play.

MIKE: Mr. Eckert, that air conditioner you sold me is a real loser. It blows hot and cold, whistles "Dixie" all

night, drips on my carpeting, and does everything but cool.
I'm fed up with it.

EDDY: Gee, I know you've had a little trouble with—

MIKE: A *little* trouble? That thing's been a royal pain.
It's a piece of crap. You took me for four hundred dollars
on that lemon—not to mention all the time and frustration
of getting repairs in your shop.

EDDY: I wish you wouldn't say I "took" you—we've
been very cooperative in servicing that unit for you.

MIKE: Yeah, and it still needs a complete overhaul.
It's just not cooling at all—aside from all that noise.

EDDY: Well, we'll take it back into the shop and—

MIKE: Oh no you don't! Not that "shop" routine again.
You're getting more use out of this machine than I am.
You've had enough cracks at repairing this thing. Now I
want my money back.

EDDY: I'm sorry, but we don't give refunds.

MIKE: You robbed me of four hundred dollars and
now you won't refund my money?

EDDY: I did not "rob" you. We just have a policy of
no refunds.

MIKE: No wonder they call you "Fast Eddy." Look,
I have a right to a refund.

EDDY: What makes you think so?

MIKE: Because you gypped me. No one has to pay
good money for worthless junk.

EDDY: Have you checked the warranty on that Arctic
Blast? It says that we are responsible *only* for making repairs
and replacement of defective parts. That's your only remedy
under the warranty—not a refund. As I've said, we'll stand
by the warranty and take your machine back to the shop
again—

MIKE: For the fifth time? Where does this runaround
end—with me sleeping in your shop all summer? I'm sick
of repairs. Either you refund my money or—or—I'll put a

big sign in my window: "Fast Eddy sells lemon air conditioners!"

EDDY: That's foolish. But all I can do is offer further
servicing under your warranty.

MIKE: All warranties are lies, just like your whole
business. Well, okay, I'll show you—I'm going to put up
that lemon sign today!

EDDY: Go ahead. Make a fool of yourself.

MIKE: I will. Goodbye.

Mike Keller has succeeded in cutting off his nose to
spite his face. He stomps out of Fast Eddy's having gained
nothing and having committed himself to something rather
foolish: putting a "lemon" sign in his window—as if that
could win him anything but the ridicule of his neighbors.
(A "lemon" sign disparages a product, to be sure, but it
also implies that the sign maker is a sucker!)

Where did Mike Keller go wrong? First of all, he entered Fast Eddy's raring for a fight. Without so much as a
hello, he rattled off a bunch of gripes and declared he was
fed up. He branded the merchandise "a piece of crap." Mike
was understandably frustrated by the repair-shop runaround; however, by getting belligerent he succeeded only
in putting Eddy on the defensive—a position that was bound
to work against Mike's best interests.

Many consumers psych themselves up this way. They
take whatever injustice has been done as a personal affront,
when in fact there may simply have been a clerical mistake
or a computer foul-up. It's usually more productive—and
relaxing—to begin with the assumption that the other side
is open to reason and will be accommodating. Should the
assumption prove false, there'll be plenty of time for righ-
teous indignation.

Second, Mike let his frustration and resentment be
directed against Eddy personally. He accused Eddy of

robbing and gypping him. Probably the single hardest lesson for the angry consumer to learn is that shouting matches and name-calling accomplish very little. By abusing an adversary in a personal way, you needlessly bring his self-respect into play against you; now he's resisting you for personal as well as business reasons. So even if you convince him of the rightness of your position, he'll still be bent on vengeance for your personal slights.

Third, Mike had no real ultimatum to deliver—no punch. About all he could muster was his threat to put a "lemon" sign in his window, and that gesture lowered his reputation almost as much as it did Fast Eddy's.

Powerlessness is the downfall of most consumers. There comes a point in a person-to-person confrontation when you have to stop being Mr. Nice Guy and stick it to the other fellow where it hurts. Unfortunately, at this critical moment consumers find themselves at a loss for words. They don't think they have any real power, so they grow reckless and make idle threats or self-defeating ones (as in Mike's case), and wind up out on the street feeling impotent and a little foolish.

Let's compare Mike's disastrous confrontation with Susan's. She visits Fast Eddy's the very next day.

SUSAN: Good morning, Mr. Eckert. Do you remember me?

EDDY: Yes, of course, Miss Phelps. Is everything okay with that air conditioner now?

SUSAN: I'm afraid not. That's why I dropped by—to see what we can work out together.

EDDY: Well, we're here to serve you, Miss Phelps. We'll take that unit back into the shop until we get it right.

SUSAN: I appreciate your offer, Mr. Eckert, but don't you think it's about time we both faced facts? The problem isn't one that can be repaired. Your men have proven that with their repeated attempts. The problem, Mr. Eckert, is this Arctic Blast unit. It's got so many defects that it just isn't doing what air conditioners are supposed to do. Let's face it, Mr. Eckert, I've gotten a lemon.

EDDY: Well, let's give my boys another chance, eh?

SUSAN: Honestly, Mr. Eckert, I've really gone the limit on this unit. Nothing has made it work so far, and in the meantime I've been deprived of my money's worth. I don't think I should have to put up with any more attempted repairs. So I'd like you to take the unit back and refund my money.

EDDY: I wish I could, Miss Phelps, but Fast Eddy's has a policy against giving refunds.

SUSAN: Why?

EDDY: Why? Well—it's just always been our policy.

SUSAN: But surely you can make an exception when something you sell turns out to be a lemon?

EDDY: I'm afraid not. We do, of course, stand prepared to fix the—as you call it—lemon. But we can't take it back once you've already accepted it.

SUSAN: Mr. Eckert, I hereby revoke my acceptance.

EDDY: What do you mean, you revoke your acceptance?

SUSAN: I mean just what I said. When you first delivered the Arctic Blast, I accepted it. But now that I see you can't fix it, I revoke my acceptance. The air conditioner is yours again—not mine.

EDDY: What makes you think you can decide all this on your own?

SUSAN: The Uniform Commercial Code.

EDDY: The *what?*

SUSAN: The Uniform Commercial Code—it's the law in this state. When a consumer gets stuck with a lemon, and repairs don't help, the Code says the consumer can revoke acceptance and get a full refund on the lemon.

EDDY: Well, maybe that is the law, but I've got rights too, you know. The warranty on your Arctic Blast says all I have to do is repair parts or replace them. That's all—nothing about taking the air conditioner back and making a refund.

SUSAN: The Code won't let you get away with that. You can't force me to settle for endless repairs on a lemon. It makes no difference what the warranty says. The Code says when a product is a lemon I can revoke and get a refund—regardless of the warranty. That's the law, Mr. Eckert.

EDDY: Well, uh, why don't you let me think it over.

SUSAN: Sure. Talk to your lawyer. Ask him to check out the Uniform Commercial Code—especially sections 2-608 and 2-719.

EDDY: 2-608 and 2-719, eh?

SUSAN: That's right. Tell your lawyer a customer revoked acceptance under the Code and you'd like to avoid a lawsuit, if possible—

EDDY: A lawsuit . . . ?

SUSAN: Well, honestly, if you won't take back the air conditioner and refund my money, you'll leave me no choice but to sue you in small claims court for the full purchase price. It'll be an open-and-shut case.

EDDY: Yes, well, let's see if we can work this out without all that bother, shall we? I'll call you back.

SUSAN: I hope it won't take too long, Mr. Eckert, because every day that you delay there are incidental and consequential damages mounting up.

EDDY: Incidental and consequential . . . ?

SUSAN: The Code lets me sue you for *all* the losses your lemon caused me—not just for its purchase price. That will include the rental fee on the substitute air conditioner which you're forcing me to rent. Plus storage charges—I'm sure you don't expect me to store your lemon—it is *yours* now—free of charge. Plus the damage to my rug from the dripping. Plus—

EDDY: Okay, Miss Phelps, okay, I see your point. I'll call you back today. I'm sure we can settle this.

SUSAN: Oh, good, Mr. Eckert. I'll look forward to your men delivering a refund check and picking up that air conditioner in a day or two. Good day, Mr. Eckert.

EDDY: Yes, good day, Miss Phelps, good day.

This imaginary dialogue between Susan Phelps and Eddy Eckert dramatizes the general direction that every power play should take—although obviously no two power plays will ever be the same. In her confrontation at Fast Eddy's, Susan dealt with Eddy pretty much as a lawyer would have. Not just because she knew enough to drop a few section numbers from the Uniform Commercial Code. That helps, to be sure, but it's not the secret of a power play. The secret lies in using certain time-tested techniques when dealing with people who violate your rights.

Lawyers have long used these techniques in confrontations with their adversaries. Lawyers don't prevail merely by using a lot of highfalutin legalese; indeed, such technical talk is usually kept to a minimum. Lawyers gain the upper hand because they know how to deal with people in a manner that is tough yet diplomatic. There is no pat formula for this technique of persuasion. But if we look back over Susan Phelps's power play more closely, we can discern several key lawyer-like approaches that she used with great success.

1. *Be civil.* Susan, unlike Mike Keller, began her confrontation as politely as possible—with a "Good morning." (Even after the smoke cleared, Susan and Eddy were still able to say "Good day" to each other.) As elementary as it may sound, good manners (and a sense of humor) are enormous strengths when dealing with an adversary. Law-

yers have long known that politeness—even if in appearance only—leaves the channels of communication open between adversaries. This open-door atmosphere is useful, especially when you have to deal repeatedly with the same adversary before a settlement can be reached.

2. *Be businesslike.* Instead of getting personal, as Mike did, Susan remained cool throughout her confrontation with Eddy. Like Susan, a lawyer would never rant and rave at someone with whom he hoped to strike a deal. Noise generally betrays impotence—the fact that you have no real leverage at your command.

3. *Be reasonable.* From the moment Susan said, "I dropped by to see what we can work out together," her whole attitude signaled to Eddy: This is no big deal; you and I can handle this ourselves; we're teammates tackling this together. This sort of accommodating approach tends to put your adversary at ease (off guard, you might say!). You seem to be a reasonable person—not some crank—so your adversary feels disposed toward working things out with you. Lawyers are forever striving to reach reasonable settlements that keep clients out of full-fledged court battles. A willingness to be fair—or at least *appear fair-minded*—is critical to the successful outcome of a power play.

4. *Listen sympathetically.* Susan Phelps was a pretty good listener. She let Eddy have his say. Early on, when he offered further repairs, she even responded graciously, "I appreciate your offer"—although she was probably thinking, "What a load of bull; it's the runaround again!" Soothing remarks like "I see what you're driving at" and "I can appreciate your reasoning" (whether you agree with it or not) have a salutary effect on your adversary. They convey the impression that you're open-minded, and they invite a similarly sympathetic attitude on your adversary's part.

Having dealt with myriad people locked in seemingly intractable disputes, lawyers long ago discovered that often one person simply wants recognition for his viewpoint or for the burden he's shouldering. Lend that person a sympathetic ear and you may have given him half of what he wants; getting the other half will be that much easier.

5. *Escalate gradually.* Susan Phelps paced herself carefully. She began by simply stating her dissatisfaction with the air conditioner. Who knew what Eddy might volunteer? When Eddy offered only more repairs, rather than a refund or a new unit, Susan explained that she'd had enough repairs and asked for a refund. She didn't fly off the handle on learning of Fast Eddy's no-refund policy; instead she asked why. When Eddy failed to come up with any reason, Susan probed further to see whether he would make an exception in the case of an obvious lemon. All the while, she was looking for a reasonable concession from Eddy which would avoid the need for any legal threats. When none was forthcoming, Susan finally drew the line: "I hereby revoke my acceptance," she announced sternly.

Susan dealt with Eddy as a lawyer would have. A lawyer doesn't enter with guns blazing. He first tries to get a feel for his adversary: How strongly is the adversary committed to a particular position? Is there room for compromise? Can the whole problem be resolved without recourse to the law? If the adversary appears to be unreasonable and unyielding, the lawyer will then escalate. He will start to lay his legal chips on the table, raising probable violations of the law and potential penalties. If necessary, the lawyer may play pot-limit poker, threatening dire legal consequences unless the adversary starts cooperating.

6. *Lower the boom.* As the last stage in her steady escalation, Susan made it clear to Eddy that he was toying with a serious and costly violation of the law. To drive home her point, she hit Eddy with a few legal codewords: *Uniform Commercial Code, sections 2-608 and 2-719,* and *incidental and consequential damages.* Clearly, Susan knew

something that Eddy didn't know. She knew about a source of leverage that is beyond most consumers (like Mike Keller). This obvious knowledge of where the real power lay increased her clout with Eddy; it transformed her suggestion of a lawsuit into a most plausible threat, which Eddy could not afford to ignore. (Incidentally, in Chapter 4 you will be learning everything Susan knew about the Uniform Commercial Code and how it protects you against getting stuck with a lemon.)

Lowering the boom by invoking the law is, of course, part of a lawyer's stock in trade. It's always persuasive to marshal the power of the state on your side of an argument. The real stakes in any confrontation—e.g., money damages, lawyer's fees, wasted time—become painfully clear once one side starts invoking the sanction of the law.

7. *Leave some breathing space.* Susan was careful not to back Eddy up against the wall when he said he would have to think over her demands. She immediately suggested that he consult his lawyer. As a practical matter, Eddy may have wished to do exactly that. Even if he had no intention of incurring legal fees over this dispute, he still needed some breathing space to review everything Susan had said and make up his mind on his own. The breathing space allowed Eddy to save face by eventually saying he was acting "on advice of counsel" (whether that was true or not).

Even lawyers won't push their luck when an adversary is yielding, because being overaggressive can backfire. The adversary may be goaded into stubborn resistance, despite the fact that his goose is cooked.

We may speculate without much difficulty on the outcome of Susan Phelps's power play. Fast Eddy was soundly shaken. Accustomed to outwitting the Mike Kellers of the world, Eddy found himself up against a cool customer who talked a tough and intimidating language. What customer ever walked into Fast Eddy's and demanded a right of revocation under section 2-608 of the Uniform Commercial Code? Nice little Mike Keller type customers just don't talk that way. Oh, they may rant and rave, but a thick skin is all you need to handle them. Susan Phelps's codewords pierced that skin and created some real doubts: What if she's for real? What if she sues me? What if I have to pay for her other losses besides the price of the air conditioner? Why do I have a headache all of a sudden? That's the disquieting effect that Susan's codewords had on Eddy.

Suppose that before giving in and avoiding further trouble, Eddy does consult a lawyer. He will learn that, yes, Susan Phelps is basically correct. The Uniform Commercial Code (which, as we will learn in Chapter 4, has been adopted in every state but Louisiana) does give consumers the right of revocation when they get stuck with an unrepairable lemon. In addition to recouping the purchase price, a consumer is entitled to collect any extra damages caused by the lemon—including storage costs until the seller takes the lemon back. Since Susan has acted reasonably and with restraint, the lawyer will advise Eddy not to waste money defending against a winning lawsuit. Thus, curiously enough, the final touches to Susan's power play come not from Susan but from Eddy's lawyer!

2

How to Plan and Execute a Power Play

The Power Play System

Bully for Susan Phelps, you may be thinking. Somehow she was able to walk into a store and sound off about the Uniform Commercial Code and consequential damages. And she was civil and reasonable and sympathetic and whatever else a lawyer is supposed to be. But how is the average consumer supposed to be as sharp as Susan Phelps? (She's probably a Radcliffe Phi Beta Kappa who's translated *War and Peace* into twelve different languages and holds the world record in the javelin throw.)

Okay, your point's well taken. Let's step back for a moment and put the power play into proper perspective. That way you'll get a handle on it and see how you, too, can play as hard and as well as Susan did. In a nutshell, the power play system follows three basic guidelines:

1. Know your legal rights.
2. Recognize your adversary's soft spot.
3. Put pressure on that soft spot in a power play.

With a little help from us, and some studying on your

part, you can master all three precepts and deal with your adversaries like a lawyer.

Step 1 requires reading the chapter in this book that is relevant to your problem. Are you, like Susan Phelps, the frustrated owner of a lemon (be it an air conditioner, a new car, a food processor, etc.)? Then read Chapter 4, "Defective Products." You'll come away knowing everything Susan knew. Is your landlord threatening to evict you because you complain too much? Check out Chapter 11, "Overpowering Your Landlord." Is your new home falling apart? Read Chapter 3, "Warranty Protection for New-Home Buyers." And so on.

In the appropriate chapter, you will learn your legal rights. While we've tried to make our explanation as nontechnical as possible, we don't baby you with easy generalizations. We give you hard legal specifics: the chapter and verse of state and federal laws, and the reasoning behind precedent-setting court decisions. (Some chapters even have special appendixes in the back of the book listing key laws and cases in your state.) Like Susan Phelps, you'll be putting all this nitty-gritty information to work in your own power plays.

After learning your rights, the second step in the power play system is pinpointing your adversary's *soft spot*. The soft spot is your adversary's legal Achilles' heel—that point where the law makes him vulnerable to pressure from people like you. Often the soft spot will become apparent to you as you discover what your rights are, because almost every right you possess relies on a corresponding duty—or potential liability—on your adversary's part. (For example, Susan Phelps's right to revoke gave rise to Fast Eddy's duty to take back the lemon or incur liability to Susan for its purchase price, plus other potential damages.) These duties, liabilities, legal sanctions, etc., are the *X's* that mark your adversary's soft spot.

Frequently the soft spot will be fear of a costly legal battle. In many instances, you'll learn that your adversary may be liable for double, treble, or even quadruple damages, or perhaps up to $10,000 in penalties. A good number of laws allow the victorious consumer to collect his attorney's fees from the other side, thereby inflating the potential loss your adversary faces.

There are other kinds of soft spots. For example, what businessman relishes the threat of being investigated by a government agency, such as the Federal Trade Commission? In Chapter 9 we'll see that a bill collector who makes harassing phone calls to you can have his telephone service suspended or even terminated. Knowing this, you can see that the bill collector's business lifeline is exposed—a soft spot indeed. Squeeze it hard enough and you can put the bill collector out of business.

After you've learned about your rights and the soft spot, you're ready to prepare for step 3: putting pressure on your adversary's soft spot in a power play. Out of all the legal principles you learn in the chapter you read, select those that cover your particular problem. Apply them in your own mind to the problem you face. Ask yourself logically what outcome these principles dictate. Play devil's advocate with yourself; try to anticipate how your adversary may react to the legal principles you expect to raise in your power play. How will he try to get around your points?

You won't be entirely on your own in this planning stage. Throughout each chapter we have provided helpful hints labeled *power play pointers*. These are lawyer's tips on how to translate the law you're learning into the real-life give-and-take that occurs in a personal confrontation. The power play pointers help you to anticipate and counter ploys that your adversary is likely to spring on you. They teach you how to use the law as both a sword and a shield—

attacking your adversary with the thrust of your rights, while defending yourself behind a wide array of legal protections.

For example, Chapter 10 discusses many prohibitions on what a creditor can legitimately ask a woman who is applying for credit. He cannot inquire, for instance, about her marital status. Following this section of Chapter 10 comes a power play pointer that suggests ways in which to handle improper inquiries from creditors—e.g., the creditor who asks, after writing down your name, "Is that 'Miss' or 'Mrs.'?"

Our power play pointers are not intended as predictions of exactly what you will encounter when you confront your adversary. Considering all the variations that can occur in a person-to-person confrontation, there is no way that we can feed you, word for word, what you should say as well as what your adversary will respond. Were we to undertake such a feat of clairvoyance, you might be tempted to memorize dialogue from the book, only to find, embarrassingly, that your adversary doesn't read "his lines" as expected.

Instead, you should simply absorb the thrust of the power play pointers, without feeling any obligation to memorize them. *They are not scripts for you to act out.* Their true function is to provoke your imagination—to let you see how the law can be taken off dusty shelves and brought to life in the midst of your everyday problems. If you pause at each pointer, and even in between, to reassess your own problem, chances are you'll dream up even better ways in which to disarm your adversary with all the legal weaponry you're picking up in the course of the chapter. Above all, relax and enjoy the power play pointers and every nuance they conjure up for you; half the fun of a power play is savoring it in advance.

Another important step in preparing for a power play

is to determine your priorities. What do you want to get out of your adversary? Are your demands realistic, or are you shooting for the moon? In Susan Phelps's case, rejection of the prcduct and a full refund were realistic demands. Susan had already been through the whole repair-shop routine several times over. She would have been asking for too much, however, had she tried to reject the air conditioner the moment it first malfunctioned. At that point it would have been reasonable to insist that the store live up to the warranty and service the product. The whole point of a power play, remember, is to vindicate your rights—to gain your just deserts—not to force the other side to grant something you're not entitled to.

When it comes to carrying out a power play, there is no set of stage directions for you to follow. No two power plays will ever be exactly alike, even for similar violations of your rights. (The power play between Susan and Eddy was just an illustration—not a model against which all other confrontations must be measured.)

A power play is simply a conversation with a definite goal. You know what the goal is, and you control how to go about accomplishing it. Initially, use as little pressure as possible. You will often be pleasantly surprised to discover how quickly reputable businesspeople accommodate your legitimate requests. (Don't be disappointed if your power play turns out to be unnecessary; just keep it handy, because no doubt you'll need it again soon.) Should you start encountering resistance, then escalate gradually, as Susan Phelps did, until you finally have to lower the boom and lay down the law.

Bear in mind that you can adjust the force of your power play to suit your personality and the nature of your relationship with your adversary. For example, you may be less hard-nosed in a confrontation with your boss than you would be when dealing with the parents of a neighborhood vandal. While the legal power at your command is always ready to be tapped—like a good head of steam— you alone can decide how much to release, how swiftly, and in what sort of blasts.

In any power play you will find it effective to employ the seven lawyer-like techniques that worked for Susan Phelps: (1) be civil; (2) be businesslike; (3) be reasonable; (4) listen sympathetically; (5) escalate gradually; (6) lower the boom; and (7) leave some breathing space.

The Strategic Use of Codewords

The key to a successful power play is the strategic use of codewords. They are the jabs and hooks—maybe even the knockout punch—of a power play. Every time you use a codeword well, you go one up on your adversary; so even if you don't kayo him, you're likely to beat him on total points.

Why are codewords so potent? First, they establish you as someone to be reckoned with, because you obviously know your legal rights. You can believe that as soon as Susan Phelps announced to Fast Eddy that she was revoking her acceptance under the Uniform Commercial Code, his estimation of her shot up about fifteen points.

Second, codewords unnerve your adversary by implying that you know how to get at his soft spot. Take the codeword *Regulation B,* which you'll be learning about in Chapter 10. Regulation B is a complex set of federal rules prohibiting discrimination against women in the granting of credit. Merely by alluding to Regulation B in a creditor's office, you are subtly reminding him that the transaction you and he are engaged in happens to be subject to close governmental scrutiny and severe legal sanctions.

Third, codewords intimidate your adversary by warning him that he's heading for legal trouble. No one likes to be confronted with the possibility that his misconduct may have serious legal consequences. That spells lawyers, investigations, and court hearings—not to mention money.

Fourth, and most important, codewords are real conversation-stoppers. They tend to leave your adversary sitting there with his mouth half open. After all, what is a merchant like Fast Eddy supposed to say when Susan Phelps tells him that the Uniform Commercial Code takes precedence over an ineffective warranty? The only thing he can say is just what Eddy said: "Well, uh, why don't you let me think it over" (which is a face-saving way of saying "Boy, you've got me over a barrel on that one"). So, besides being authoritative, codewords let you gain a decisive psychological edge over your adversary.

In the course of each chapter's power play pointers we suggest some ways in which to drop codewords. Again, our aim is not to feed you lines from offstage, but merely to illustrate when and how codewords may work well for you.

To coach you further, we conclude each chapter with a *codeword glossary*. The glossary contains our choice of the most potent codewords you've learned about in the chapter. Each codeword in the glossary is followed by a capsule definition (to refresh your memory) and then, where appropriate, the codeword's *legal citation,* the official designation of where a particular law or regulation or court case can be found in the law books.

A citation acts rather like a stamp of approval, validating both the existence and the authoritativeness of a particular law or case.

For example, the codeword glossary to Chapter 8 (on auto leasing) includes *Consumer Leasing Act,* which is followed by this explanation: "The federal statute that requires detailed prerental disclosures by auto lessors and severely limits the size of balloon payments. This law can be found in section 1667 of title 15 of the United States

Code." The last sentence provides the legal citation for the Consumer Leasing Act. If you (or, for that matter, your adversary or his lawyer) go to a law library, locate the set of law books containing the United States Code (the basic federal statutes of this country), pull out the volume containing title 15 of the Code, and turn to section 1667 of title 15, you will find the official legal text of the Consumer Leasing Act. (By all means, follow this procedure if you have a yen to read the original text of any of the laws we discuss.)

The legal citations to court cases look a bit different from the citations to statutes. That's because court decisions are published in consecutively numbered volumes called *law reporters.* Federal court decisions are generally published in the Federal Reporter or the Federal Supplement. State court decisions are published in regional reporters, covering several adjacent states. For example, the Southern Reporter contains decisions from courts in Alabama, Florida, Louisiana, and Mississippi. If you look at the codeword glossary for the very next chapter (on warranty protection for home buyers), you will see that the first codeword listed is the name of a state court decision, *Barnes* v. *Mac Brown and Company.* This codeword is followed by a brief explanation and a legal citation: "This is a leading 1976 Indiana case, found in volume 342 of the North Eastern Reporter, Second Series, at page 619; it extended warranty protection to buyers of a used home." (Don't let "Second Series" throw you. Most reporters have a first and second series of books; the former simply contain older cases, while the latter contain more recent ones.)

After you have read the chapter on your problem and evaluated your situation in light of it, consult the codeword glossary. Select the codewords that are bound to be most relevant in your upcoming power play. Your choices will be dictated by what you've just finished reading about your rights; also, the power play pointers may have tipped you off to codewords that will help you. On a sheet of white paper, type out the codewords you choose; make sure you get their legal citations down correctly.

You will take this list of codewords with you to the power play. Basically, there are four different ways in which you can use it when you're up against your adversary. First, the list serves as handy reminder notes, should you forget any point that you intended to raise.

Second, your written codewords allow you to counterpunch quickly if your adversary tries to call your bluff. Suppose he turns on you abruptly and demands: "The Consumer Leasing Act? What the devil is the Consumer Leasing Act?" No doubt, he fully expects some mealymouthed reply like "I read about it somewhere in the newspapers." To which he's dying to respond: "Oh, 'somewhere in the newspapers,' eh? Listen, don't believe everything you read in the papers."

You'll be able to deftly avoid this sort of damaging exchange by immediately referring to your list: "The Consumer Leasing Act happens to be a federal statute that's enforced against dealers like yourself. It's section 1667 of title 15 of the United States Code, if you want to take that down!" That'll be enough to shut your adversary up—or send his legal lackey scurrying into the library to dig up title 15 (that is, assuming your adversary wants to pay his lackey for this little treasure hunt).

Third, you can rather dramatically put your adversary on formal notice of the law by literally handing him your piece of paper during a power play. Suppose you bought a defective product using a credit card, winding up with both a lemon and a bill. In Chapter 4 you will learn that you don't have to pay the credit card company's bill for a defective product because of a federal law called—rather cryptically—Regulation Z. After referring to the codeword glossary at the end of Chapter 4, you could type out: "Regulation Z—title 12 of the Code of Federal Regulations, section 226."

When you return to the store and find the person who sold you the defective product, you can say: "I'm not paying my credit card bill for this product you sold me, because it's defective. You might as well take this thing back, since you're not going to be paid by the credit card company." If the salesperson balks, you're in a perfect position to say: "Look, I have a legal right not to pay this bill under federal Regulation Z. Here's the name and citation of the law." Hand the salesperson your codeword sheet; then hand him the lemon.

Fourth, your list of written codewords can enable you to nip in the bud any tricks your adversary is likely to pull. (We alert you to many of these tricks in our power play pointers.) Suppose you are a female employee seeking to be paid as much as male coworkers who perform the same job you do. In Chapter 6 you will learn that you have the legal right to equal pay for equal work. You will also be warned (in a power play pointer) of a typical ploy the boss may pull on you if you ask him for equal pay: "Well if you insist on it," he'll say, "I'll just have to *lower* the men's pay till it equals yours!" As Chapter 6 explains, the boss is violating the law, because he is required to *raise* your salary to the men's level—not lower their salaries. The federal court case that upholds this rule (*Marshall* v. *Hodag Chemical Corporation*) is listed in the codeword glossary for Chapter 6.

You would write down the name and citation of the Marshall case and take it with you when you ask the boss to give you pay equal to the men's. Then if he says he'll have to lower their pay, you will be ready with a cool word of caution: "That's not what I'm asking for, and you know it. Besides, what you're suggesting doesn't jibe with federal law, and that could mean a ten-thousand-dollar fine. Before you do anything, you'd better have a look at the federal court decision, *Marshall* v. *Hodag Chemical Corporation.* Here's a copy of the legal citation for the case."

Don't be surprised if you get a few glazed looks when you start scoring direct hits with codewords. They work rather like depth charges in submarine warfare—sinking in slowly and then knocking your adversary off kilter. Not that you should bank on your adversary's rolling over and playing dead the moment he hears your codewords. These words won't work instant magic, so they shouldn't be uttered like some fearful curse.

In fact, the most effective way to utter codewords is in a low-key, almost offhand manner. You can often do this by posing innocent-sounding rhetorical questions—that is, questions to which you know the answers, as your adversary can plainly guess. "By the way," Susan Phelps might have asked Fast Eddy, "are you sure your repairs-only policy squares with the Uniform Commercial Code? My understanding is that the Code calls for refunds when repairs become pointless."

This approach is obviously much more casual than the one Susan actually used, but it could have proven equally effective. Slipping codewords into rhetorical questions is like introducing termites into a house. The codewords chew away at your adversary's confidence. You gain the edge over him, not in a dramatic coup, but through the steadily gnawing doubts you've created in his mind. You, of course, must be the ultimate judge of the codeword style that best fits both your personality and the circumstances of your power play.

Since your codewords and legal citations will rub your adversary's nose in the law, don't be surprised if he inquires, "What are you, some kind of lawyer or something?" You should, of course, answer no. "Then why should I believe all this stuff you're telling me about the law?" he may well retort. "Oh, listen, don't take *my* word for it," you should respond without batting an eye, "by all means, talk to your lawyer. He'll confirm that what I've told you is really the law."

Don't be afraid of making such a candid concession. In fact, it may turn out to be one of the most potent tactics in your power play. First of all, your candor reinforces your credibility. Any consumer who welcomes the opinion of his adversary's lawyer must be pretty sure of what he's talking about. Second, your adversary is going to have to start paying money once his legal man enters the picture. Lawyers hardly even answer the telephone nowadays unless their fee meter is ticking away. So you're already making your adversary wonder, "What's this whole mess going to cost me?"

Third, and most important, your adversary's attorney is an unseen ally of yours in the power play. That may sound strange. But remember: *a power play is not a bluff.* It is based on very real rights and safeguards which the law guarantees. So if your adversary consults his attorney, your demands are not going to be dismissed. The lawyer will sense immediately that you're getting some solid advice from somewhere, because you sure know how to cite legal chapter and verse to support your demands. The lawyer's advice to your adversary is likely to be: "This guy's no fool. He's making a plausible legal argument here—one that could cause you serious trouble. Can't you figure out a way to make him happy, before this thing gets blown out of proportion?" After receiving pressure on two fronts, chances are your adversary will try to strike a fair deal with you.

We would like to offer some final advice to readers who may feel a bit embarrassed at the prospect of uttering codewords in a forthright manner. It's understandable that you might at first be self-conscious about asserting yourself so boldly. Like most consumers, you're not accustomed to throwing around the kind of weight that the power play system affords. With a little practice, however, and some good results, you'll grow comfortable standing up for your rights.

In fact, we bet you'll start to feel justifiably proud of yourself—and with good reason. The power play system is not just another in the currently popular schemes of psychological one-upmanship, where you pretend to possess powers that are not truly yours. Trying to live up to such a hyped-up system can leave you feeling uncomfortably like a con artist or impostor. The power play system is founded on very real powers *that already belong to you under the law*. This book simply reveals what is rightfully yours today. By demanding your just deserts, you'll be acting as a tough-minded citizen—a sort of "private attorney general." Whether or not you do so will depend largely on your temperament. Are you the kind of person who gives up his rights without a fight? Or are you the kind of person who, all his life, has been waiting for the chance to look some antagonist dead in the eyes and say, "Not so fast, my friend. Do you realize that under the law of this state . . ."

3

Warranty Protection for New-Home Buyers

Two weeks after you move into your new house, the bathroom door starts sticking. You complain to the builder, and he sends over a carpenter to plane down the door. Fair enough. Then you notice a crack opening up in the caulked space between the bathtub and the wall. Again you complain, and the same carpenter comes over and caulks up the crack. But it reopens within a week; in fact, the entire floor is separating from the wall. Cracks begin to split the wall itself. Incredible as it seems, your new house is coming apart at the seams! All of a sudden, the builder becomes less accommodating. He no longer sends over a carpenter. Indeed, he eventually stops even taking your calls. You face the scary fact that you've been stuck with a $48,000 lemon, and the builder refuses to give you any lemon aid.

A farfetched horror story? Not at all. Complaints about shoddy construction in newly built homes are rising at an alarming rate across the country. The defects range from flooded basements and sagging roofs to paper-thin walls in a Florida condominium and New Jersey tap water that bubbles like soda.

According to a front-page exposé in the *Wall Street Journal* (September 28, 1978):

> *Private home inspectors say they are regularly seeing glaring defects in brand-new homes. One inspector, Phillip Monahon of Massachusetts, says that 20% of new homes he has inspected have had "serious defects" requiring more than $500 to fix. A few years ago the Department of Housing and Urban Development inspected a test sample of new homes and found that 24% were defective. . . . Reports of complaints like these are pouring into the Better Business Bureau in Washington at a record rate. . . . Concern about defective housing is likely to grow as more problems are found in the record 1.5 million single-family homes started last year and the 1.3 million that are expected to be started this year.*

Until fairly recently the buyer of a new home had little legal protection against a slipshod builder. Indeed, the law helped builders to evade dissatisfied buyers under the doctrine of caveat emptor (let the buyer beware). It was up to the home buyer to protect himself against getting stuck with a lemon. The law treated him as though he were the builder's equal in terms of expertise and business savvy. Presumably, the buyer was capable of inspecting the land and the house and determining whether they were satisfactory and suited his needs. He was not entitled to expect anything from the builder-seller unless the latter specifically made assurances or guarantees—which he hardly ever did. Once the buyer had accepted the house, no matter how naively, caveat emptor allowed the builder to slip out scot-free through the back door (assuming it had not collapsed with the rest of the house!).

This deplorable state of the law offended many judges, especially as giant legal strides were being taken to protect consumers against defective merchandise. Arkansas Supreme Court Justice George Smith reflected the misgivings of many of his judicial brethren when he observed in 1970: "One who bought something as simple as a walking stick or a kitchen mop was entitled to get his money back if the article was not of merchantible quality. But the purchaser of a $50,000 home ordinarily had no remedy even if the foundation proved to be so defective that the structure collapsed into a heap of rubble."

In the last twenty years—chiefly during the 1970s—there has been a dramatic widespread reversal in the law governing the duties and liabilities of new-home builders. This unheralded revolution occurred in courtrooms across the country, where judge after judge rejected caveat emptor as a cruel legal anachronism. The reasons for rejection were summed up well by the Wyoming Supreme Court in the 1975 case of *Tavares* v. *Horstman:*

> *Since World War II homes have been built in tremendous numbers. There have come into being developer-builders operating on a large scale. Many firms and persons, large and small operators, hold themselves out as skilled in home construction and are in the business of building and selling to individual owners.*
> *Developers contract with builders to construct for resale. Building construction by modern methods is complex and intertwined with governmental codes and regulations. The ordinary home buyer is not in a position, by skill or training, to discover defects lurking in the plumbing, the electrical wiring, the structure*

*itself, all of which is usually covered up and not open
for inspection.*

*A home buyer should be able to place reliance on
the builder or developer who sells him a new house.
The improved real estate the average family buys
gives it thoughtful pause not only because of the base
price but the interest involved over a long period of
time. This is usually the largest single purchase a family
makes for a lifetime. . . .*

*It ought to be an implicit understanding of the
parties that when an agreed price is paid that the house
is reasonably fit for the purpose for which it is to be
used—that it is reasonably fit for habitation. Illusory
value is a poor substitute for quality. There is no need
for the buyer to be subjected to the harassment caused
by defects and he deserves the focus of the law and its
concern.*

What the Wyoming Supreme Court—and dozens of
other state courts—substituted for caveat emptor is a new
legal doctrine known as the *implied warranty of habitability*.
Under this doctrine, new homes are covered by a warranty
not unlike that which comes with consumer goods. To date,
the warranty-of-habitability concept has been adopted by
thirty-four states: Alabama, Arkansas, California, Colorado, Connecticut, Delaware, Florida, Idaho, Illinois, Indiana, Kentucky, Louisiana, Maryland, Michigan, Minnesota, Mississippi, Missouri, Nebraska, New Hampshire, New
Jersey, New York, North Carolina, North Dakota, Ohio,
Oklahoma, Oregon, Pennsylvania, Rhode Island, South Carolina, South Dakota, Texas, Vermont, Washington, and
Wyoming. (The official name of the legal authority establishing the warranty rule in each of these states is listed in
Appendix B.)

Power Play Pointer. If you live in one of the states listed above, don't ever let a builder brush you off with the lame excuse of caveat emptor. "Let the buyer beware" is such a long-standing cliché that many builders probably assume it's still the law. But you know differently. Clue the builder in the moment he suggests that you accepted your house—good, bad, or indifferent—and now you have to live with it. Just tell the builder, in an appropriately funereal tone, that caveat emptor is dead in your state. Should his disbelief require production of the death certificate, just give him the name and citation of the legal authority in your state (see Appendix B).

Suppose your state is not among the thirty four that have already adopted the implied warranty. You can still rely on the warranty as it prevails in other states. It's entirely likely that more and more states, including yours, will be jumping on the warranty bandwagon in the near future, judging by the rapidity and unanimity with which courts are dumping caveat emptor in favor of the new warranty. Courts in your state will probably be guided by decisions already reached in other states. So proceed on the assumption that when the proper test case arises in your state, the court will adopt implied warranty protection for new-home buyers. Just tell the builder that an overwhelming majority of states now support warranty protection; as-yet-uncommitted states will undoubtedly follow this progressive lead.

Unlike the warranty on most consumer goods, the implied warranty of habitability doesn't come printed on a card attached to your new house. It doesn't have to; no magic words are required, no special promises between you and the builder. The implied warranty is automatically imposed by law on your transaction with the builder. That's because state courts and legislatures have decided that, as a matter of sound and equitable public policy, the standards embodied in the warranty ought to be made a binding part of every agreement for the construction or sale of a new house.

Power Play Pointer. When complaining to your builder, be prepared for a shell game. He may point to the sales contract or deed on your house and ask smugly, "Where is this warranty you keep harping on? It's not written down here anywhere."

"You're right," you can concede without a qualm, "it's not. But then, it doesn't have to be. State law imposes it, whether you wrote it down or not. That's why it's called an *implied* warranty."

What legal protection does the new implied warranty of habitability give to you? Basically, it makes the builder-seller of a new home accountable to you for producing a structure that is—to borrow some language from the Wyoming Supreme Court—"reasonably fit for the purpose for which it is to be used—that is reasonably fit for habitation."

The concept of *habitability* is pivotal to the operation of the new warranty. How well constructed does your new house have to be in order to qualify as being legally habitable? Generally speaking, the house should be:

—free from defects caused by faulty workmanship, improper engineering standards, and inadequate materials;

—free from defects caused by faulty installation of plumbing, electrical, heating and cooling systems; and

—free from major construction defects (i.e., any damage to the load-bearing portions of the house—the foundation, walls, floors, beams).

As an Illinois appeals court has explained,

*The primary function of a new home is to shelter its
inhabitants from the elements. If a new home does not
keep out the elements because of a substantial defect
of construction, such a home is not habitable within the
meaning of the implied warranty of habitability.
Another function of a new home is to provide its
inhabitants with a reasonably safe place to live, without
fear of injury to person, health, safety, or property. If a
new home is not structurally sound because of a
substantial defect of construction, such a home is not
habitable.*

Many cases have arisen over flooded basements. Sometimes the builder chose an unsuitable site—like directly over
an underground spring—or failed to supply proper drainage
or to waterproof the cellar. An equal number of cases were
based on sewer problems. Because the builder didn't con-
struct a big enough septic tank, or built the tank on ground
higher than the house or failed to connect sewage-disposal
pipes securely, sewage backed up into the new houses,
ruining floors and furnishings and, not incidentally, causing
a stinking mess. In all these cases, the defects and their
aftermath rendered the new houses legally nonhabitable under the implied warranty.

Power Play Pointer. Whenever you discover—or even
suspect—that your new house may be defective, notify the
builder immediately. Needless delay can result in the loss
of legal remedies later on—like the ability to sue the builder
for money damages. So call the builder right away, especially if it's an emergency. Confirm your call in a letter, sent
to the builder via certified mail, return receipt requested.
You'll then have proof that the builder was on notice of the
defect as of a certain date.

In order to get a varied picture of typical conditions that violate the implied warranty of habitability, let's take a gloomy tour of several recent new-home disasters, all of which involved breaches of warranty.

Hot and cold running Alka Seltzer. When Henry and Barbara MacDonald first turned on the faucets in their New Jersey home, they expected clear, drinkable water. Instead, they were confronted with water that fizzed like Alka Seltzer. The pipes knocked when the water ran, and soon the plumbing fixtures, as well as the family's laundry, exhibited chocolaty brown stains. A month after the MacDonalds moved in, their washing machine conked out; the dishwasher followed suit four months later. All of these mishaps were traced to the implausible presence of methane gas in the well that the builder had drilled. Because of this defect, the builder had breached the warranty.

Buckled floors. Shortly after Carmela Centrella moved into her new home on Long Island, the oak floors began to buckle. This disfigurement was due to flooding that had occurred during construction. The builder was responsible for this breach of warranty.

Paper-thin walls. George and Lili David may have thought someone was throwing a surprise housewarming for them when they moved into their new condominium apartment in Bar Harbor Islands, Florida. Actually, the walls of the apartment were so thin—in violation of official specifications for the building—that the Davids could literally hear every word spoken and sound made by their neighbors in the adjacent condominiums. This condition violated the warranty of habitability.

Leaks. Jean Gay's new house in Montesano, Washington, was plagued by numerous defects that made it legally nonhabitable. Right off the bat, the roof sprang so many leaks that a hundred tin shingles were required to repair it temporarily. Electrical problems developed after water leaked across the main electrical control panel for the house. The furnace regularly overheated and would not turn on and off automatically. The exterior paint used was so thin that the outside of the house had to be repainted.

The well ran dry. Less than two weeks after Mr. and Mrs. William Krol moved into their new Maryland home, they decided to throw a dinner party. Unfortunately, on the afternoon of the party, while preparations were underway, the house ran out of water—the well just stopped. The Krols survived the evening, largely by the grace of friendly neighbors who donated water, not to mention stoic guests whose self-restraint or early departure avoided taxing the bathroom facilities. For the next six months the Krols were forced to survive on water supplied by neighbors' hoses. Incredibly enough, when the Krols sued the builder who had constructed the well, the trial court granted judgment for the builder. On appeal, however, the case was reversed and sent back for a new trial. The appeals court rejected the notion that the implied warranty of habitability could possibly "expire after the first flush"!

In all of these cases, the defects in question were not obvious to the unsuspecting buyer at the time of his purchase. Bear that in mind, because the implied warranty won't protect you from your own stupidity. You can't overlook a gaping hole in the wall and plead ignorance later on. While you're not expected to know about the intricacies of unseen pipes, wires, and beams, etc., you should be aware of defects which a reasonably diligent search would have revealed.

In order to amount to a breach of warranty, a defect in your new house must be substantial; it must directly and seriously affect living conditions. Minor defects aren't covered by the warranty. The builder isn't obligated to deliver a *perfect* house—just one that is *reasonably fit* to live in.

Compare two recent Florida cases, both involving condominiums. In a 1972 case, there was a breach of warranty when the condominium's air-conditioning system broke down. Five years later, however, another air-conditioner case went against the condominium buyers. Mr. and Mrs. William Roudebush had complained that their condominium was rendered nonhabitable because of the noise made by the air conditioner. The evidence they presented, however, fell short of establishing a breach of warranty. Judge Joseph McNulty explained:

> *The warranty involved is that the condominium unit was reasonably fit for the ordinary or general purpose intended, namely, as living quarters. A breach thereof, therefore, would be that it is not so fit; and the test of the breach is an objective one, i.e., whether the premises met ordinary, normal standards reasonably to be expected of living quarters of comparable kind and quality. There was no evidence on behalf of the Roudebushes which went to this test. They merely tended to show that, as to their sensitivity to noise, the premises were uninhabitable. (It appears, for example, that while admitting the noise was undetectable during normal conversation sounds, it was most disturbing to them in the still of the night.) No showing was made, nor was there a basis for comparison to establish, that their sensitivity to noise was not hypersensitivity, but was that of reasonable persons—a burden resting with them as plaintiffs. The subjective, "personal satisfaction" test is not enough.*

Power Play Pointer. Heed the plight of the Roudebushes. Before you decide that defects in your new house violate the warranty, ask yourself as objectively as you can:

Would a reasonable person, moving into a house similar in kind and quality to mine, conclude that the house failed to meet ordinary living standards which might normally be expected of it? If the answer is yes, then you can be pretty sure you're not in the Roudebush situation and you've got a genuine breach of warranty. Don't let the builder sweet-talk you by minimizing the defects and emphasizing your persnicketiness. Just keep reiterating your firm conviction that "no reasonable person would pay what I've paid and tolerate a house where the chimney is caving in/the base-ment floods." Appealing to the builder's sense of reason and fair play can't hurt. He may even agree to live up to the warranty.

Warranty protection has generally been confined to the *first occupants of brand-new houses*—that is, houses that are being planned for construction (say, by a tract devel-oper, who agrees to build the buyer's house based on an existing model home); houses that are under construction (regardless of what stage of completion they may be at when sold to the buyer); houses that are completed and ready for their first occupants.

This limitation to first purchasers is not absolute, how-ever. Several states extend warranty protection to subse-quent purchasers of new houses. For example, warranty statutes in Minnesota and New Jersey cover original and subsequent purchasers for the life of the warranty. In Con-necticut and Maryland the warranty statutes crack down on cagey builders who may try to evade their responsibilities by arranging to sell a new house to one person who, it is understood, will quickly resell it—the scheme being to in-sulate the builder from the second buyer by means of the original dummy buyer. It's the builder who winds up a dummy. He remains liable to the subsequent purchaser for breach of warranty, just as though the subsequent sale had been the original one.

Even more significantly, the highest courts of three states have recently extended warranty protection to purchasers of previously occupied homes. The Rhode Island Supreme Court did so in the 1974 case of *Casavant* v. *Campopiano;* the Indiana Supreme Court did the same in the 1976 case of *Barnes* v. *Mac Brown and Company;* and two years later Colorado's Supreme Court followed suit in *Duncan* v. *Schuster-Graham Homes, Inc.* The new houses in these cases had been occupied for anywhere from one to three years before a second set of occupants moved in. Soon enough these new owners discovered defects that had not been apparent when they bought the used houses. Despite their not being original purchasers, the new owners were covered by the warranty, under which the builder remained accountable to them. Whether more and more courts will follow the lead of Colorado, Indiana, and Rhode Island will probably depend on the circumstances in each new case.

Power Play Pointer. Don't let a builder off the hook just because you're not the original owner of your home. Although the law would currently seem to be on the builder's side, this legal area is expanding rapidly, mostly in favor of buyers. A builder can't be at all positive of what a judge might decide; depending on the circumstances, the builder could be held liable to you for his slipshod work despite the occupancy of the owner who preceded you. So if you wind up arguing with the builder over his responsibilities, emphasize those factors that point to the builder as the culprit: for example, the house is still relatively new and therefore wouldn't ordinarily have deteriorated as much as it has; the defects are the kind that would normally result from poor construction, rather than misuse by prior occupants; the defects were not at all evident when you bought the house, indicating that the builder's mistakes had not yet manifested themselves. Keep placing the burden squarely on the builder's shoulders. That way the issue will remain focused on what *he* is going to do to carry out *his* responsibility, instead of *who* caused this defect.

How long does the implied warranty last? The answer varies somewhat from state to state. By statute in both Connecticut and Maryland, the warranty expires, generally speaking, after one year; Minnesota's and New Jersey's statutes set three different time limits—one-, two-, and ten-year periods—depending on the category of defect (see Appendix B). In other states the warranty will generally run for what judges call a "reasonable time, in light of all the circumstances." That probably means two years or so— enough time for any defects attributable to the builder to manifest themselves.

Power Play Pointer. Reasonableness is the key legal term here. Try to deal with the builder on that basis. Impress on the builder that the defect you're complaining about is what the law calls a *latent* (or hidden) *defect*. This latent defect took its own sweet time to manifest itself—perhaps not until six months or a year or more after you moved in. It's not your fault that the trouble reared its head so late. Argue that it would be only reasonable for the builder's warranty to extend to your particular problem.

In the 1976 Indiana case mentioned earlier, *Barnes* v. *Mac Brown and Company,* the latent defect didn't show up until three years after the house had been built. Then the Barneses (who were the second owners) discovered that the basement leaked because of a large crack around three of the walls. The Mac Brown Company was held liable to the Barneses for breach of warranty.

Can a builder escape his responsibility to you through some legal loophole in his contract with you? Maybe, but he's going to have a tough time trying. Here's why. The implied warranty was imposed by judges across the country to safeguard home buyers. It embodies a carefully thought-out judicial response to a widespread consumer rip-off. Therefore, judges are extremely reluctant to let builder-sellers get around the warranty's protection simply by using some tricky legalese in a contract or deed.

Nevertheless, builders will try. Indeed, they already have—unsuccessfully—in a number of cases. The device generally employed—and one you should beware of—is a *disclaimer clause* in your contract with the builder-seller. A disclaimer is a legal loophole that basically says you're not entitled to warranty protection, or else it limits the builder's liability to you in case of a breach of warranty. Courts are virtually unanimous in rejecting the validity of these disclaimers. The usual grounds for rejection are: (1) the disclaimer was not worded plainly enough to alert the buyer to exactly what he was losing; and (2) the disclaimer is contrary to "public policy" (i.e., judges don't approve of it).

The only kind of disclaimer that might legally deprive you of warranty protection is one that sets forth clearly, conspicuously, and in detail, just what degree of protection you are giving up by accepting the disclaimer. For example, your contract with a builder might state that you, the buyer, are not relying on the builder for any warranty that the house will be free from defects caused by faulty workmanship and defective materials; or defects caused by faulty installation of plumbing, electrical, heating and cooling systems; or major construction defects in the structure of your house. If your contract has a disclaimer clause which is that specific, *don't sign it;* you'll be hard pressed later on to say you didn't understand what you were giving up.

Power Play Pointer. Any disclaimer clause you encounter is likely to be much more subtle than the one just suggested. It's exactly this kind of subtle, ambiguous clause that you can fight—and beat. Remember, courts won't let a builder trick you out of warranty protection.

Suppose your contract with the builder says that you accept the house "as is" or "in its present condition." Two weeks after you move in, so does an inch of sewage—your septic tank backs up into the house. When you demand that the builder make immediate repairs on the sewage system, he hems and haws, and points out that you took the house "as is," without any warranties.

No way! As the Missouri Supreme Court said of a similar situation: "We do not believe a reasonable person would interpret the disclaimer as an agreement by the purchaser to accept the house with an unknown latent structural defect." You just tell the builder that his "as is" clause won't take him half as far as he thinks. Tell him: "Your 'as is' clause is way too broad. No court in this country would let that monster swallow up the implied warranty. All your disclaimer does is alert me to obvious defects— not the kind of latent defect that went wrong here."

You could say the same sort of thing if, for example, the builder's disclaimer read: "There are no warranties on this house." Once again, this disclaimer is too highly generalized. It doesn't specifically let you know that you're waiving your rights under the implied warranty. Therefore, no court will enforce such an unwitting waiver against you.

The key point for you to bear in mind—and repeat whenever necessary—is that this implied warranty is imposed *by law*—that is, by courts and legislatures—not by written contracts or deeds. You have a right to warranty protection, which you can lose only if the builder's disclaimer is detailed and clear and you knowingly agree to it.

Now that you understand your warranty rights, how do you get what you're entitled to? The ultimate sanction when all else fails is, as might be suspected, a lawsuit. *A builder-seller who breaches the warranty can be held liable to the buyer for money damages.* Roughly speaking, there are seven elements that go into the making of such a lawsuit:

1. You bought a house from the builder-seller. (You may not have to be the original buyer, as we've already seen.)

2. You had no particular expertise in the construction of houses.

3. The builder held himself out as being competent in matters of house construction.

4. The house contains a substantial defect.

5. That defect was caused by the builder's improper design, materials, or workmanship.

6. The defect made your home fall below those minimum standards of habitability that courts now require (i.e., there was a breach of warranty).

7. As a result, you have suffered a loss.

If these elements are established in court, the builder will be liable to compensate you for your loss. The amount of that loss is generally calculated in one of two ways: either the amount of money it would reasonably cost you to repair the defect, or the difference between the market value of the house with and without the defect (i.e., the decrease in market value caused by the defect). Thus, if repairs to a leaking roof cost $1,700, the builder could be held liable for $1,700. If a crack in the foundation wall decreases the market value of the house by $5,000, that would be the amount you could recover from the builder.

In addition, you can usually recover the amount of any secondary damage that the defect may have caused you, such as personal injury, property loss, or hardship and inconvenience. For example, a leak in the roof, a flooded basement, or a sewer backup may ruin your floors, walls, furniture, etc.; impurities in the well water may permanently stain your clothing and linens. If this damage was caused by the breach of warranty, the builder will be liable for it.

Power Play Pointer. Short of suing the builder-seller for damages, what can you say or do to get your rights from him? Confront him with your knowledge of his soft spot—namely, his potential liability to you for breach of warranty. Use the prospect of a costly lawsuit and a big money judgment as leverage to pry the necessary repair work out of the builder.

To prepare for this confrontation, gather enough information so that you can impress on the builder exactly what he stands to lose if you drag him into court. Consult another contractor and get a written estimate of how much it would cost to fix the defect(s) in your house. Compare that figure with the decrease in market value attributable to the defects in your house. (You can get an estimate of the decrease from a real estate broker.) The latter figure will often exceed the former by a considerable amount (maybe even thousands of dollars). If so, use the big dollar figure as a measure of the builder's potential liability; it'll sober him up to how much he stands to lose by continuing to ignore you. (Don't forget to tote up any other damages you've suffered as a result of the defects, such as ruined furnishings. Add on this amount to the figure you're using.)

Make an appointment to meet with the builder. A good place would be the scene of the crime—your house! Explain to the builder that you want to try one last time to work things out with him before you "take legal action." Make it clear to the builder that you are prepared to sue him for breach of the implied warranty of habitability unless he cooperates with you. He may, of course, argue that no law has been broken. In that case, you'll have to use what you've learned from this chapter to convince the builder that his workmanship does fall below prevailing legal standards.

Go right for the builder's soft spot. Inform him just how high you think his liability might run. For example, you might say: "Real estate brokers have informed me that the market value of this house has dropped by at least ten thousand dollars because of the defects. You're the one who's going to foot that bill if I have to sue you, because you're responsible for the *decrease in market value*. I'm prepared to hold off on any legal action for a reasonable time, so long as you take all the steps necessary to make this place legally habitable."

You are now leaning on the builder's soft spot. The decrease in market value probably amounts to far more than it would cost the builder to fix your house. So you've given the builder a real cash incentive—unpalatable though he may find it—to cut his losses. Either he performs more construction work at his own expense or he runs the risk of having to pay for large price fluctuations in the real estate market. Chances are, if the cost of meeting your demands is less than the potential legal liability, the builder will be persuaded to choose what is for him the lesser of two evils.

When the builder comes around to your way of thinking, make sure he commits himself to take specific steps— no more vague promises. Set up a detailed work schedule with periodic deadlines so that you'll be able to gauge how work is progressing. You may have to renew your threat of a lawsuit if steady progress is not made.

Codeword Glossary

Barnes v. *Mac Brown and Company* This is a leading 1976 Indiana case, found in volume 342 of the North Eastern Reporter, Second Series, at page 619; it extended warranty protection to buyers of a used home.

Casavant v. *Campopiano*   This is a leading 1974 Rhode Island case, found in volume 327 of the Atlantic Reporter, Second Series, at page 831; it extended warranty protection to buyers of a used home.

cost of repairs   One measure of the builder's liability for breach of warranty.

decrease in market value   The other measure of a builder's liability, based on the difference between the market value of the house with and without the defect.

Duncan v. *Schuster-Graham Homes, Inc.*   This is a leading 1978 Colorado case, found in volume 578 of the Pacific Reporter, Second Series, at page 637; it extended warranty protection to buyers of a used home.

implied warranty of habitability   The legal principle that assures the buyer of a home that is reasonably fit to live in (for the legal citation for the case or statute that upholds this principle in your state, see Appendix B).

latent defect   The kind of hidden defect that a builder will generally be held responsible for, despite any disclaimer in the contract or deed.

money damages   Compensation for losses caused by breach of the implied warranty of habitability.

4 *Defective Products*

Of all the complaints consumers have, none is voiced more often or louder than: "It doesn't work!" After all, you work hard to earn your money, and you expect that money to buy a product that works.

In this chapter we will examine some strong power plays you can use against the people who sell defective merchandise. We will pay special attention to defective automobiles, since the problem occurs so frequently.

We shall also look at the problem of buying a defective product on credit. Since another company becomes involved —a credit card company or a finance company—you will need specially tailored power plays.

Getting a Refund on a Lemon

You just bought a brand-new space-age food processor from Foodglow, Inc. You unpack it, put all the pieces together, turn it on, and drop in a carrot, but instead of grinding it up, the machine grinds to a halt. About all your food processor can process is a marshmallow.

You take the machine back to Foodglow. They try to fix it. But the repairs just can't get the machine to operate properly. What you have is a lemon.

Indeed, one of the best-selling consumer products on the market today is the lemon. The seller may call it a food processor, or a camera, or a car, or anything else. But you know exactly what it really is. And when you get stuck with one of them, be prepared for a lot of aggravation.

The problem is that no one wants a lemon—including the store that sold it to you. They don't want it back. They have your money and would prefer to keep it that way. (Of course, if you bought on credit you can withhold payment, as we shall see later in this chapter.) Our goal, therefore, is to use a power play to get you your money back.

In order to determine your rights when you buy a defective product, we must break down all consumer products into two categories. In the first category are all products sold without any promises by the seller to do anything if the product turns out to be defective. Products sold "as is" fall into this category. (Another way of saying "as is" is an accompanying statement that "This product is sold without any implied warranties." If the product came with this statement on it, without any promise as to quality or workmanship, then it would be the equivalent of an "as is" product.) If you buy an "as is" product, expect to have no remedy if it goes kaput. What you bought is what you got, and no power play is going to help you.

Products in the second category come with a promise that the product will work. Sometimes this promise is spelled out in a warranty. Sometimes it is not written out at all. Under the law of all the states (except Louisiana), every product sold (with the exception of products sold "as is") has an *implied* warranty that it will do what it's supposed to. So, whether you have a written warranty or an implied warranty, the seller is promising you that the product you bought will work as you, a reasonable person, expect it should.

We will look at your rights if you buy any product with the promise that it will work (i.e., not sold "as is") and discover that it is defective. This covers 99 percent of all purchases, since in general only used or heavily discounted products are sold "as is."

Every state, with the exception of Louisiana, has adopted a law called the Uniform Commercial Code. The Code defines the rights and obligations of sellers and buyers of products. We will utilize this law in creating our power play.

When you buy a product, pay for it, and take it home (or take delivery of it), you have *accepted* the product. When you discover that the product does not do what it is supposed to, you want to send it back to the people you bought it from, i.e., reject it. In the law, this is called *revoking* your acceptance. Revocation is simply canceling your prior acceptance of the product. Once you have rejected the product, you can properly demand your money back.

When can you revoke the acceptance of a product? The Code tells us that revocation is proper if the defect in what you bought "substantially impairs its value" to you. An example will help you understand what this term means.

On November 30, 1972, Mr. Schumaker went to Ivers music store to buy an electric organ. On Ivers's recommendation, Mr. Schumaker bought a Story Clark Magi organ. The organ cost $1,119.72.

Approximately two weeks after the organ was delivered, one of the bass pedals stopped working. Shortly thereafter another bass pedal gave up, and then two keys on the keyboard followed suit. Mrs. Schumaker contacted Ivers, who sent a serviceman out. Repairs were made. The result was that now every octave on both keyboards had one key that did not work. Further calls were made, but the organ was simply a lemon. The Schumakers tried to get their money back, but Ivers refused. Then the Schumakers went to court.

The South Dakota Supreme Court decided *Schumaker v. Ivers* in 1976. The court pointed out that under section 2-608 of the Uniform Commercial Code, the Schumakers could properly revoke their acceptance of the organ if the defects in the organ "substantially impair[ed] its value" to them. The court then went on to point out that "[a]lthough the term 'substantial impairment' may not be susceptible of being precisely defined, surely it connotes more than merely minor, easily repairable defects in the goods." When the defect goes directly to the function of the product, then "substantial impairment" exists. And an organ on which some keys do not play is clearly substantially impaired. Therefore, the Schumakers were entitled to return the organ and get their money back in full.

If you use common sense you will be able to decide whether your purchase is substantially impaired. Remember, minor defects do not substantially impair a product. A scratch, for example, is not substantial. The problem we are dealing with is the real lemon. This is the mixer that can't mix, the television set that can't receive a channel or two (or receives them poorly), the toaster that won't pop up the toast, the typewriter that won't hit the letter *e*, and so on. If the problem goes to the ability of the product to do what it is supposed to, then it is substantially impaired.

Now, let's assume you purchased a product which you discover is substantially impaired. What should you do? The answer is that, under the law, you must try to get it fixed. Under most warranties repairs are provided. If you have no warranty, you still must give the seller a chance to fix the problem. If repair or replacement works, fine. You are happy. But, since we are dealing with lemons, repairs are not likely to help. One of the main characteristics of a lemon is that it keeps breaking down.

How many shots does the repairman get before you can revoke your acceptance? There is no magic number. In the case of the Schumakers' organ, the repairman was out three times and couldn't fix it. We recommend that you give the seller at least two chances to fix the product, more if you are tolerant.

Many of you will buy a product with a warranty that says your *only* remedy if the product is defective is to get it repaired. Does that mean you are stuck going back and forth to the repair shop with your lemon? Absolutely not. The law does not expect you to keep trying a remedy which does not work. Section 2-719 of the Code says that when a limited remedy fails "of its essential purpose," then you can revoke your acceptance. What this means is that if the product can't be repaired after a reasonable number of attempts, you can send it back and demand return of the purchase price. *That is true even though the warranty says you have the right only to get the product repaired.*

For example, let's assume you bought a substantially impaired washing machine. The warranty says that if the machine is defective your only remedy is to have it repaired —no cash refunds. You've tried repairs a couple of times, and the washing machine just won't work right. This is the time to use section 2-719 of the Uniform Commercial Code. The section says that you can disregard the warranty! You gave repairs a chance and they didn't work. You are well within your rights to refuse to continue going back and forth to the repair shop. You have the right to get your money back.

One final point before we explain how to revoke acceptance of a product. Under the Code, you must revoke within a reasonable amount of time after discovering that the product you bought is substantially impaired. You cannot keep using the product for months and then claim it is defective. The fact that you were using it will tend to show that the product was functioning.

Even if you are not using the product, don't put off revoking your acceptance. The longer you wait, the weaker your case will be. So long as you are trying to get the product repaired, you don't have to worry. But once you have given up, get back to the store and revoke!

Now you know that you have the right to revoke acceptance of the product you bought and that you should not put off doing it. How do you revoke an acceptance? Quite simply: walk into the store and say: "I revoke the acceptance of this product, which I bought here." Better still, write it down on a piece of paper and hand it to the person who sold you the product. That's it. You have now revoked your acceptance. Return the product and demand your money back—it's that simple.

Power Play Pointer. Let's assume you bought a TV set. A week after it's delivered, it breaks down. You give the repairman four cracks at repairing it, but it keeps going on the fritz. You have had enough. You visit the store and inform the manager: "I want to return the TV and get my money back." The manager is pleasant and suggests that a repairman be sent out again. You say: "I've had the repairman out four times and that's enough. I want my money back." The manager is likely to tell you it's not store policy to give cash refunds. He may take out a warranty card, point to it, and say: "Look at the warranty. Our only obligation is to repair the TV set." Your answer is: "Under the *Uniform Commercial Code,* if the repairs don't work, I don't have to keep trying. I hereby revoke my acceptance of the TV. I offer to return the TV set and I demand my money back." Be prepared to back up your demand with the appropriate sections of the Code from the codeword glossary.

We would recommend that as a precaution you revoke your acceptance in writing. It is not absolutely necessary, but if at some later time you go to court, you should have some concrete evidence that you revoked your acceptance and when the revocation occurred. Consider, therefore, preparing the following note:

> *[Insert date]*
>
> *I hereby revoke my acceptance of the [insert product] I bought at [insert name of store]. The product is substantially impaired and acceptance is being revoked pursuant to section 2-608 of the Uniform Commercial Code. I offer to return the product in return for the money I paid.*
>
> *[Signature]*

Make a copy of the note and keep it for your records.

When you go to the store to revoke your acceptance, hand the salesperson the note.

Sometimes sellers don't want to take the product back, despite your revocation. As we mentioned earlier, even the seller of a lemon doesn't want it back. If this occurs, you may be tempted to dispose of the product. Do not take your anger out on the product. Under the law, you have an obligation to take good care of that product so long as it is in your possession. We will provide you with an additional power play to help you convince a skeptical salesperson to take the product off your hands. And, as you will see, you may be able to charge the *seller* with any costs you incur in keeping that product in good condition.

Under section 2-715 you are entitled to collect *incidental* and *consequential damages* if you are sold a substantially impaired product. Here are examples of these damages.

Incidental Damages

Mr. Rodrigues bought some furniture from R. H. Macy & Co. Here is how a court later described what happened: "There was long delay and when finally delivered, the furniture did not conform to what [Rodrigues] had ordered. It would take pages to recount the further delay, inspections, phone calls, letters and general frustration which [Rodrigues] suffered in attempting to consummate the sale and furnish his home. And during this time, Macy's exhibited almost total indifference to the plight of this customer."

Mr. Rodrigues had not yet paid for the furniture. However, since it was in his home he had accepted it. He decided, therefore, to revoke his acceptance. He returned the furniture to Macy's. However, Mr. Rodrigues was not done yet. He went to small claims court to sue Macy's for the incidental damages he had suffered. Here is what the court said:

> [*Section 2-715 of the Uniform Commercial Code*]
> states ". . . *Incidental damages resulting from the seller's breach include expenses reasonably incurred in inspection, receipt, transportation and care and custody of goods rightfully rejected . . . and any reasonable expenses incident to that delay. . . ." The incidental damages listed are not intended to be complete but merely illustrate the kinds of incidental damages contemplated by the statute. . . . The court finds that* [*Mr. Rodrigues*] *suffered incidental damages of $150*

*for the care and custody of the [furniture] and for
handling and securing [its] return. . . . [Mr. Ro-
drigues] shall have judgment of $150 . . . with
interest . . . and cost and disbursements.*

In another example of incidental damages, the product
sold was a dog. A Labrador dog named Zein, to be precise.
Mary Wade put an ad in the St. Louis *Post Dispatch* advertising Zein for $300. The ad said Zein was a duck hunter.
Leonard O'Brien bought Zein.

To make a long story short, Zein did not like to go
into the water. As the court pointed out, "Zein was very
shy. She would go into the water but she was slow to go
into the water. Zein was not an aggressive hunting dog.
Labradors have to hit the water with great eagerness." The
court had no problem concluding that a hunting dog which
tiptoes into the water is substantially impaired.

As incidental damages, the court awarded O'Brien $90,
which was the cost of putting Zein up in a kennel after he
had tried to revoke his acceptance of the dog.

Consequential Damages

Unlike incidental damages, which arise when you suffer losses keeping or transporting the defective product,
consequential damages are your losses resulting directly
from the product itself. For example, in one case, *Belcher
v. Hamilton,* Ralph Hamilton bought a freezer from John
Belcher. The freezer kept breaking down and despite repeated efforts could not be made to work properly. Each
time it broke down all the food in the freezer spoiled.
Twice Hamilton lost over $400 in food. He sued Belcher
and collected the cost of the lost food as consequential damage.

Power Play Pointer. If you have problems convincing the seller to allow you to revoke your acceptance, remind him of your right to collect incidental and consequential damages. What damages you might have depends on what your purchase was. We have given you some examples. Be creative. Think how your particular defective product might cause you some losses. For example, do you have to rent a product to replace the one that was defective? The rental costs could be consequential damages. Might there be storage charges that could be considered incidental damages? When you have prepared yourself, be prepared to explain to the seller that "Under the *Uniform Commercial Code,* you are liable for *damages* I suffer because this product is defective. Unless you want to really lose a lot of money, I suggest you allow me to revoke my acceptance and give me my money back." Then give the seller examples of the types of damages you might claim.

We feel this power play will give you a solid chance to get your money back. However, if by some chance the seller is really obstinate, feel free to use the Uniform Commercial Code in small claims court. In Appendix A we explain how this court works. Prepare yourself for court by reviewing the appropriate sections from the codeword glossary so you can sound like a lawyer when you speak to the judge.

Defective Automobiles

In the preceding section we looked at your rights if you buy a lemon. Now we want to apply those rights to a specific problem: automobiles. We are devoting a separate section to this problem because Detroit is the birthplace of the lemon. Odds are, if you buy a lemon it will have an internal combustion engine.

We will not be supplying you with any additional power play pointers. The exact same principles discussed in the preceding section apply here. What we will do is give you more examples to help you decide when to revoke your acceptance when an automobile is causing the problem. Also, the cases we discuss will be part of the codeword glossary, to give you extra power when dealing with a car salesman.

Does the Uniform Commercial Code apply to motor vehicle purchases? Absolutely. Just read what one judge wrote when confronted with a tale of woe from a new-car buyer:

> *The facts present the complaint of an ever-increasing number of consumers who purchase new automobiles but who are thereafter unable to get necessary and satisfactory adjustments made on their new cars. In many cases these highly mechanized machines with so many moving parts will require careful alterations before they will run as smoothly as they should. The question we must consider is just how long the buyer must wait and how many unfulfilled promises may be made before he is entitled to revoke his acceptance of an automobile and be returned the purchase price. Our sympathies lie with those who repeatedly return their cars for repairs or service, then get them back in almost the same condition as when the complaints were originally registered. Sympathies aside, the law, ever just, provides a remedy for the situation where such a purchaser seeks to revoke his acceptance after receipt of and payment for the goods purchased.*

It is that remedy which we will look at now.

You will remember from the previous section that in order to revoke your acceptance you must meet certain requirements. They are: (1) the automobile must be substantially impaired; (2) the seller must have been given a reasonable chance to repair it; and (3) you must revoke your acceptance within a reasonable amount of time. Let's look at these requirements as they apply to automobiles.

Substantial Impairment

Motor vehicles are complicated pieces of machinery. There is a host of possible problems. The question is, what problems *substantially* impair the vehicle? One court which had the task of deciding this issue suggested that the "test ultimately rests on a common-sense perception of substantial impairment." In trying to make sense out of past court cases, the court found that there were various classifications into which particular defective cars fit. "Minor defects not substantially interfering with the automobile's operation or with the comfort and security it affords passengers do not constitute grounds for revocation. On the other hand, if the defect substantially interferes with operation of the vehicle or a purpose for which it was purchased, a court may find grounds for revocation. Indeed, substantial impairment has been found even where the defect is curable, if it shakes the faith of the purchaser in the automobile."

Your basic case of substantial impairment can be found in *Stream* v. *Sportscar Salon, Ltd.* The problem was that the engine was losing oil—so much oil, in fact, that the engine stopped. Tests showed the engine did not have sufficient compression. A new engine was installed, but the same problem developed. The buyer decided he had had enough and revoked acceptance of the car. The court concluded that the car was substantially impaired. The buyer got his money back.

In another case, *Zoss* v. *Royal Chevrolet, Inc.*, no single problem was very serious. Here's a rundown: imperfections in the exterior finish, the built-in burglar alarm going off for no reason, squeaky emergency brake, faulty window weather-stripping, water leak through hole where rearview mirror was attached, frayed carpeting, a front-end rattle, and other similar minor problems. Put them all together and you have a rotten car. The court decided that "[h]ere many of the non-conformities [i.e., defects] were not in and of themselves substantial. However, the cumulative effect of all the non-conformities so impaired the value of the [car] as to constitute substantial impairment to [the buyer]."

In most cases common sense will tell you when you have a substantially impaired vehicle. While a loose molding or a cracked battery is annoying, it is not substantial. It is the kind of problems the law expects you to get repaired. You can't demand your money back. But, from the examples we have discussed, you should be able to identify those problems that are substantial, those that turn a car into a lemon.

A Chance to Repair

Under the law, you must give the seller a chance to repair your car before you revoke your acceptance. There are no firm and fast rules dictating how often you must visit the repair shop before you can cancel the sale. Here's a typical case, *Stofman* v. *Keenan Motors, Inc.*

On March 9, 1972, a couple bought a car. The next day they returned it because it was vibrating. Repairs were made. On March 20 the car stalled. A fuel pump was replaced. On three other occasions the car stalled and minor adjustments were made. On April 16 the car stopped in traffic and had to be towed to the dealer. The fuel pump was replaced again. The following day the couple revoked acceptance of the car.

The court was confronted with a car dealer who claimed that "its willingness to repair the car free of charge rendered [the couple's] return of the car unjustifiable and unnecessary." To which the court responded: "Admittedly, a merchant-seller must be given a reasonable opportunity to correct defects in a product, but we believe that [the dealer] had more than ample opportunity to make these changes over the course of six weeks during which [the couple] brought the car in for service and specified the particular defects about which [they] were concerned."

Most new-car warranties try to limit your remedy for a defective car to "repair and replacement of parts." That's just what the Ford Motor Company tried to do in the case of *Riley* v. *Ford Motor Co.* Here's what Ford's warranty said: "[Ford warrants] to the first retail purchaser . . . that the Selling Dealer, at his place of business, and using new Ford parts or Ford authorized remanufactured parts, will repair or replace, free of charge . . . any of the following parts that are found to be defective. . . ." That was the only promise Ford was willing to make.

Mr. Riley bought a Ford having such a warranty. He encountered these problems: noise in the rear end, air conditioning did not work, speed control did not function, power seats became inoperative, the radio aerial functioned spasmodically, the rear seat did not fit, headlight panels were not synchronized, the cigarette lighter was missing, the transmission did not function properly, gear shift lever would not function, and the left door would not close properly.

Riley gave Ford a couple of chances to repair the Ford. Finally Ford sent a Technical Service Representative, who road-tested the car and recommended further repairs. Riley had had enough. As the court said, "[Riley] believed he had a better idea." He revoked acceptance of the car.

The court had no problem concluding that the car

was substantially impaired. The problem was that Ford claimed its only obligation was to repair and replace defective parts. But the court pointed to section 2-719 of the Uniform Commercial Code, which says that if a remedy provided by a seller does not work, the buyer can disregard it. In this case, Riley did give Ford a reasonable chance to repair the car. They could not do it. The remedy of repair and replacement had failed. Thus, under section 2-719, Riley was free to revoke acceptance of the car. And that is exactly what he did. The court ordered Ford to give Riley back the full purchase price of the car.

In each of the two cases we have discussed, the car buyer gave the seller at least two chances to repair the car before giving up and revoking acceptance. It's difficult to formulate a general rule for deciding when to give up on repairing or replacing parts. About the best rule is found in the case of *General Motors Corp.* v. *Earnest,* where the court said: "The seller does not have an unlimited time for the performance of the obligation to replace and repair parts. . . . This is not more than saying that at some point in time, it must become obvious to all people that a particular vehicle simply cannot be repaired or parts replaced so that [it] is made free from defect." When you reach that point in time, you have given the seller a chance to repair. You can disregard your warranty and revoke your acceptance.

Timely Revocation

You can't buy a car, have problems with it, drive it for six years, and then return it for your money back. You must revoke your acceptance within a reasonable time after having discovered that the car is substantially impaired.

From the cases we have read, this general rule is clear: so long as you are trying to get the car fixed, you don't have to worry about a delay in revoking your acceptance. The problem arises if you use the car after it has been repaired and then decide to revoke. Such use of the car would imply that the car was functioning properly.

We have read cases where a car buyer did not revoke acceptance of the car for over a year and encountered no problem in court. For example, in one case a car buyer did not revoke his acceptance until almost fourteen months after buying the car. However, a court hearing the case decided that "it is significant that [the buyer] was in almost constant touch with the dealer concerning the condition of the vehicle, relying on the dealer's continued assurances that the automobile would be repaired satisfactorily. When it became apparent to the buyer that repeated attempts at adjustment had failed, he unequivocally notified [the dealer] that he was revoking his acceptance. Under the circumstances of this case, involving an almost continuous series of negotiations and repairs, the delay in notice . . . was not unreasonable."

If you feel you have a lemon, do not wait to revoke your acceptance. Any delays can be costly. Once you have made up your mind, go directly to the dealer and revoke.

Damages

We saw in the preceding section that if you revoke acceptance of a product you are entitled to claim any damages you suffered from having received defective goods. What sort of damages are you likely to have if the defective product is a car?

The most obvious damage is loss of the use of the car. If you have to pay for alternate transportation, such as a rental car, you could properly claim that cost as incidental damages. For example, in the case of *Riley* v. *Ford Motor*

Co., the cost of alternate transportation amounted to $403.43, and that is what he was reimbursed for by the court.

Repairs which you had to pay before you revoked your acceptance would also be recoverable as damages. For example, in *Durfee* v. *Rod Baxter Imports,* the buyer spent $116.30 trying to repair his Saab before he gave up and revoked acceptance of the car. The court awarded him $116.30 as incidental damages.

Finally, incidental damages such as the cost of registering the car, parking it while it is out of service, having it towed, and other such losses suffered should be recoverable.

Sometimes car makers try to take away your right to incidental or consequential damages. After all, they don't want to open themselves up to the possibility of having to pay your damages. For example, in the Durfee case we just discussed, the warranty on the car specifically recited that the seller would not be liable for any incidental damages. The court nonetheless awarded damages of $116.30. How could they do that? The answer is that the court disregarded the attempt by the seller to limit his liability for damages. "To withhold incidental damages from a buyer revoking acceptance is to make cancellation of the contract a less than adequate remedy. . . . In these circumstances, [the buyer] is entitled to recover both his purchase price and incidental damages."

The authority for the court's action comes from good ol' section 2-719 of the Uniform Commercial Code. Under this section you have the right to disregard any attempt by the car dealer to limit your remedies.

Codeword Glossary

Belcher v. *Hamilton*   A state court case found in volume 475 of the South Western Reporter, Second Series, at page 483. The seller of defective goods is responsible for any consequential damages the buyer may suffer.

consequential damages   A monetary loss suffered by a buyer as a result of having purchased defective goods. These damages are authorized by section 2-715 of the Uniform Commercial Code.

Durfee v. *Rod Baxter Imports, Inc.*   A state court case found in volume 262 of the North Western Reporter, Second Series, at page 349. The buyer of a defective automobile is entitled to incidental damages. A car dealer cannot take this right away in a warranty.

incidental damages   A monetary loss suffered by a buyer as a result of having purchased defective goods. These damages are authorized by section 2-715 of the Uniform Commercial Code.

revoking acceptance   The legal term used to describe a consumer's right to return a defective product (see Uniform Commercial Code, section 2-608).   ·

Riley v. *Ford Motor Co.*   A federal court case found in volume 442 of the Federal Reporter, Second Series, at page 670. An example of a case where a car company tried to limit a car buyer's recourse for a defective car to repair and replacement of parts. This limitation was disregarded and the buyer could revoke his acceptance (see Uniform Commercial Code, section 2-719).

Rodrigues v. *R. H. Macy & Co., Inc.*   A small claims court case found in volume 391 of the New York Supplement, Second Series, at page 44. The buyer of defective goods (furniture in this case) may recover incidental damages to cover the cost of storing and transporting the defective goods ($150 in this case).

substantial impairment   The legal term used to describe the condition of a product which gives rise to the right to return the product and get your money back.

Uniform Commercial Code   The basic law governing sales in every state except Louisiana. Pertinent sections include:

    section 2-608   A buyer's right to revoke acceptance of substantially impaired products.

    section 2-711   The buyer of a substantially impaired product who revokes acceptance has the right to get the purchase price back from the seller.

    section 2-715   A buyer who revokes acceptance of defective goods has the right to incidental and consequential damages.

    section 2-719   Any attempt by the seller of defective goods to limit your remedy to repair or replacement of parts, or to limit your right to incidental or consequential damages, may be invalid.

Up Against a Finance Company

Buying on credit has its virtues and its drawbacks. One of its virtues is that you get the product before you have fully paid for it. If the product is defective you have leverage over the seller: you can revoke your acceptance and then you don't have to pay whatever is still owing. However, the folks who sell on credit are not fools. They don't like debtors to have leverage if a product proves defective. And, as we shall see, for a long time the law has helped counterbalance the leverage a credit purchase gave you. Let us explain.

    Let's assume you owe us $10. You are the debtor. We are the creditor. We take your IOU and sell it to a fellow named Bill for $9. You now owe Bill the $10, instead of us. We get less money, only $9, but we don't have to worry about collecting from you. Under the law, Bill has the right to collect the $10 from you, going to court if necessary. In legal jargon, Bill is called a *holder in due course*. He is a person to whom a debt has been transferred. So far there are no problems.

But let's complicate the situation a bit. Let's assume you owe us the $10 because we sold you an electric toothbrush that we promised would work well for at least a year. You took the toothbrush home and plugged it in; it exploded. You call us up to say you won't pay us the $10 because the electric toothbrush didn't work. We tell you that you don't owe us the $10 anymore. You now owe Bill.

You call up Bill to complain. Bill says he doesn't care about the toothbrush, he has an IOU and he wants to collect on it. If Bill goes to court, he can collect on that IOU. As a holder in due course, he can collect even though you may have a perfectly legitimate reason for not paying. So far as the law is concerned, your complaint is against us, the folks who sold you the toothbrush. Bill is innocent, and he's entitled to be paid.

You don't need much imagination to see how this holder in due course rule can be abused to cheat consumers. Obviously, selling goods on credit helps the seller sell more goods. But he becomes vulnerable, since if the goods prove to be defective you have the simple remedy of not paying for them. If the seller can sell your obligation to pay to someone else, then, under the holder in due course rule, you have to pay regardless of whether the merchandise is defective or not. *You have to pay that holder in due course even if the goods are defective.* Your only remedy is to sue the seller in court to get your money back. And in many cases that is simply not economical. Attorney's fees can be higher than the cost of what you bought. And sometimes the seller will simply go out of business, leaving you with no one to sue.

This may sound technical but, believe us, the holder in due course rule was used to rip off consumers every day. Here, for example, is an actual case.

John Hatch went to buy a used car. The used-car salesman, Mr. Compact, took Hatch to the American Consumer Discount House, where Hatch signed some papers to get the car on credit. The total price of the car was $1,512. Needless to say, the car, despite its warranty, did not work at all. The dealer refused to fix it. Hatch went to American Consumer Discount House, the people who had financed the car purchase, and was told: "This is your baby. . . . We gave you a personal loan." Hatch couldn't use the car. The dealer wouldn't fix it. And American Consumer sued Hatch for the money he owed. According to Hatch, "my home and all of my possessions were up for a sheriff's sale. They repossessed the car. They sold it to me for $1,512, and about a month later they sold the same car for $300 because it wasn't in good shape."

According to the Federal Trade Commission, such abuse of the holder in due course rule was especially prevalent in the sale of courses of training or instruction, furniture and appliances, home improvements, automobiles, carpeting, alarm systems, and swimming pools. However, the problem can appear whenever you make a credit purchase.

The problem remained serious until 1975, when the Federal Trade Commission passed a Trade Regulation Rule, which went into effect on May 14, 1976. It's called "Preservation of Consumers' Claims and Defenses," and here's how it works.

The Rule applies to purchases of consumer goods or services. It does not cover commercial purchases.

The Rule applies to all credit agreements. The only exceptions are purchases on a credit card (that problem is discussed in the next section) and purchases costing over $25,000 (get a lawyer before you buy).

Here's how the Rule operates. It requires that every consumer credit purchase agreement have the following clause in the agreement itself:

Notice

Any holder of this consumer credit contract is subject to all claims and defenses which the debtor could assert against the seller of goods or services obtained pursuant hereto or with the proceeds hereof. Recovery hereunder by the debtor shall not exceed amounts paid by the debtor hereunder.

This clause becomes part of the contract itself. Under the clause, your rights are protected against the holder in due course. Thus, regardless of whom your debt is sold to, you can raise the same claims and defenses you had against the seller.

For example, assume you buy a car on time. The installment contract must have the clause in it. If the car salesman sells the contract to a finance company, the clause will remain in the contract. Now let's assume the car is a lemon. You decide to revoke your acceptance and stop paying for it. You have the right to refuse to pay the finance company. The finance company stands in the same position as the seller. You are free, therefore, to use the rights we explained earlier in this chapter against the finance company.

There is one exception to this Rule. You remember that earlier in this chapter we explained that under certain circumstances you can sue the seller of defective merchandise for incidental and consequential damages. Under the Federal Trade Commission Rule, you cannot sue the finance company (the holder in due course) for any damages. All you are entitled to recover is the amount you have already paid to either the seller or the finance company. Of course, you are still free to sue the *seller* for damages if you want. But the finance company will not have to pay any damages.

Just to make sure you understand this Rule, let's take one final example. Let's assume you buy a $1,000 piano on time. You pay $100 down and agree to pay $100 a month for nine months. The piano company sells the installment contract to Acme Finance Co. The piano is "substantially impaired" and you revoke acceptance. If the finance company comes after you, you can properly claim that you have revoked acceptance and no longer owe any money. You are then free to sue the seller for any incidental or consequential damages you suffered. You could also sue the seller for your down payment. However, since you have the piano and the finance company can't get your money, you are in a good position to negotiate a settlement.

In this situation, the seller was the person who gave you credit. He then sold the credit agreement to somebody else. Often credit is extended in a different way. The seller does not give you the credit and then sell the credit agreement to a finance company. Instead, he puts you in touch with someone who lends you money. For example, in the case of John Hatch, the used-car dealer didn't give Hatch credit for the purchase. Instead, he took Hatch by the hand to American Consumer Discount House. They gave him the credit by giving him the money to pay the used-car dealer. This situation is called a *purchase-money loan*.

The Trade Regulation Rule applies only to certain purchase-money loans. Specifically, it applies only if the seller is affiliated with, or refers you to, the person who gives you credit. For example, automobile sellers frequently establish organizations to give car purchasers credit. If you finance a car purchase using such an affiliated finance company, the Trade Regulation Rule applies. Likewise, if the seller refers you to a particular finance company for credit, the Rule applies. In both situations there is a formal or informal relationship between the seller and the creditor. And in both cases you can treat the creditor as if he were the seller should you get defective merchandise.

That leaves one situation in which the Rule does not apply. If you go out and get your own purchase-money loan without any help from the seller, then the old holder in due course rule applies; if you have a problem with your purchase, the creditor won't care. He doesn't know what you bought with your money, and he shouldn't be responsible if it is defective. And that is exactly what the law says. So if you go to a bank and borrow $5,000 and then go out and buy a car, the bank is not governed by the Rule. They will want their money regardless of what happens to the car.

Power Play Pointer. Use the leverage the Federal Trade Commission has provided you with. If you believe you have a substantially impaired product, follow the rules we have already discussed to revoke your acceptance. In addition, you will have to notify the creditor, the person you owe the money to, that you have revoked your acceptance.

If the seller is the same person who gave you credit, you need only notify the seller that you have revoked your acceptance. If the seller claims that as the creditor he is entitled to get paid regardless of the condition of the merchandise, simply refer him to the Federal Trade Commission Trade Regulation Rule. For example, assume you bought a radio on credit from Sound, Inc. Each month you pay Sound, Inc., an installment. Sound, Inc., is the creditor. If the radio is defective, you can revoke your acceptance. If Sound, Inc., claims that as the creditor you must pay regardless of the condition of the merchandise, just say: "The *Federal Trade Commission* has decided that I don't lose any of my rights because I bought on credit." Be prepared to refer to the Trade Regulation Rule if necessary to drive your point home.

In some cases the person to whom you owe the money will not be the person from whom you bought the merchandise. This can occur when the seller transfers your debt to a finance company. It can also occur when the seller directs you to a finance company that lends you the money to buy the merchandise (a purchase-money loan). In either case, you will have to notify the creditor that you have revoked your acceptance with the seller. We suggest you do this in a letter sent to the person to whom you owe the money. Here's what the letter might say:

> *Dear Sir:*
>
> *I am revoking acceptance of [describe product] bought at [insert name of store] since it is substantially impaired. Under the Federal Trade Commission's Holder in Due Course Rule (16 Code of Federal Regulations section 433.1) I am asserting my rights under sections 2-608 and 2-719 of the Uniform Commercial Code. Please contact me so that we may resolve this matter quickly.*
>
> > *Sincerely,*
> > *[Signature]*

We suggest you send the letter by certified mail, return receipt requested. You should also keep a copy of the letter for your records.

You should now be in a good position to negotiate a settlement. Remember, since you have revoked acceptance of the product, it is technically not your property. Be prepared to return it in exchange for your money. And be sure to take good care of the product until it is returned.

Codeword Glossary

Federal Trade Commission   A federal agency that protects consumers' rights and that issues Trade Regulation Rules and enforces the Rules. A list of Federal Trade Commission Regional Offices is in Appendix E.

holder in due course   The person or company to which a debt is transferred.

purchase-money loan   Money lent to you on credit so you can buy a product.

Trade Regulation Rule   Found in volume 16 of the Code of Federal Regulations in section 433.1, this Rule gives you the same rights against a holder in due course as you had against the seller.

When You Charge a Lemon

The future is in plastic. Credit cards, to be precise. In fact, for most of us the future is now. Our wallets and purses are filled with multicolored wafers of plastic which can translate into dinners, airplane trips, and products. We all know the dangers of credit cards. Mother warned us about spending money we didn't have. But there are some advantages also. As we shall see, buying on credit can help you out when what you bought does not measure up to what you thought you bought.

Advertisers of credit cards are quick to tell us the advantage of having ready credit. When you see that once-in-a-lifetime buy, a hundred-dollar television perhaps, and you have only ninety dollars, just use your credit card. What the advertisements do not tell us is what you can do when you get home, plug in the TV, and blow out your circuit breaker. There you sit, in the dark, when eventually the bill from the credit card company arrives. One TV: $100. You write out your check in the dark, knowing that your credit card company does not care about your TV problems. Or do they? As we shall see, whether they like it or not, they must care about your TV.

In 1975 changes were made in the Truth in Lending Act that were designed to protect users of credit cards. Congress saw the potential for abuse in credit card transactions and sought to protect the consumer. One of the regulatory changes was designed to protect a hapless hypothetical TV purchaser.

Before we get to the specifics of how this law helps you, we should provide a definition. What is a credit card? Obviously, the big companies such as Master Charge, American Express, Diners Club, Visa, and the like issue credit cards. But what about cards issued by the local department store, the florist, or the supermarket? The answer is that all of these are credit cards. In fact, any card, plate, coupon book, or similar device with which you can buy something now and pay for it later is a credit card for our purposes.

Now let's assume you bought a product or a service and paid for it with a credit card. Perhaps you bought a sofa and paid with a credit card. Or maybe you had your television set repaired and paid the serviceman with a credit card. If you have a problem with the product or service, the Truth in Lending Law is for you. Here is how the law works.

If you buy a product or a service from a nearby store using a credit card and that product or service turns out to be defective, you do not have to pay your credit card bill. It sounds simple, and it is. There are some restrictions, as we shall see. But this rule is still an extremely effective tool for dealing with shoddy products or services.

The first restriction is that the product or service you purchased must have cost at least $50. Small purchases simply do not get the protection of this law.

Second, the place you bought the product or service from must be located in the state in which you live (which is where your credit card bill is sent). If it is not within your state, it must be within one hundred miles of where you live. Thus, for example, if you live in New York City and buy a product in Newark, New Jersey, this regulation will help you, since Newark is less than one hundred miles from New York City.

There is one situation in which you do not have to worry about these distance restrictions. If the person you bought the product or service from also, directly or indirectly, is owned or franchised by the credit card issuer, then the distance restrictions do not apply. For example, assume you live in Los Angeles. You are on a trip and use your Mobil credit card to get your car fixed at a franchised Mobil dealer in Ohio. The regulation applies to you. Even though you are not in your state or within a hundred miles of your home, you fit into the rule, since Mobil issued the credit card and also franchises the dealer from whom you bought the service.

Under the law, if you buy a product or service and find it is defective, you must first make a good-faith attempt to resolve the dispute. Thus, you must go back to the store from which you bought the product or service and honestly try to get satisfaction. (If the store is far from where you live, a letter will do.) For example, if the service was not properly performed, ask that the serviceman be sent out again. If a product is defective, either get a new one or get your money back. Remember that you are legally required to act in good faith before you can refuse to pay the bill.

Let's assume that despite all the good faith you can muster, the store just can't repair or replace the defective product. What you have is a lemon. Earlier in this chapter we explained what your rights are if you buy a lemon. You know that if the product is "substantially impaired" you have the right to return it and get your money back. In this case, since you used a credit card, you don't have to get any money back. You just have to get the credit card company to stop billing you for the product. And that is exactly what the Truth in Lending Law helps you do.

Under Regulation Z of the Truth in Lending Act, you have the right not to pay a credit card company for your purchase of a defective product costing over $50. All you have to do is notify the credit card company that the product they are billing you for is defective. That's all there is to it. Then it's up to the store from which you bought the product to work out a resolution of the problem with you.

Power Play Pointer. Write a letter, following this basic format.

[Insert date]

Dear Sir:

On [insert date] I bought a [insert product] from [insert name of store]. My credit card number is [insert your number]. I have made a good faith attempt to resolve a problem resulting from a defect in the product purchased. I have not been able to resolve the problem and request that pursuant to section 226.13 of Regulation Z my account not be billed for the amount of the purchase. The amount is [insert the cost of the product].

Sincerely,
[Signature]

Bring the letter to the store. Show it to the person who sold you the product. Tell him that if you don't get your money back, you will send the letter off to the credit card company. The letter speaks for itself. However, you may want to add: "If I send this letter off, the credit card company won't pay you. If you want to get the problem resolved, you might as well just settle it now." If the problem is not resolved, send the letter off to the credit card issuer.

The ball is now in the store's court. So far as the credit card issuer is concerned, they will not pay the store. So far as you are concerned, you will not pay the credit card issuer. That means the only loser is the store, and sooner or later they are likely to get in touch with you. Under the law, you and the store are left to work out your dispute on your own. Once it is worked out, the credit card issuer will abide by the resolution (either billing you or dropping the particular charge entirely).

We have already explained what your rights are if you buy a defective product. Use those rights. And take advantage of the added leverage the Truth in Lending Law gives you. Since you have not paid for the product yet, the seller will be anxious to come to a quick settlement.

One problem may be bothering some of you. You are used to paying your bills on time. You value your credit rating. Will the fact that you are not paying for the defective product or service adversely affect your credit rating? Under the law, the answer is no. The store is not permitted to report you to any person as a delinquent until the dispute is settled. And the dispute can be settled only if you agree to a settlement with the store or a judge decides who is right. So using this law should not adversely affect your credit rating.

This power play, designed to force a store to resolve your dispute, can fail if the credit card issuer goes after you to pay your bill. Under the law, they are supposed to wait until you have resolved your problem with the store. However, in the event they do not follow the law, you may need some help to get them off your back.

Credit card issuers who violate the law can be sued.

Under the law, you are entitled to collect from $100 to $1,000, depending on how big your purchase was. In no case can you collect less than $100. Thus, if a credit card issuer notifies you that they do not care what problems you are having, they want to get paid, they have violated the law and you can sue them. You could use small claims court, since for most purchases you will be suing for only $100. But still, $100 for a night at court is not bad! Check Appendix A to see how to sue in small claims court.

When you go to small claims court, be sure to bring along the copy of the letter you sent to the credit card issuer notifying them of the defect in the goods or services you purchased. Bring along any evidence to show that the credit card issuer is refusing to accept your excuse for not paying. Tell the judge that under section 130 of the Truth in Lending Act you are suing for a minimum award of $100.

Codeword Glossary

Regulation Z   Regulations found in volume 12 of the Code of Federal Regulations at section 226 that were issued under the Truth in Lending Act.

Truth in Lending Act   A federal law found in title 15 of the United States Code at section 1601. The Act gives the Board of Governors of the Federal Reserve System authority to issue regulations to protect users of credit cards.

5 Employment Problems of the Working Woman

"What do you want to be when you grow up?" Little boys are asked that question all the time. They respond dutifully: a fireman, a policeman, a lawyer, a doctor, an astronaut, etc. They know they can be whatever they want to be, at least in their youthful imaginations. Little girls don't have to worry about what they want to be when they grow up. No one ever asks them. Everyone knows. Little girls grow up to be mothers of little boys and little girls.

Some little girls apparently have grown up wanting more. They have wanted to be firefighters and police officers and lawyers and doctors and astronauts, etc. They have also wanted to be welders, and pursers on ships, and filmmakers, and do all the other jobs traditionally thought of as "men's work." With the help of some important laws and a lot of perseverance, they have succeeded. This chapter is about the laws they used and how you too, using these laws, can grow up to be whatever you want.

The relationship between an employer and employee (or prospective employee) is uniquely sensitive. In many

79

businesses, the employer—the very person who is denying you your rights—is the person with whom you must work each day. The person who is denying you your rights is writing out your paycheck. Is it any surprise, therefore, that many women are reluctant to assert their rights because they fear that their employer will retaliate by firing or demoting them?

The first type of discrimination we shall examine involves getting a job. Here there is little danger of retaliation by an employer, since you obviously can't be fired or demoted if you didn't get the job in the first place.

The second and third types of discrimination we discuss involve problems you may encounter on the job: unequal working conditions and sexual blackmail. We will provide you with the tools to rationally persuade your employer to stop discriminating against you. We believe you can use diplomatically applied pressure to get your rights. Properly used, our power plays should not result in retaliation by an employer. However, we recognize that some employers may be greatly intimidated by a well-informed woman. The chance of retaliation always exists. So we begin our discussion by pointing out that retaliation is against the law. The law specifically prohibits an employer from taking any action against you as a result of your asserting your rights under the law. Thus, if you are fired or demoted because you exercised your rights, the employer can be ordered to reinstate you to your old job. In addition, the court can order that you receive back pay to compensate you for the time you were out of work or in a poorer job. These legal protections are by no means guaranteed, and getting your rights if you are the victim of retaliation is a slow and uncertain process. The law does not work quickly and retaliation is hard to prove. You are in the best position to judge whether your employer will retaliate if you assert your rights. Balance the risk involved against the likelihood and importance to you of getting your rights and decide whether the risk is worth taking.

Title VII of the Civil Rights Act

The primary source of protection against job discrimination is Title VII of the Civil Rights Act of 1964. When this law was just a bill pending before the House of Representatives, it was not meant to deal with sex discrimination. Only at the last minute was the word *sex* included as an illegal basis for discrimination. Back in 1964, few foresaw what impact the inclusion of a single word would have on the rights of women.

The basic purpose of Title VII is stated in section 703(a):

> *It shall be an unlawful employment practice for an employer—*
>
> *(1) to fail or refuse to hire or to discharge an individual, or otherwise to discriminate against any individual with respect to his compensation terms, conditions, or privileges of employment, because of such individual's race, color, religion, sex, or national origin; or*
>
> *(2) to limit, segregate, or classify his employees or applicants for employment in any way which would deprive or tend to deprive any individual of employment opportunities or otherwise adversely affect his status as an employee because of such individual's race, color, religion, sex or national origin.*

This broad prohibition against sex discrimination has some exceptions. First, the law itself does not apply to all employers. Second, there are some limited situations in which sex may be taken into account by an employer.

Title VII applies only to employers having at least 15 employees. This represents a sharp reduction over the requirements when the law first went into effect (a minimum of 100 employees). As the number of employees required for coverage by the law has decreased (to 75 in 1966; 50 in 1967; 25 in 1968; and 15 in 1973), the number of businesses to which the law applies has increased. Although Title VII has been around since 1964, you may very well be applying for a job or work at a business which became subject to the law only in 1973 (a business with only 20 employees, for example).

The only other requirement is that your job be in an "industry affecting commerce." Roughly translated, this means that the business must in some way affect the movement of goods or services across state lines or international borders. Don't worry too much about this requirement. The way the courts have interpreted it, most sizable businesses "affect commerce" in some way. In one case the owner of an office building claimed he was not engaged in commerce, but the court pointed out that his elevators carried mailmen delivering the mail from out of state, and the cleaning people used detergents made in other states. You get the picture. As a practical matter, most businesses somehow affect commerce.

Even if you work for a small business which does not affect commerce, you are not out of luck. Most states have laws that are very similar to Title VII. These laws do not require that a business affect commerce before employees can receive protection. Thus, if you are not covered by Title VII, contact your state or local human rights commission. (The addresses are in Appendix C.)

If your job, or prospective job, *is* with a business (1) having 15 or more employees and (2) affecting commerce, you have the protection of Title VII. There remains one situation in which an employer covered by Title VII may nonetheless take sex into account in making employment decisions. It's called the *bona fide occupational qualification* (BFOQ) exception. Common sense generally dictates when this exception applies. Consider whether, as a woman, you would expect to get a job as a model for men's clothing. Should a man be entitled to claim sex discrimination if he didn't get a job as a wet nurse? Of course not. In each of these cases, *the gender of the job applicant is a legitimate qualification for properly performing the job.* Therefore, legally speaking, sex is a BFOQ for the modeling and wet-nurse jobs.

Title VII permits employers to consider the sex of a person when considering him or her for a particular position for which sex is a BFOQ. While common sense normally dictates when an occupational qualification is bona fide or phony, sometimes the line is not so easy to draw. We will look at specific examples of BFOQs.

While all this talk about BFOQs and "affecting commerce" may sound imposing, it really is not. Just remember the basic requirements in order for you to be covered by Title VII's protection:

1. 15 or more employees;
2. the employer's business somehow affects commerce; and
3. sex is not a BFOQ.

If the job you are applying for—or have—is with a covered employer, you have Title VII on your side. If you want to make absolutely certain you have the protection of Title VII, contact your nearest office of the United States Equal Employment Opportunity Commission (EEOC). This agency helps enforce Title VII and will be able to tell you whether you are covered. (A list of regional EEOC offices is in Appendix D.)

Getting a Job

In 1975 a federal judge observed: "Title VII is a vital instrument in the long struggle to establish the right of prospective employees to be hired on the basis of merit and not turned away at the hiring gate by the scourge of . . . sex discrimination. We have moved far from the days when the employer, in his absolute judgment, without any accountability, could hire or fire at will." For many employers, however, it is still difficult to accept the fact that they do not have total freedom to pick and choose whom they will hire. They cling to the idea that they can use their sixth sense to make hiring decisions. Sixth senses have a way of reflecting stereotyped notions about men and women. It is just this kind of discrimination in hiring that Title VII tries to control.

There are two ways in which sex discrimination during job hunting can occur. First, an employer simply bases his decision not to hire you on the fact that you are a woman. Second, an employer establishes hiring rules that, though they appear fair, actually have the effect of discriminating against women. For example, a rule providing that all plumbers must be at least six feet tall *regardless of sex* may sound fair on its face. However, if a woman could prove that the *impact* of the rule is that few women qualify because women tend to be shorter than men, she may make out a case of sex discrimination. Only if the employer could justify the rule on the basis of some real business necessity would the rule be permitted to stand—for example, if he could prove that to be a good plumber you must be at least six feet tall, the rule might be justified.

If you are confronted with an employer who has established a rule that appears nondiscriminatory but that has the result that few women, if any, qualify for the job, we sug-

gest you contact the nearest EEOC office. (See Appendix
D.) We do not feel a power play is likely to work against
an employer who has established a rule that appears fair
but that in reality discriminates. You will probably need the
help of the EEOC or a lawyer to convince an employer
practicing this type of subtle discrimination that he is violating the law.

But now let's look at the first kind of discrimination—
the kind that occurs most frequently. In these cases, the
employer clearly takes sex directly into account when making an employment decision. The United States Supreme
Court in the landmark decision of *McDonnell Douglas
Corp.* v. *Green* explained the basic requirements necessary
to prove this kind of sex discrimination in hiring: (1) you
are a woman; (2) you applied and qualified for a job for
which the employer was seeking applicants; (3) despite
your qualifications you were rejected; and (4) after your
rejection, the position remained open and the employer
continued to seek applications from persons with your qualifications. This is your classic case of sex discrimination.
There are variations on the theme. But every case shares
one basic element: the employer based his decision, at
least in part, on your sex.

Power Play Pointer. Most employers know better than
to come right out and say "We don't hire women for this
job." Usually they will simply turn down your job application with no explanation. This is where the Supreme Court's
test from *McDonnell Douglas Corp* v. *Green* comes in very
handy. If you apply for a job opening and don't get the job,
and the position remains unfilled or is filled by a man, you
have a case of sex discrimination. Use the McDonnell case
as leverage to get the employer to give you a reason why
you were not hired. Tell him that if the reason you were not

hired was your sex, he has violated the law. The burden is now on the employer to come up with an explanation for his employment decision.

While the McDonnell case is useful, many employers know about the case. They know better than not to give you a reason for not hiring you. And they know that sex should not be one of the reasons. So they create some other excuse which sounds fair.

Consider the case of *East* v. *Romine, Inc.* Cora East was a welder in Savannah, Georgia. On April 24, 1969, she applied for a welding job at Romine, Inc. She did not get a job. Later during the same year, Romine did hire welders on nine occasions. All nine welders hired were men. There was no evidence that Cora East was not qualified as a welder. Rather, the employer claimed that her past employment record was not good.

The court applied the Supreme Court's *McDonnell Douglas* criteria: "As a woman, Ms. East is in a group protected by Title VII. She formally applied for a welding job and was at least presumptively qualified on the basis of an application which showed a long history of welding work. Romine, Inc. accepted applications whenever they came in, and Ms. East was not offered a job. Lastly . . . Romine hired nine welders within six months after East made her application." The Court concluded Cora East had made out a case of sex discrimination.

That left the question of whether Cora East's past employment record was a proper ground for refusing employment. Here the court made an important point.

The evidence in the case went purely to East's prior work record. There was no comparative evidence introduced as to the work histories of the nine men hired in the subsequent six months. . . . If someone

*is hired, and if there is more than one applicant for the
position, then the decision as to which person to hire is
necessarily a comparative process. Introducing
evidence as to only one person does not explain how
some other person was chosen. . . . The employer
cannot merely say that he looked into her record with
other employers unless he also engages in the
complementary enterprise of making the same check
upon the persons he did hire when those persons were
males and the applicant who alleges discrimination is
female.*

Thus, Cora East had the right to have her qualifications
judged by an objective standard. Was she more or less
qualified than the men hired for the job? The requirement
of an objective standard in hiring makes it impossible for
an employer to simply dismiss your job application because
"you're not qualified."

Power Play Pointer. The most frequently used device
for discriminating against women job applicants is the subjective judgment. "You're not qualified." "Your work record
isn't very good." "You don't have enough experience." What
are you supposed to say when told this? The answer is found
in *East* v. *Romine, Inc.* If a man was hired for the job, you
have the right to know why he was better qualified than
you. You have the right to an objective evaluation. The employer cannot hide behind a subjective evaluation. You are
within your rights to ask: "Why was Joe, whom you hired,
better qualified than I was?" And if Joe was not better qualified than you, you have a case of sex discrimination.

Sometimes an employer refuses to hire women because
he believes that women *as a whole* cannot perform the job.
Unlike the case where Cora East was refused a job because

the employer thought she was not fit, this situation arises when the employer believes that all women are not fit. He believes that there is a particular qualification for the job that calls for a man. This is what we referred to earlier in this chapter as the bona fide occupational qualification, or BFOQ. A couple of examples will help explain when such an occupational qualification is bona fide and when it is not.

Let's assume you are applying for a job in a men's prison. There are two job openings. One is for a correctional counselor, where your task would be to maintain security. The other job is as a cook.

If you choose to apply for the correctional counselor's position, the prison could legally refuse to hire you simply because you are a woman. The reason, as explained by the United States Supreme Court, is that "a woman's relative ability to maintain order in a male, maximum security, unclassified penitentiary . . . could be directly reduced by her womanhood. . . . The employee's very womanhood would thus directly undermine her capacity to provide the security that is the essence of a correctional counselor's responsibility." It's not that the job is dangerous. Rather, the sex of the jobholder directly affects the ability of the jobholder to do the job. That makes sex a bona fide occupational qualification. At least, so concluded the Supreme Court.

However, would sex be a BFOQ if you applied for the position of cook, where your responsibility is not security but rather preparing food? New York State's Department of Correctional Services thought it was. They refused the job of cook to a woman because she was a woman. They claimed the job was too dangerous. After all, "it is dangerous for a female to work alone in a prison during the early morning hours and [the prison authorities] are not willing to risk the consequences. . . ."

In this case, however, the court ordered the prison to hire the woman cook:

> *Title VII rejects . . . this type of romantic paternalism [i.e., protecting women by excluding them from dangerous jobs] as unduly Victorian and instead vests individual women with the power to decide whether or not to take on unromantic tasks. Men have always had the right to determine whether the incremental increase in remuneration for strenuous, dangerous, obnoxious, boring or unromantic tasks is worth the candle. The promise of Title VII is that women are now on equal footing. We cannot conclude that by including the bona fide occupational qualification exception Congress intended to renege on that promise.*

In order to help you understand just how narrow the BFOQ loophole is, here are some examples of jobs for which sex was found *not* to be a BFOQ.

Lifeguard. A hotel operator refused to hire a female lifeguard, claiming that "most of its guests who use the pool are male and that the additional duties of the lifeguard are such that only male applicants could perform them." The additional duties involved cleaning the locker rooms and the pool area. The Equal Employment Opportunity Commission decided that the hotel had not established a BFOQ. "It is obvious that, if a male can clean the women's locker room, a female can clean the men's locker room." As to a female's ability to clean the pool, the Commission dismissed this claim by pointing out that the hotel "has produced no evidence that all or substantially all females are unable to perform the duties."

Lifting Boxes. A woman applied for a job which required lifting boxes. She was refused because the employer felt young women should not (and could not) lift boxes. The Commission decided the employer "has introduced no evidence concerning the lifting abilities of . . . female applicants. [He] assumes on the basis of a 'stereotyped characterization' that women cannot in general lift boxes, while all men are treated as if they can. . . . It is clear that using class stereotypes denies desirable positions to a great many women perfectly capable of performing the duties involved. Upon the evidence . . . the Commission finds [the employer's] contention that the job classification falls within the bona fide occupational qualification exemption is without merit."

Power Play Pointer. Employers like to be protective. They may genuinely feel they are helping you. Chances are, however, that they have just stereotyped women and cannot imagine them doing dangerous, strenuous, or "unladylike" work. If confronted with an employer who suggests that the job you are applying for is too dangerous, do not respond with: "But I want to do dangerous work." This is likely to reinforce the employer's paternalistic instincts. Instead, try this response: "The *Equal Employment Opportunity Commission* has decided that the danger or strenuousness of a job is not a *bona fide occupational qualification.*" This response places the emphasis on your *right* to work, as opposed to your *desire* to work. Desires are easy to sidestep. Rights are not.

Ship Purser. In another case, a steamship company refused to employ female pursers. The company claimed there were not separate toilet and shower facilities on the ships. The Commission pointed to the law, 29 Code of Federal Regulations section 1604.(a)(1)(iv), which specifically provides: "[t]he fact that the employer may have to provide separate facilities for a person of the opposite sex will not justify discrimination under the bona fide occupational qualification exception unless the expense would be clearly unreasonable."

Finally, there is the case of the company that refused to put a woman in a job which required her to, among other tasks, take customers on plant tours, take customers to football games and to dinner, and take customers on hunting trips. The reason the company gave for not hiring women was that male customers would not go on hunting trips with female managers unless they were "built like Raquel Welch." The Commission refused to consider the bra size of a woman job applicant to be a BFOQ. The fact that customers or coworkers would prefer to have a man in the job is not a legitimate basis for discriminating against women. In fact, this type of stereotyping is just what the law is designed to prohibit. On pages 102–103 we explain your rights if your employer violates the law. You will find additional power plays to help you get your rights.

Working Conditions

Physical Surroundings

Title VII's prohibition of employment discrimination covers working conditions. This does not mean that every woman employee is entitled to good working conditions. Title VII doesn't guarantee good treatment, only equal treatment for both men and women. So you must ask yourself this question: Am I, a woman, working under poorer conditions than men working for the same employer and doing the same type of work? If the answer is yes, chances are your employer is violating Title VII.

A good example of women's right to equal working conditions is found in *Laffey* v. *Northwest Airlines, Inc.*

The problem was different working conditions for men and women flight attendants. Women were required to remain under a weight limit; men were not. Women shared rooms on stopovers; men had single rooms. Women were not permitted to wear glasses; men were. Women had to use luggage of a specific size, color, and brand; men had no limits on the type of luggage they could use. Women could not exceed 5 feet 9 inches in height; men could be up to 6 feet tall. Women were not permitted to marry; men were. Women had to stop flying at age 32; men had no age limit. We could go on and on. In each and every one of the differences mentioned above, the court found a violation of Title VII. Men and women were being treated differently and there was no acceptable reason.

Power Play Pointer. Many employers are not aware that working conditions are covered by the law. Your initial step in the power play is to explain the law to your employer. Explain why you believe you are working under conditions less desirable than those of male employees. In most cases, your employer's explanation for the inequality of working conditions will be economic: he can't afford to upgrade your environment. One solution might be to have you switch places with the men who have better working conditions. There may be a practical reason why this cannot be done. If there isn't, and your employer refuses to allow the change, you know you have an employer practicing sex discrimination.

Your next step is to explain why you believe you have a right to equal working conditions. Be prepared to explain that the law prohibits treating men and women employees differently and that working conditions are covered by the law. Your authority, remember, is Title VII of the Civil Rights Act. Refer to the law if necessary. For example, you might say: "Under *Title VII* of the Civil Rights Act, I know I have the right to working conditions equal to those being provided to the men doing similar work." Your employer then has a choice. He can agree with you, in which case you can make plans for better working conditions, or he can say you are wrong. If he thinks you are wrong, be prepared to refer to *Laffey* v. *Northwest Airlines, Inc.* Suggest that he take a look at the case. You know that the case backs up the point you are making.

The Laffey case is not only a good example of unequal working conditions, it is also an example of a *class action* situation. When Laffey sued Northwest Airlines, she sued not only for herself but also on behalf of all female flight attendants at Northwest. Therefore, the court's decision applied to the entire class of female flight attendants. Northwest was not dealing with a single person. And the court's decision had a stunning impact on Northwest's operations. For Northwest, Laffey was no laughing matter.

A class action is possible if you and your female co-workers are suffering under the same discriminatory working conditions. Whenever you are not the only victim in the company, consider organizing the other women and bringing a class action.

Power Play Pointer. The class action poses a real threat to any employer. The increased leverage that the action provides you can be used effectively in a power play. No rational employer will disregard the possibility of a class action.

You can raise the possibility of a class action by pointing out that there are other women in the business who are also being discriminated against. You might then say: "We are thinking about bringing a *class action*." If your employer tries to test you by asking what a class action is, tell him. You know that it's a court case brought on behalf of all the women employees being discriminated against by your employer. If he tries to dismiss the idea of a class action, be prepared to refer to *Laffey* v. *Northwest Airlines, Inc.* The case is a good example of a class action used to remedy unequal working conditions. The case also happens to be very long and detailed. Any employer or lawyer who looks at it will quickly realize that it would be better to settle your case than even risk the possibility of being the defendant in a case such as *Laffey.*

You should also be thinking about the possibility of organizing the other women in your business. A request to see your employer signed by many female employees will not go unnoticed. And if enough women want to join in, think about hiring a lawyer.

Sexual Blackmail

Hollywood is not the only place where women are taken advantage of sexually in return for glib promises that their names will be in lights. The problem of sexual blackmail on the job may exist anywhere and anytime a man has the power to hire or fire a woman.

When we say sexual blackmail on the job we mean the situation in which a male employer (or supervisor) requires sexual relations with a female employee as a prerequisite to continued employment or advancement on the job. Some people call this sexual harassment. We don't believe this type of economic rape is merely harassment. It is blackmail and we shall call it that.

We have seen that Title VII of the Civil Rights Act of 1964 prohibits discrimination against women with respect to "terms, conditions, or privileges of employment." Is sexual blackmail a "condition of employment" prohibited by Title VII? Surprisingly, that question was not squarely dealt with by the courts until 1975. And when the courts confronted the issue, they could not agree on the answer.

Some courts saw peril in banning sexual blackmail:

The attraction of males to females and females to males is a natural sex phenomenon and it is probable that this attraction plays at least a subtle part in most personnel decisions. This natural sexual attraction can be subtle. If the [woman's] view were to prevail, no superior could, prudently, attempt to open a social dialogue with any subordinate of either sex. An invitation to dinner could become an invitation to a federal lawsuit if a once harmonious relationship turned sour at some later time. And if an inebriated approach by a supervisor to a subordinate at the office Christmas party could form the basis of a federal lawsuit for sex discrimination if a promotion or a raise is later denied to the subordinate, we would need 4,000 federal trial judges instead of some 400.

We do not know what sort of Christmas parties are held in federal courthouses. We also don't know what this judge's idea of "an invitation to dinner" is. We do know that the approach taken by that judge has not been followed by most other courts. Let's look at two recent cases.

The first case is *Tomkins* v. *Public Service Electric and Gas Company.* A woman applied for a job at Public Service Electric and Gas Company of New Jersey and was hired in April of 1971. She worked well, and in August of 1973 began working as a secretary to a supervisor. On October 30, 1973, Ms. Tomkins claims, her supervisor invited her to have lunch with him at a nearby restaurant "in order to discuss his upcoming evaluation of her work, as well as a possible job promotion." According to the court's findings, here is what happened at the lunch: "He made advances toward her, indicating his desire to have sexual relations with her and stating that this would be necessary if they were to have a satisfactory working relationship. When [Helen] attempted to leave the restaurant, the supervisor responded first by threats of recrimination against Helen in her employment, then by threats of physical force, and ultimately by physically restraining Ms. Tomkins."

Ms. Tomkins complained about the incident to management. She was transferred to another position, which, she claimed, was inferior. After a series of bad evaluations, she was fired in January of 1975.

Ms. Tomkins went to court claiming she was the victim of discrimination. The case finally reached the United States Court of Appeals for the Third Circuit, which decided she had a valid claim under Title VII. The court pointed out that had Ms. Tomkins merely been subjected to sexual advances, without more, Title VII would not have been violated. However, since Helen's job was contingent on giving in to the sexual demands, the demands became a "condition of employment" and Title VII was therefore violated.

Power Play Pointer. Established facts are extremely important in making out a case of sexual blackmail. A supervisor who is practicing blackmail is not likely to solicit favors from you in a letter. There will be no record of what he has proposed to you. Therefore, *you* must make that record. Every time the supervisor makes an advance, write down what happened and when in a private "blackmail diary." If there were any witnesses, write down who they were. The more detailed your records, the more credible your complaint will be later on.

Power Play Pointer. If a potentially serious blackmail problem seems to be developing, contact your state or local human rights commission (the addresses are in Appendix C). Get a copy of their complaint form. The next time an employer or supervisor attempts to pressure you, give him the form and say: "The next time you bother me, this form is going to be filed. Sexual blackmail is against the law, and if I file this complaint you will be in big trouble." The fact that you have a complaint form will tell the blackmailer that you mean business because you have visited your local human rights commission.

Remember also that the case of *Tomkins* v. *Public Service Electric and Gas Company* clearly holds that sexual blackmail violates the law. If you like, write down the name of the case (using the official citation from the codeword glossary) on the complaint form. Tell the sexual blackmailer to look up the case, because if he doesn't stop, he's going to find himself a defendant in a case. And you might remind him that the whole sorry story of his sexual frustrations will be spread out in cold print in the law books.

In order for your employer to be held liable under Title VII, he must have known that an employee of his is committing sexual blackmail against another employee. If the employer himself is doing the blackmail, he has "actual" knowledge. In many businesses, the person running the company does not know what is happening in the rank and file. To hold the employer liable for sexual blackmail by one of his employees, you must understand when an employer is liable for the acts of an employee.

In *Barnes* v. *Costle,* the man accused of sexual blackmail was, ironically, an employee of the Environmental Protection Agency's equal employment opportunity division. A woman employee claimed that:

> [S]hortly after commencement of her employment
> . . . the director initiated a quest for sexual favors by

> *"(a) repeatedly soliciting her to join him for social activities after office hours, notwithstanding her repeated refusal to do so; (b) by making repeated remarks to her which were sexual in nature; (c) by repeatedly suggesting to her that if she cooperated with him in a sexual affair, her employment status would be enhanced." She states that she "continually resisted his overtures . . . and finally advised him that notwithstanding his stated belief that many executives 'have affairs with their personnel,' she preferred that their relationship remain a strictly professional one." Thereafter, she charges, the director "alone and in concert with other agents of the Agency, began a conscious campaign to belittle her, to harass her and to strip her of her job duties, all culminating in the decision . . . to abolish her job in retaliation for her refusal to grant him sexual 'favors.' "*

Confronted with these facts, the court had no problem finding sexual blackmail. A trickier question was whether the Environmental Protection Agency was responsible for the acts of one of its employees. As one judge hearing the case put it:

> *The employer or higher supervisor is not in the best position of anyone to know whether an employee has been unjustly damaged on her job. The sexual advance of a supervisor toward an employee is seldom a public matter; and the distinction between invited, uninvited-but-welcome, offensive-but-tolerable and flatly rejected advances ordinarily does not fall within the special ability of the employer or higher supervisor to discern. However,* once a complaint of offensive advances has been made, the employer's role becomes far more serious. *[Emphasis added.]*

The key question is just how serious that role is. In the case of the Environmental Protection Agency, the court concluded that "generally speaking, an employer is charge- able with Title VII violations occasioned by discriminatory practices of supervisory personnel." However, the court was careful to point out that "should a supervisor contravene employer policy without the employer's knowledge and the consequences are rectified when discovered, the employer may be relieved from responsibility under Title VII." In this case, the Environmental Protection Agency abolished the job held by the sexually victimized woman. Thus, the EPA chose to rectify the problem not by disciplining the supervisor but rather by abolishing the woman's position. In this situation, the employer, the EPA, could be held respon- sible for the acts of the supervisor.

Power Play Pointer. The trick now is to make your employer aware that he is responsible for the sexual black- mail being committed by a supervisor. Many employers will simply tell you, "Boys will be boys." They won't take your problem seriously. Your job is to make the employer realize that if he fails to do something he has violated the law. Come right out and say: "Sexual blackmail is against the law. It violates *Title VII* of the Civil Rights Act. If you don't do something about it, you will be violating the law."

If your employer still doesn't want to get involved, he will probably say: "I can't be responsible for what my supervisors do." A claim of "I'm not responsible" is the call for *Barnes* v. *Costle.* Remember that this case has decided that an employer *is* responsible for the sexual blackmail of an employee if he fails to do something about it. Be prepared to refer to the Barnes case. Once you have explained the case to your employer, there is no way he can duck his responsibility without running a risk. And why should he run a risk for an employee?

Title VII Remedies

You will not always be able to solve your problems on the job simply by pointing out that sex discrimination is occurring. You may have to go the next step and explain to an employer why it is in his interest to give you your rights.

Under Title VII, if you sue your employer for sex discrimination, the court has broad authority to force your employer to give you your rights. However, before you can go to court you must give an administrative agency a chance to settle your complaint through "conference, conciliation and persuasion." Only if that step does not work can you bring your case to court.

Under the law, the administrative agency that gets the first crack at remedying your problem is your state or local human rights commission. In Appendix C we list all the state commissions that have been approved to handle complaints under Title VII. (If there is no agency in your state, then the place to file a complaint is the nearest office of the Equal Employment Opportunity Commission. This is a federal agency charged with enforcing Title VII.) Under the law, you must file your complaint within 180 days of the discriminatory action. This is an extremely important rule. *If you do not file within 180 days, you may lose your right to complain.* So contact your state or local agency and find out exactly what complaint procedures must be followed and the deadline for filing a complaint form.

If you feel you have been the victim of sex discrimination, you have a choice. You can immediately file an official complaint. Alternately, you can threaten your employer (or prospective employer if you were turned down for a job), saying you will file a complaint if he does not remedy the discrimination. There are pros and cons for both approaches.

Many companies feel betrayed if an employee goes to an outside agency to file a complaint before airing the grievance inside the "shop." They like to pride themselves on their ability to handle complaints in-house. This is especially true of larger corporations that have employee-relations departments. Also, the threat of bad publicity and a legal action that an official complaint to a state agency poses may permanently mark you as a complainer. Your future in the company may be limited.

On the other hand, there are dangers in talking to the employer without first having filed a complaint. The biggest danger is that the employer will retaliate before you have had a chance to file. Assume, for example, that you complain about sexual blackmail. You get fired; then you file a complaint. Your employer may argue that you filed the complaint because you were fired, not because of any sexual blackmail. You will have to prove that your firing took place because you complained to your employer about sexual blackmail. If you had a complaint to your state agency already on file before you were fired, you would have an easier time proving that your discharge was in retaliation for exercising your rights.

We cannot suggest whether you should file an official complaint and then talk to the employer or vice versa. We recommend that you contact your state or local human rights agency and discuss it with a representative. Consider all the pros and cons and then decide for yourself.

In the event you decide to file an official complaint and then discuss the problem with your employer, your power play will be based on your willingness to withdraw your complaint if the employer agrees to remedy the sex discrimination. However, if you decide to talk first to your employer before filing an official complaint, your power play will use the leverage of the threat to file.

Power Play Pointer. Visit your state or local human rights commission and speak to a representative. Say that you do not want to file a complaint yet, but you want them to record the fact that you visited the office and discussed your rights. Get a copy of the complaint form. When you speak to your employer, take it along and show it to him. Tell him that you visited the human rights commission to discuss the problem, but have not yet filed a complaint. Tell him that the commission recommended that you file a complaint but you would prefer to work it out without the necessity of a formal proceeding.

Using this procedure, you cut the risk of retaliation. Your employer knows that you have been to see the human rights commission. If you are fired or demoted, he knows you will be able to prove you were complaining about a denial of your rights. This procedure may protect you against the possibility of retaliation.

In the event that you file a complaint with your state or local human rights agency and no resolution is attained, the next step is to file your complaint with the federal Equal Employment Opportunity Commission. Your state or local agency will tell you how to go about doing this. If the EEOC cannot reach a settlement, they will notify you that you have the right to bring your employer into court. We are not going to explain the exact steps that you must follow; your state or local agency can explain that to you in detail. For our purposes, the important question is what a court can do to your employer. After all, our goal is to help you convince your employer to give you your rights *without having to go to court.* If an employer knows what may happen to him if you do go to court, he will, we hope, see the light and give you your rights.

Section 706 of Title VII explains what your remedies

are if you go to court to sue your employer, claiming sex discrimination. In essence, the section says that a court can do just about anything to remedy the discrimination. The court can order you to be hired, or reinstated if you were fired; order that back pay be awarded to you; order that the employer stop a particular employment practice; order that an employer start a particular hiring practice; order that an employer establish an affirmative-action plan to hire more women, etc.

In most cases, the court will fashion a remedy to deal with the particular facts of a case. This remedy might involve one or more of the options available under section 706. For example, if you were discriminated against because you were not hired for a job, the court might order that you be hired and award you back pay, i.e., the salary you would have received had you been hired when you applied for the job. In addition, the court could order that you now be given seniority measured as of the day you applied for the job. Exactly how much the court gives you depends on what the judge believes is needed to fully remedy the discrimination you have suffered. Let's look briefly at some of these remedies in action.

Back Pay. Under title 42 of the United States Code, section 2000e 5(g), you are entitled to receive back pay. In *EEOC* v. *Ford Motor Company*, the court computed the amount of the back pay by "reconstructing the probable employment history of each woman [discriminated against], assuming she had been hired for one of the positions. . . ." Assume, for example, that you were wrongfully denied a job which paid $12,000 per year. You were unemployed for two years. A court could order the employer to pay you the amount you would have earned had you been hired. In this case, the amount would be two years at $12,000 per year, for a total of $24,000.

Hiring Order. If you have been denied a job in violation of the law, in addition to back pay, the court can order that you be hired.

Affirmative-Action Order. Where, for example, you are the victim of sexual blackmail, the court can order the employer to take specific steps to avoid any further harassment. Such an order might include establishing a specific policy prohibiting sexual blackmail. Or the court could order that an offending supervisor be transferred—whatever steps are necessary to stop the sexual blackmail.

Attorney's Fees. In the event you are forced to hire a lawyer to bring your case, and you ultimately win, the court has the authority to order your employer to pay your attorney's fees.

Power Play Pointer. If you have explained your rights to an employer and he still is not impressed enough to give them to you, then you will need additional firepower. You will have to explain what will happen to the employer if you exercise your rights.

Explain to the employer that you have the right to back pay and/or an affirmative-action order. Explain why the employer has nothing to gain and everything to lose by discriminating against you. For example, if you are wrongfully denied a job, you might say: "Under *Title VII*, if I have to go to court you will be ordered to hire me and I will be entitled to *back pay*. You will be forced to pay me for work I have not performed. You'll save a lot of money by simply hiring me now."

If you are being denied equal working conditions, point out that a court will simply order the employer to equalize the conditions. For example, you might say: "I know I have the right under *Title VII* to get a court order requiring you to improve my working conditions. Why go through all the trouble of a court case?"

All these references to back pay and court orders will clearly mark you as someone who takes her rights seriously; someone who is likely to follow through with a court case. And that is exactly the message you are trying to convey. Remember, an employer who won't give you your rights when you ask for them must be convinced that it is in his interest to give you your rights.

The credibility of a threat to go to court is substantially increased if your employer knows that you don't need a lot of money to hire an attorney. There are attorneys who will take sound cases knowing that if they win their attorney's fees will have to be paid by the employer under court order. Use this fact to emphasize the seriousness of your purpose: "I've been told I should get an attorney. They say that under *Title VII* you have to pay my attorney if I win the case, so attorneys are actually after me to bring this case. I don't want to, but if you won't help me, I'll have no choice."

Perhaps the most effective remedy available for enforcing Title VII is the class action. This is a legal procedure in which all the women subjected to essentially the same discrimination by an employer bring a case as a class. A court can issue an order that will benefit all the affected women. For example, if you brought a class action against your employer, claiming that all the women who work there have poorer working conditions than the men, the court could order that all the women employees get better working conditions. The potential impact on the employer from a class action is tremendous.

Power Play Pointer. If you're dealing with larger businesses, the magic codeword is *class action*. For such businesses, one employee does not pose a great threat. They can absorb the cost of some damages, and if they have to hire you they will. However, when you say *class action* big problems appear in an employer's imagination. If you win your case, the employer will have to remedy the discrimination as it affects all women employees of the company who are victims of discrimination. That can result in huge damage awards as well as court orders to change working conditions for all women in the company. If you feel there are other women in the company who have been subjected to the same discrimination you have, the mere mention of class action will be a mighty power play. You can raise the possibility quite innocently: "I was speaking to some other women and they mentioned something called a *class action*. They suggested we get together and get a lawyer to start an action like that." Behind that innocent suggestion lurks a nightmare to most employers. However, if you are past the point of being coy, come right out and say: "Look, I fully intend to bring a *class action* on behalf of the other women employees who are being discriminated against. If I win, and I believe I will, you are going to have to change the way everything is done around here. It's going to cost you a great deal. Check with your lawyer. Let me know your decision by next week so I can tell my lawyer what to do." If your employer does not respond he is a fool and nothing short of a court case will get you your rights.

Executive Order 11246

In addition to the remedies available under Title VII, some of you will qualify for a remedy available under Executive Order 11246. These orders are issued by the President. They lay down the rules that must be followed by those departments of government under the control of the President.

Executive Order 11246 provides you with a potentially devastating power play. As one corporate executive told us: "Say the words 'Executive Order 11246' and we stand up and salute." Why? Because under this Order you have the power to threaten most companies with the possible loss of a large part of their business. Does any employer have a softer soft spot than the possibility of losing business? We don't think so.

This law applies to businesses that have contracts with the United States Government. For example, the law would apply to a clothing manufacturer who, as part of his business, sells uniforms to the United States Army. Most large businesses have some contracts with the government and are covered by this law. If your employer is among them, you have an additional source of firepower for your power play.

While the goal of the Order is very similar to that behind Title VII, the method of attaining the goal is very different. The Order applies *only* to businesses which have contracts to provide goods or perform services for the United States Government. The Order requires that, as a term of the contract, a business must agree not to discriminate. Thus, the leverage used by the government to insure nondiscriminatory employment practices is its option to choose which businesses it will give contracts to and on what terms.

The basic requirements of the Order apply to any business having a contract with the government worth at least $10,000. If a business to which the Order applies subcontracts any work, the subcontractor also must comply with the Order. As a practical matter, most large businesses have some contracts with the government. Indeed, many count on government contracts as an important source of income.

The Order prohibits discrimination with this language: "The contractor will not discriminate against any employee or applicant for employment because of . . . sex. . . . The contractor will take affirmative action to ensure that applicants are employed, and that employees are treated during employment, without regard to their . . . sex. . . . Such action shall include, but not be limited to the following: employment, upgrading, demotion, or transfer; recruitment or recruitment advertising; layoff or termination; rates of pay or other forms of compensation; and selection for training including apprenticeship."

This is very sweeping language. It parallels the prohibitions found in Title VII. But what makes the Order dynamite is the potential sanctions in the event a business is found to be in violation of the Order. They go from a reprimand up to blacklisting the company from any further contracts with the Government.

You cannot bring a legal action against an employer for violating the Order, as you can in the case of Title VII. The enforcement of the Order is left to the Secretary of Labor; he has created the Office of Federal Contract Compliance (OFCC) to do the job. You have the right to file a complaint with OFCC, using their official complaint form (see pages 110–111). We suggest that you contact the nearest office and get a copy of their complaint form. You can also use the opportunity to verify that your employer is covered by Executive Order 11246.

Power Play Pointer. No employer is entirely sure how far the Office of Federal Contract Compliance will go to enforce Executive Order 11246. *No employer wants to find out.* Indeed, the mere fact that you have heard of the Order puts you in a class by yourself. Add to this the fact that you know of the Office of Federal Contract Compliance and your employer knows you are a threat to be reckoned with.

To fully appreciate just how soft your employer's soft spot is, just put yourself in his position. Imagine that an employee comes in and says: "I am being discriminated against in violation of *Executive Order 11246.* If this discrimination is not rectified, I will contact the *Office of Federal Contract Compliance* and lodge a formal complaint. As you know, under the law the Office is required to investigate all complaints. When they see what is going on here, there is a good chance you will lose all the business you have with the United States Government." What would you do if faced with this credible threat? Are you going to risk a large part of the company's business over one complaint of sex discrimination? No! You will hire the woman or improve the working conditions or stop the sexual blackmail. You are not going to risk the profit margin of the business over one claim of discrimination. All you have to do now is be the employee who walks into the employer's office and says: "I am being discriminated against in violation of *Executive Order 11246* . . ."

Codeword Glossary

affirmative-action order Authorized by title 42 of the United States Code, section 2000e-5(g). A court can order an employer to take affirmative steps to remedy a discriminatory policy.

attorney's fees Authorized by title 42 of the United States Code, Section 2000e-5(k). If you win a court case charging sex discrimination, the court can order the employer to pay your attorney's fees.

back pay Authorized by title 42 of the United States Code, section 2000e-5(g). A court can order an employer to pay you the salary you would have received had you not been discriminated against.

Barnes* v. *Costle A leading federal court case found in volume 561 of the Federal Reporter, Second Series, at page 983. It holds that an employer is responsible for sexual blackmail committed by a supervisor if the employer has knowledge of it.

bona fide occupational qualification (BFOQ) Those situations in which an employer may properly take sex into account in making an employment decision.

OMB Approval No. 044R-1588

U.S. DEPARTMENT OF LABOR EMPLOYMENT STANDARDS ADMINISTRATION Office of Federal Contract Compliance Washington, D. C. 20210	COMPLAINT OF DISCRIMINATION IN EMPLOYMENT UNDER GOVERNMENT CONTRACTS

INSTRUCTIONS: Only complaints of discrimination in employment by companies working under Government contracts are filed on this form. The act of discrimination must be based on RACE, COLOR, RELIGION, SEX, or NATIONAL ORIGIN, and the complaint must be filed within 180 days of the discriminatory act. Other types of discrimination are not handled by this office. Fill in the form, making one copy for yourself and one official copy. The official copy of the form must be typed or printed legibly and signed by you.

YOUR NAME		TELEPHONE NO.	SOCIAL SECURITY NO.	
STREET ADDRESS		CITY	STATE	ZIP CODE

MAIL THIS FORM TO:

NAME, ADDRESS & ZIP CODE OF THE COMPANY INVOLVED

U.S. DEPARTMENT OF LABOR
EMPLOYMENT STANDARDS ADMINISTRATION
OFFICE OF FEDERAL CONTRACT COMPLIANCE
WASHINGTON, D. C. 20210

FOR WHICH GOVERNMENT AGENCY IS THE COMPANY UNDER CONTRACT?

GIVE THE EXACT DATE OF THIS DISCRIMINATION

DISCRIMINATION FOR	WHAT DID IT INVOLVE? *(Check only the most apparent factor)*			
☐ RACE OR COLOR	☐ HIRING	☐ LAYOFF OR RECALL	☐ EMPLOYEE BENEFITS	☐ DISCHARGE
☐ RELIGION	☐ PROMOTION	☐ TRANSFER	☐ WAGES	☐ TRAINING OR APPRENTICESHIP
☐ SEX	☐ DOWNGRADING	☐ JOB ASSIGNMENT	☐ SEGREGATED FACILITIES	☐ OTHER *(Explain below)*
☐ NATIONAL ORIGIN				

THE COMPLAINT:	*Tell the full story of this act of discrimination. Show all dates, places, and the names and titles of persons involved.*

☐ Continued on the other side.

Form CC-1
Dec. 1974

THE COMPLAINT *(Continued from page one)*

_____

Additional pages may be attached to this form. *Please put your name and S.S. No. at the top of each page.*

I certify that the information given above is true and correct to the best of my knowledge or belief. (A willful false statement is punishable by law: U.S. Code, Title 18, Sec. 1001)	YOUR SIGNATURE	DATE

DO NOT WRITE BELOW THIS LINE

The complainant has reaffirmed this complaint in my presence.
This complaint is now the basis of an investigation under EXECUTIVE ORDER 11246 and/or EXECUTIVE ORDER 11375.

NAME OF INVESTIGATOR	TITLE	SIGNATURE

AGENCY OR DEPARTMENT CONDUCTING INVESTIGATION	DATE INVESTIGATION STARTED

GPO 888-156

class action   Authorized by Rule 23 of the Federal Rules of Civil Procedure. It established the right of a woman to sue an employer on behalf of all other similarly situated women employees who are being discriminated against.

East v. Romine, Inc.   A leading federal court case found in volume 518 of the Federal Reporter, Second Series, at page 332. An employer can refuse to hire a qualified woman only if he can show that the man hired for the job was better qualified.

Equal Employment Opportunity Commission (EEOC)   The federal agency authorized to prosecute cases of sex discrimination.

Executive Order 11246   Under this Presidential Order, the federal government can cancel a government contract with any business that is practicing sex discrimination.

hiring order   Authorized by title 42 of the United States Code, Section 2000e-5(g). An employee who has been wrongfully refused a job, or has been wrongfully fired, may get a court order requiring that she be hired.

Laffey v. Northwest Airlines, Inc.   A leading federal court case found in volume 374 of the Federal Supplement at page 1382. An employee improperly denied equal working conditions may sue in a class action (see glossary, above) on behalf of all other women employees.

McDonnell Douglas Corp. v. Green   A decision of the United States Supreme Court found in volume 411 of the United States Reports at page 792. A landmark decision listing the requirements to make out a case of sex discrimination in hiring.

Office of Federal Contract Compliance (OFCC)   The federal agency established by the Secretary of Labor to handle violations of Executive Order 11246 (see glossary, above).

state and local offices of human rights commissions

Agencies charged with the responsibility for enforcing Title VII (see glossary, below).

Title VII Located in title 42 of the United States Code at sections 2000e through 2000e-17. The basic federal law which prohibits sex discrimination in hiring and working conditions.

Tomkins v. Public Service Electric and Gas Company
A federal court case found in volume 568 of the Federal Reporter, Second Series, at page 1044. Sexual blackmail violates the law.

6   *A Working Woman's Right to Equal Pay*

If Jack and Jill had been paid to fetch a pail of water, they each should have been paid the same wage. And if Jill broke her crown when she came down, she should have been entitled to the same medical benefits as Jack was. That is the gist of the Equal Pay Act.

In the preceding chapter we saw how Title VII of the Civil Rights Act of 1964 can be used by women to demand equal access to the job market. Having secured a job, however, many women find they are getting paid less than men doing similar work. Employers, the vast majority of whom are men, often believe that women work to keep busy while men work to support a family. Using this stereotyping, they have justified paying women less than men. This may soothe the ego of men working side by side with women. It may make economic sense for the employer. But it does not help a woman's ego, or her budget. Furthermore, it is simply not fair, and the working woman does not have to put up with it.

Let's assume a woman named Gail sells bedding in a department store. Across the aisle, Jim sells household appliances. Jim gets $5 per hour. Gail gets $4 per hour. Every day Gail looks across the aisle knowing that every hour Jim has earned one dollar more than she has. Gail wonders why she is getting less money. She thinks she works as hard as Jim does. She thinks she should get as much as Jim does. In principle, the law agrees.

The Equal Pay Act was passed by Congress on June 10, 1963. The goal of the Act was summarized by the Court of Appeals for the Third Circuit in the case of *Shultz* v. *Wheaton Glass Company:* "The Act was intended as a broad charter of women's rights in the economic field. It sought to overcome the age-old belief in women's inferiority and to eliminate the depressing effects on living standards of reduced wages for female workers and the economic and social consequences which flow from it." In order to reach its goal, the law requires equal pay for equal work.

The problem with this law is that while it may be easy to decide what equal pay is, comparing jobs to determine if they are equal is very difficult. If Jim and Gail are both considered salespeople, then perhaps their jobs are equal. But if Jim is an appliance salesperson and Gail is a bedding salesperson, maybe they actually have different jobs.

In this chapter we will show you how to compare your job with that of a man working with you who is getting paid more. You will learn what tests to apply to decide whether the jobs are equal. Do not look forward to any magical scientific equation for comparing jobs. We are examining a law that is not noted for its clarity or exactness. However, we will be giving you a number of examples, and we hope that from these you will learn what equal pay for equal work means. But before we do that, we must make sure the law covers you.

The Equal Pay Act is a federal law. Under the Constitution, the Act can apply only to employers whose business somehow affects commerce. Thus, if what you or your employer does has no effect outside of the state in which you work, the federal government has no authority to regulate how much you get paid. However, just about any activity that brings you in contact with another state or a foreign country will be enough to impose the requirements of the Equal Pay Act on your employer. For example, if you put the postage on letters going outside your state, you are involved in "commerce" and your employer must abide by the Act.

If you work for any large business, chances are you have the protection of the Equal Pay Act. If you work in a smaller business, we suggest you contact the nearest office of the Wage and Hour Division. This agency is part of the Department of Labor and is charged with enforcing the Equal Pay Act. Check the telephone directory under "United States Government, Labor, Dept. of" for the nearest office. A representative at the Wage and Hour Division should be able to tell you if you are covered by the Act.

If you discover that the Act does *not* cover you, do not despair. Almost all states have enacted laws that parallel the federal Equal Pay Act. These state laws do not require the employer to be engaged in interstate commerce. Just contact your state or local human rights commission for further information on the law in your state (a list of the commissions is in Appendix C).

Equal Work

Under the Equal Pay Act, you have the right to equal pay for equal work. This right sounds simple, and in principle it is. The problem is in finding an equation by which to compare jobs to determine if they are equal. The law understands that few people perform exactly the same jobs, and the law does not require equality (despite its name). Instead, it establishes four criteria by which jobs should be compared. If under each of these criteria the jobs pass the legal test of "equality," then, for purposes of equal pay, they are equal. The four tests are: equal skill, equal effort, equal responsibility, and similar working conditions.

Before we examine each of these criteria in depth, there are some general principles that apply regardless of the particular criteria being compared. First, the law recognizes that "jobs that require equal skill, effort, and responsibility in their performance . . . are usually not identical in every respect." Do not worry if your job and the job you are comparing it to are in some ways different. The question is, how different? As we examine each of the criteria for comparing jobs, you will quickly see that jobs need not be exactly the same in order for the requirement of equal pay to apply.

Second, what jobs are called does not determine whether they are equal. Just because an employer calls one job "administrative assistant" and another job "typist" does not mean the jobs are unequal. Job titles frequently do not reflect the job being performed. The Equal Pay Act compares what two workers *do,* not their job titles.

Power Play Pointer. A favorite ploy of employers trying to get around the Equal Pay Act is to change titles of jobs and thereby make them unequal. Do not be fooled. If an employer tries to dismiss your demand for equal pay by pointing to your job title and saying it is different from the title held by a man, just respond: "The *Equal Pay Act* compares jobs, not job titles. Let's compare what we do."

Finally, remember that you are comparing similar jobs, not jobs that require similar skill, effort, and responsibility. If you work all day typing and a man sitting next to you sharpens pencils all day, and he gets paid more, the Equal Pay Act will not help you. He may be using less skill and effort, but his job is not even similar to yours.

Now let's examine the four criteria for comparing jobs to determine if equal pay is required. Remember, you are comparing your job with one held by a man. If a woman is getting paid more than you for doing the same job, the Equal Pay Act does not care. The law protects you only from discrimination *based on sex*. Discrimination between people of the same sex is not prohibited.

Equal Skill

The equal pay requirement applies only to jobs that require equal skill in their performance. Skill includes consideration of such factors as experience, training, education, and ability. Absolute equality is certainly not required. However, your job and the job you are comparing it to must require essentially the same skills.

Take two people, one male and one female, who are typists in an office. The woman types on a standard electric typewriter. The man uses one of the new computerized typewriters that require additional training to use. The two jobs are not equal, since additional training is required for one of the jobs.

However, suppose a man and a woman in an office are both typists and both jobs require them to spend two thirds of their time on typing and related matters, but the remaining third of the time is spent on other tasks, not necessarily the same. For example, let's assume the man operates a calculator and the woman does the office copying. Both employees are essentially typists, but does their "other work" require different skills justifying a wage differential?

The answer, according to the regulations issued by the Secretary of Labor, is that "if there is actually no distinction in the performance requirements of such jobs so far as skills utilized in these tasks are concerned," the jobs require the same skill. Only if operating a calculator requires a higher degree of training, education, or ability would the jobs be different. Thus, the general rule is that jobs that are essentially the same, in this case typing, will not become different merely because the typists perform additional different duties—unless these additional duties require clearly different levels of skill. Ask yourself whether the additional duties being performed by the man require additional experience, training, education, or ability. If the answer is no, then the jobs require equal skill.

Power Play Pointer. Employers like to point to minor differences between jobs to justify paying higher wages to a man. The simple fact that the man is performing some different work during part of the day does not justify a higher wage. You must look at what the work actually is to decide whether greater skill is required over what you are doing. Thus, if an employer responds to your request for equal pay with "But Jim also has to sharpen the pencils/ sweep the floor/close the windows/change the typewriter ribbons," just respond, "Under the *Equal Pay Act,* those additional duties don't require additional skill. You don't need training to do it. Therefore, you can't justify paying more to Jim."

Equal Effort

In addition to requiring essentially the same skill, the jobs must require essentially the same effort. Effort is measured in terms of the amount of physical or mental exertion needed for the performance of the job. This requirement does not mean you must exert the same *kind* of effort as your male counterpart, only the same *amount.*

Suppose that a male checker employed by a supermarket is required to spend part of his time carrying heavy cartons or replacing stock, which involves lifting heavy items. You too are a checker, and you devote an equal effort during your checking operation. But you also do work requiring some dexterity, such as rearranging displays of spices and other small items. The difference in kind of effort required of you and the male checker would not make your efforts unequal. Both jobs require additional effort above just checking out groceries. In this case, the additional work requires about the same amount of effort.

Thus, effort cannot be measured in terms of how much sweat is required. Mental exertion can be compared to physical exertion. Based on the court cases that have tried to cope with this rather difficult equation, so long as both jobs are essentially the same, minor additional duties requiring different types of physical or mental effort will not render the jobs unequal.

Power Play Pointer. Employers frequently, and quite honestly, fail to understand that in some situations physical and mental effort can be equated for purposes of determining whether equal pay is required. Review the effort required for your job and the job you are comparing it to. Does the man do some physical work which you don't do? If the answer is yes, be prepared to explain why the mental effort you exert balances the physical effort exerted by the man. Thus, if the employer says that Jim lifts boxes or carries typewriters, or does other physical work, you should be prepared to say: "That's true, but I also perform other work that requires extra mental effort. It is a different kind of effort, but under the law, they can be equated." Remember, your authority for this rule is the Equal Pay Act. You should be ready with your codeword glossary authority, since many employers will simply not believe that physical and mental effort can be equated.

While physical and mental effort can be compared, you must be performing some mental effort to balance off your male coworker's physical effort. If that coworker is in fact performing additional physical effort and you are not performing a corresponding physical or mental effort, he would be entitled to a higher wage. For example, let's assume that on an assembly line the man at the end of the line is required, as part of his job, to lift the assembly and place it on a pallet. You work on the line with other men and women, getting pay equal to yours and not doing extra lifting. In this situation, a wage differential between you and the man at the end of the line would be permitted, since he is expending extra physical effort. However, a wage differential would not be permitted for workers on the line with you who are expending about the same physical effort as you are.

Here is a good guideline to use to determine if two jobs require equal effort. Look at the wages of other people performing your job and the job you are comparing it to. Are the wages usually the same? If, in the field in which you work, the salaries for the two jobs are usually equal, then you have excellent evidence that equal effort is required. (This same rule of thumb could be applied to the other criteria. However, when the question is how "hard" you work, this type of comparison is especially useful.)

For example, you work in a factory as a fine sander of wood. A man working next to you does rough sanding. He gets paid more than you do. Do the jobs require the same effort? One good way to bolster your case is to look at other rough and fine sanders in your business or in similar businesses. If you find that rough and fine sanders usually get paid the same, you have excellent evidence to show equality of effort.

Equal Responsibility

In addition to equal skill and effort, jobs that require equal pay must also entail equal responsibility. The regulations say that "responsibility is concerned with the degree of accountability required in the performance of the job, with emphasis on the importance of the job obligation."

This is an extremely vague requirement. How does one define "responsibility"? The answer, the cases tell us, is to look for specific tasks that have accountability. Say there are four salesclerks in a shoe store. One of the clerks has the authority to approve checks given as payment. That clerk could receive higher wages based on the additional responsibility he or she has.

However, the regulations tell us that "there are situations where one employee . . . may be given some minor responsibility which the others do not have (e.g., turning out the lights in his department at the end of the business day) but which is not of sufficient importance to justify a finding of unequal responsibility." Thus, additional responsibilities must be significant before they will justify a wage differential between male and female employees.

Power Play Pointer. Because the requirement of equal responsibility is so vague, it is a favorite criterion used by employers to justify wage differentials. Remember, though, that responsibility means real accountability, and minor additional duties do not count. So if your employer says: "Look, Jane, I'd give you what Jim is getting but I have to pay Jim more because he has the additional responsibility of changing the date on the calendar each morning," you can confidently respond: "Under the *Equal Pay Act,* that's not enough of an additional responsibility to justify paying him more than what I get. There has to be serious responsibility, not something minor like changing the calendar."

Similar Working Conditions

The final requirement for equal pay is that the conditions you work under must be similar to those under which your male coworker toils. A bricklayer who is working on a patio should not be paid the same as a bricklayer standing on a scaffold pointing the bricks on the fifty-seventh floor of a skyscraper. The jobs are essentially the same, but the working conditions certainly are not.

In general, the regulations say that the standard must be applied in a flexible manner. "In determining whether the requirement [of similar working conditions] is met, a practical judgment is required in the light of whether the differences in working conditions are the kind customarily taken into consideration in setting wage levels. The mere fact that jobs are performed in different departments of an establishment will not necessarily mean that the jobs are performed under dissimilar conditions. This may or may not be the case."

While the regulations generalize, this is one case in which generalizing is necessary. The variety of possible working conditions is great. About the only realistic standard to apply is this: Are workers normally paid more for working under the conditions your male coworker works under, as opposed to the conditions you work under? If the answer is yes, then the male worker would be entitled to a higher wage. The assumption would be that the higher wage results from the more difficult working conditions and not from the fact that the worker is a man.

In general, the courts that have tried to decide what "similar working conditions" means have concluded that the term should have a specialized meaning tailored to the particular business involved. For example, in the industrial-worker field, *working conditions* generally refers to hazards faced on the job. As the United States Supreme Court has said in the case of *Corning Glass Works* v. *Brennan:* "Working conditions encompasses two sub-factors: 'surroundings' and 'hazards.' 'Surroundings' measures the elements, such as toxic chemicals or fumes, regularly encountered by a worker, their intensity, and their frequency. 'Hazards' takes into account the physical hazards regularly encountered, their frequency and the severity of injury they can cause."

Thus, similar working conditions must be viewed in the light of the particular job you have. Do employers in your particular field generally take differing working conditions into account in setting wages? There is a simple method for coming up with the answer. Assume you think your job takes the same effort, skill, and responsibility as Jim's. However, Jim works in another part of the building. Compare the wages of your immediate coworkers with those in Jim's area. If, across the board, there seems to be a wage difference, chances are the reason is dissimilar working conditions. However, if you discover that women get paid less than men regardless of where they work, then you have a good case of violation of the Equal Pay Act.

Equal Pay

Since you are entitled to equal pay for equal work, the question often arises as to what pay includes. After all, there are many ways to be compensated for your work. And if you are doing the same work as a man but he gets double time for work on Saturday while you get only time and a half, you are hardly getting "equal pay."

Under the Equal Pay Act, *pay* generally includes all payments made to or on behalf of an employee as remuneration for employment. The regulations tell us that "vacation and holiday pay, and premium payments for work on Saturdays, Sundays, holidays, regular days of rest, or other days or hours in excess or outside of . . . regular days or hours of work are remuneration for employment. . . ." Thus, when you compare your pay with a man doing "equal work," look for equality in all forms of pay.

At this point in our discussion we should not be surprised if some of you are wondering whether using this law is worth the effort. We certainly agree that comparing equal skill, effort, and responsibility appears difficult and computing equal pay can be confusing. However, we think that when you see some practical applications of the law you will agree that it is not really so difficult to use.

The case of *Usery* v. *Johnson* provides a good example of an attempt to compare jobs to determine if they are equal. In this case, the employer was a department store. The employees who believed they were not getting equal pay for equal work were women clerks employed by the store. They claimed that male clerks were getting paid more for doing the same work.

The facts showed that clerks, both male and female, "waited on customers, marked prices on goods, stocked shelves, took telephone orders, wrote out charge slips and operated the cash register. In addition, they cleaned and straightened shelves, and, to varying degrees, obtained stock from the warehouse upstairs."

The clerks were generally assigned to different departments. Duane worked in stationery and furniture; Ellen in books, toys, and teaching aids; Almae in stationery; Marla in stationery and furniture; Jeanette in arts and crafts; and Robert in stationery and furniture.

The problem was that Duane and Robert, the two male clerks, were paid more than Ellen, Almae, Marla, Jeanette, and the other female clerks. The women contended that they were performing equal work and should have been paid the same as the men. The department store claimed that Duane and Robert performed "additional duties" in connection with their furniture-department "responsibilities."

In deciding whether the jobs were equal, the court looked at the skill, effort, and responsibility required of the men and women clerks. The first test involved skill. Did Robert and Duane utilize greater skill in their jobs that would justify a higher wage? The court said no:

> *The skill required of each of the clerks in the selling of merchandise was substantially the same whether the goods sold were furniture items or items from any other department at the store. . . . Many of the female clerks had much more experience in sales clerk duties than did either of the two males at the time the males were hired, and even among the female clerks, experience appeared to play a very minor role in determining wage rate. . . . There was, though, testimony at [the] trial that the selling of furniture, a duty performed by both male clerks part of the time, required certain abilities not required in the selling of other items at the store, such as stationery items or goods from the arts and crafts department. However, the fact that a janitor at the store . . . assembled and sold furniture part-time as well as the fact that certain female clerks were involved in selling furniture items, indicates that whatever additional abilities were required in selling furniture were unsubstantial to performance of the primary functions of all the sales clerks.*

Thus, while arguably furniture sales required greater skills, the facts indicated otherwise.

The next comparison was made on the basis of effort. And once again the court found substantial equality. The way the court approached the question of effort should be instructive:

With respect to physical effort, evidence . . . indicates that both male clerks were sometimes involved in carrying and moving items into the furniture department. . . . The time consumed in moving and carrying these items by the male clerks was insignificant [only about 10 percent of the total time spent at the job], and there was no indication that they were required to physically lift heavy furniture items and carry them down flights of stairs from the warehouse to the furniture department. In addition, several of the female clerks stated that they too went up to the warehouse to obtain supplies on occasion, although most of the items carried by the female clerks were lighter than many furniture items.

The court also had no problem finding equality of mental effort, since selling furniture and arts and crafts supplies required about the same effort. The fact that clerks selling furniture often went through catalogues with customers was not significant.

As to responsibility, the final criterion, the court found that it did not vary substantially from one department to another. In fact, "each clerk was responsible to make sure that customers were waited on and were satisfied with the service they received, that sufficient stock was available in his or her department, that items of merchandise were properly marked, that sales were figured correctly and that correct change was given." The fact that furniture is bigger than books and craft items did not result in substantially greater responsibility.

Thus, the court found the female clerks were performing substantially the same jobs, and since they were not being paid the same wages, there was a violation of the Equal Pay Act.

Before we look at another case, we want to be sure you appreciate how the court used facts to find equality among the jobs. Since it is difficult, perhaps impossible, to find absolute standards by which to compare the skill, effort, and responsibility of jobs, the court looked for evidence, much of it circumstantial, to decide whether the jobs were equal. Thus, the fact that a janitor was able to perform the job of furniture salesclerk tended to show that no particularly unique skill was required to sell furniture. And the fact that some of the women clerks worked part of their time in the furniture department also supported the conclusion that the requirements for the job of furniture salesclerk were not substantially greater than those for a salesclerk in any other department.

Power Play Pointer. If you think you are the victim of unequal pay for equal work, gather evidence tending to prove your case. Where it is possible, get written documentation. For example, where your employer prints job descriptions, keep a copy. It may prove useful. In general, keep any information tending to show equality of jobs, such as was used in the case we just discussed. When preparing to talk to your employer, go over the information you have gathered so you can back up your points with evidence.

In the next case we will look at, you will see how some employers, familiar with the Equal Pay Act, may try to avoid its impact. The case, *Marshall* v. *Hodag Chemical Corporation,* illustrates how courts will look behind such schemes.

The female employee in this case was an analytical chemist to whom the court referred by her nickname, Lottie. (Her real name was Wladyslawa Lisiecki.) She was employed in the quality control department of Hodag Chemical Corporation. About two years after she was hired, Hodag employed a man, whom the court referred to as Mike. (His real name was Miroslaw Tschaikowsky.) He was also an analytical chemist. He got $16,000 per year. Lottie got $14,200.

The court looked at the skill, effort, and responsibility of the jobs performed by Mike and Lottie and concluded they were substantially equal. But Hodag decided to change Mike's title and thereby justify giving him the higher salary. Here's what the court thought of this tactic:

> *Defendant [Hodag] did not come into compliance with the Equal Pay Act by altering Mike's duties and changing his title . . . since it failed to raise Lottie's salary at that time so as to equal the salary received by Mike. Compliance with the Equal Pay Act is not achieved by shifting the male's duties so as to make them arguably unequal to those of the female, while at the same time failing to raise the pay rate of the female. Once the Act is violated by paying different rates to persons of the opposite sexes for equal work, compliance can only be achieved by raising the rate of the lower paid sex, not by further alteration of duties.*

The court was making an important point. Under the Equal Pay Act, an employer cannot cure a violation by lowering the wage of the male employee to equal that of the female. Instead, the law specifically provides that *the female's wage must be increased to that of the male who is performing equal work.*

Power Play Pointer. Don't tolerate any employer who tries to play on your guilt feelings with "Well, if you want to complain, go right ahead. I'll just have to lower Joe's wages, and you know how much Joe needs the money." Just tell your employer, "Under the *Equal Pay Act,* if you lower Joe's wages you will be willfully violating the law, and that could mean a fine of ten thousand dollars."

Hopefully, you now have enough information and power play pointers to deal rationally with your employer. If he is reasonable, he should see the correctness, both ethical and legal, of your request for a raise. However, there are employers who are obstinate. You will need some aid to show them the light. Let us, therefore, take a look at the steps you can take, if necessary, to enforce the Equal Pay Act.

If you were to decide to enforce your rights under the Equal Pay Act, you could do so in one of two ways. First, you could file a complaint with the United States Department of Labor. The Department could, at its discretion, decide to file a case against your employer. Second, you could, on your own, simply hire an attorney to file a civil action for you.

Under the Equal Pay Act, if you prove that you were denied your right to equal pay, the court will award you your *back wages.* Thus, you end up in as good a position as you would have been had you received equal pay for your equal work. The back wages are computed by raising your salary retroactively to that of the male worker who performed equal work with you.

In addition, the court may award *liquidated damages.* Basically, these are damages to compensate you for having been discriminated against. The amount of the damages is equal to the amount of your back wages. Thus, if you are due $20,000 in back wages, the court may award liquidated damages of $20,000, meaning you would receive a total of $40,000.

Finally, the law permits a court to award *attorney's fees*. This means that if you win your case the court will order your employer to pay your attorney his fee. Some attorneys will be willing to handle your case at no charge, knowing that if they win the employer will be forced to pay. Attorney's fees can be very high and pose an added threat to your employer.

Power Play Pointer. If push comes to shove, you may have to raise the possibility of bringing a court case against your employer. Obviously, this poses a serious threat to him. Many of you will be understandably reluctant to walk into your employer's office and say: "I'm going to sue you." However, if you are prepared to go all the way, you may want to pull out the stops and confront your employer with the possibility of a court case. You might say: "I believe I should be receiving a higher salary. If you won't give it to me, I know I have the right under the *Equal Pay Act* to go to court. I know I have the right to *back wages* and *liquidated damages*. That can cost you a great deal. I hope you will see that I'm correct so we can avoid unnecessary litigation."

Many employers believe that an employee's threat to sue is just a bluff. They know how much attorneys cost, and unless you are a highly paid employee, you are not likely to have the money to pay high-priced legal talent. We suggest you mention the fact that, under the law, attorney's fees are awarded to the employee if she wins. This makes your threat to sue significantly more credible.

For example, you might say: "I don't want to take this case to court, but if I have to, I will. I will have no problem getting an attorney, since under the law, when I win you will have to pay my attorney's fees. There are attorneys waiting in line to handle cases like mine. But why give money to the lawyers? Let's settle this thing out of court."

Chances are, if you are the victim of a violation of the Equal Pay Act, other women where you work are also victims. Organizing these women into a lobbying force poses a considerable threat to an employer. Also, a group of women with a valid claim of violation of the Act are quite likely to get the assistance of the United States Secretary of Labor in prosecuting their claim. The Wage and Hour Division of the United States Department of Labor enforces this law. If you can get some women together to join in a complaint, you should consider filing a complaint.

Power Play Pointer. The threat of a number of women joining together to file a complaint with the Wage and Hour Division is formidable indeed. No employer wants the Department of Labor investigating him. We suggest you contact your local office of the Wage and Hour Division, which is a branch of the Department of Labor. Get a copy of the official complaint form. You can either file the complaint or take the form to your employer, indicating that you intend to file the complaint unless he remedies the equal pay violations. The fact that you have a complaint form from the Wage and Hour Division is sure to convince your employer that you mean business. Of course, if you get enough women to join with you on the complaint, you may want to get an attorney to represent you.

The final question we must deal with has perhaps been foremost in your mind throughout this chapter: Won't my employer retaliate against me for being a troublemaker? The answer, of course, depends on the temperament of your employer. There is absolutely no doubt that the majority of employers will not be happy to know that you know your rights. However, under the Equal Pay Act, *retaliation is against the law*. Specifically, section 15(a)(3) of the Act makes it unlawful "to discharge or in any other manner discriminate against any employee because such employee has filed any complaint or instituted any proceeding, or has testified or is about to testify in any [proceeding under the Equal Pay Act]."

Obviously, the fact that retaliation is prohibited does not mean it will not occur. Some of you will be willing to put up with the inevitable problems of being considered a troublemaker at work. However, we believe that many of you will be able to intelligently discuss your claim to higher pay with an employer without alienating the employer. We have, therefore, explained in some detail when you have a right to expect equal pay for equal work. Hopefully, this will permit you to discuss your rights with your employer in an informed way.

However, when it comes to demanding your rights, either by threatening a court case or by filing a complaint with the Wage and Hour Division, you are accepting the possibility that your future potential at work will be irreparably harmed. It is up to you to decide.

Codeword Glossary

attorney's fees Your right to have your employer pay your attorney's fees if you win your case. Authorized by title 29 of the United States Code in section 216(b).

back wages Your right to collect retroactively those wages you would have received had you been receiving equal pay. Authorized by title 29 of the Code of Federal Regulations in section 800.166.

Equal Pay Act A federal law that is part of the Fair Labor Standards Act and is located in title 29 of the United States Code in section 206. Regulations have been issued to implement the Act. These regulations are found in title 29 of the Code of Federal Regulations. The following sections of title 29 may be referred to:

section 800.121 The Equal Pay Act compares what you do, not what the jobs are called.

section 800.125 Equal skill includes consideration of experience, training, education, and ability.

section 800.127 Equal effort compares physical and/or mental effort.

section 800.129 Equal responsibility is concerned with the accountability of the jobs.

section 800.166 An employer can be fined $10,000 for violating the Equal Pay Act (see the Marshall case, below).

liquidated damages Your right to collect an amount equal to your back wages as damages. Authorized by title 29 of the Code of Federal Regulations in section 800.166.

Marshall* v. *Hodag Chemical Corporation A federal court case found in volume 16 of the Employment Practices Decisions at page 5681. An employer violating the Equal Pay Act must raise the salary of the female employee to that which the male employee is receiving. Violation of this rule is punishable by a $10,000 fine.

retaliation An employer's demotion or discharge of an employee who has asserted her rights under the Equal Pay Act. Retaliation is prohibited by section 15(a)(3) of the Equal Pay Act.

Wage and Hour Division A division of the Department of Labor that enforces the Equal Pay Act.

7 The Rights of Older Workers

Case #1—You are 52 years old. The boss says it's time you thought about taking it a little easier. Maybe you should transfer the Acme account to someone younger.

Case #2—The new X-100 copying machines are just coming off the assembly line. In a year, these machines will be the only ones the company produces. You think you are one of the best sales representatives at the company and, at sixty-three, one of the most experienced. But only the younger reps are getting training on the new machines.

Case #3—The company is having some financial setbacks. You and everyone else knows there are going to have to be cutbacks. You've been getting excellent evaluations for almost twenty years and, at 57, you're senior man in your department. Now, all of a sudden, your evaluations are "inadequate."

What all the people in these examples are getting are warning signs. Like angina pains before the heart attack, these are symptoms—in this case, of impending unemployment. But, like modern medicine, modern law has an antidote. The nitro of the older worker is the Age Discrimination in Employment Act. Use this law properly and you can work to a ripe old age.

The Age Discrimination in Employment Act was passed in 1967 with the goal of promoting "employment of older persons based on their ability rather than age: to prohibit arbitrary age discrimination in employment. . . ." *Older persons* includes anyone from age 40 to age 70. While someone aged 41 might be surprised to be an "older person," just try getting a job in our youth-oriented society. If you are over the hill at age 70, you are starting down the hill at age 40!

But before you head into the boss's office demanding your rights, let's make sure the Act protects you. We have never yet found a law that did not have exceptions, and this law is no exception. So let us begin by asking the question, who is covered by this law?

There are three requirements that you must meet to get the benefits of the Act. First, you must be at least 40 years old but not over 70. (Employees of the United States Government have no upper age limit. They have the right to be free from discrimination based on age so long as they can do the job.)

The second requirement is that your employer must have at least 20 employees for at least 20 weeks of the year. There is no requirement that all 20 employees work 20 weeks at the same time. Just ask yourself whether during the year there were, at one time or another, 20 people who worked for your employer for a total of 20 weeks.

The final requirement is the trickiest. You are covered by this Act only if the business your employer is engaged in affects commerce. This requirement has been very liberally construed. If anything your employer does somehow affects activity in another state or a foreign country, he is engaged in commerce. Most businesses buy goods from across state lines, send letters outside the state, or otherwise have some impact across a state line. Thus, unless you work in a very local business, the law will cover you. However, to be sure, we suggest you contact the Wage and Hour Division of the Department of Labor nearest where you work. The office should be listed in the telephone directory under "United States Government, Labor, Dept. of Wage & Hour Div." The staff at the office should be able to tell you whether your employer is covered by the Age Discrimination in Employment Act. If you should find out that you are not covered, ask the staff whether your state has its own law dealing with age discrimination. Many states have such laws, and they are not limited to businesses that affect commerce. If you have a state law, the staff at the Wage and Hour Division will be able to tell you how to contact the state agency that administers the law.

Those of you who are covered by the Age Discrimination in Employment Act can now ask what this Act can do for you. The answer is that the Act outlaws certain discriminatory practices. Specifically, the Act provides that it shall be unlawful for an employer:

1. to fail or refuse to hire or to discharge any individual or otherwise discriminate against any individual with respect to his compensation, terms, conditions, or privileges of employment, because of such individual's age;

2. to limit, segregate, or classify his employees in any way which would deprive or tend to deprive any individual of employment opportunities or otherwise adversely affect his status as an employee, because of such individual's age; or

3. to reduce the wage rate of any employee in order to comply with this chapter.

The key point to remember is that if you are in the

protected group of ages 40 to 70, the prohibitions listed above protect you. There is nothing in the Act that says the older you are the more you are protected. Thus, an employee who is 41 years old could not be discriminated against because of his age even though the discrimination was in favor of someone 69 years old. Once you are in the protected age group, how old you are makes no difference.

Another point to bear in mind is that an employment practice that does not discriminate *against* those in the protected age group is not prohibited. Thus, an employer's refusal to hire anyone under age 35 would be acceptable, because no one in the protected group was being discriminated against. However, the refusal to hire anyone under 42 would be a prohibited practice, since job applicants aged 40 and 41, who are in the protected group, would be subject to discrimination based on age.

Brought to its simplest form, the Act says age is irrelevant to employment decisions regarding the protected age group. However, two problems emerge. The first is that the Act does permit exceptions when age is clearly relevant to the ability of an employee to perform his or her job. This is called a *bona fide occupational qualification* (BFOQ). The second problem is more basic—how do you prove you were discriminated against on the basis of age? We will examine both of these problems in some depth.

When Age Makes a Difference

An employer may take your age into account when age is "reasonably necessary to the normal operation of the particular business. . . ." This is somewhat vague language, and the courts have had a hard time trying to decide when age is "reasonably necessary" and when it is not. There are some obvious cases, such as actors required for youthful roles, when age is clearly important. There are other situations where age is clearly not relevant. For example, to arbitrarily decide that bank tellers should not be over 40 is a prohibited practice despite a bank's desire to provide a youthful look. Likewise, recruiting receptionists only under age 35 is illegal despite the claim that a pretty face in the outer office helps morale. It is just this type of stereotyping that the Act forbids.

But in the middle are the tough cases. Let's take a look at two of them. The first, *Houghton* v. *McDonnell Douglas Corporation,* involves a test pilot named Phillip Houghton. He was hired by McDonnell Douglas in 1946 as an assistant aerodynamicist. Over the course of ten years he rose to Chief Production Test Pilot. In 1971 McDonnell Douglas had some business setbacks and decided to reduce its pilot staff. The decision on who to take off pilot status was based on age: the oldest pilots were removed from flying service first. Houghton, at 52 the oldest test pilot, was removed first.

Houghton argued that McDonnell Douglas had violated the Age Discrimination in Employment Act. McDonnell Douglas argued that age is a bona fide occupational qualification for test pilots.

The court looked at the evidence. Houghton had been examined by McDonnell Douglas's medical staff and had been found in good health and fit to fly. Houghton also presented evidence showing that older pilots tended to have better judgment and therefore fewer accidents. However, two doctors testified that the skills generally needed to fly decrease as one grows older. The doctors agreed, though, that the aging process occurs "at diverse rates and varying degrees in different persons."

After looking at the evidence, the court concluded that Houghton had clearly been removed from his job because of his age. This meant that McDonnell Douglas had the burden of showing that age was a bona fide occupational qualification. However, the company's claim that older pilots are less safe was simply not proved. The court concluded that "there was no evidence that a test pilot's ability to perform his duties, both safely and effectively, was impaired in such manner as to justify the imposition of the arbitrary age limit applied by the Company here." Since McDonnell Douglas was unable to prove that age has a direct bearing on a pilot's ability to fly, age was not a bona fide occupational qualification in this case.

Obviously, had McDonnell Douglas been able to prove that Houghton, the *individual*, was not fit to fly, they would have had no problem firing him. But in such a case age would not have been the reason for the firing. Rather, Houghton's individual inability to fly would have been the basis, and the Age Discrimination in Employment Act would not have come into issue. In this case the employer claimed that the age of a pilot affects his ability; being unable to prove this contention, they lost their case. Houghton was ordered reinstated as Chief Production Test Pilot.

Obviously, McDonnell Douglas can still fire pilots who are over 40 years of age. But the law says that age cannot be a factor in deciding whom to fire. They can fire all blond pilots if they want to; no law protects blonds. They can fire incompetent pilots; no law protects incompetents. But they cannot fire pilots on the basis of age. A law does protect older persons.

In our second case, we move from a test pilot to a bus driver and from firing to hiring. The case is called *Hodgson* v. *Greyhound Lines, Inc.* and the problem was Greyhound's refusal to hire anyone who was over 35 years of age for the position of bus driver. The bus company argued that the safest bus drivers have 16 years experience. If older drivers are hired they will have fewer years remaining to work after having gained 16 years of experience. However, by hiring younger drivers, the number of drivers on the road with 16 or more years of experience will increase. This, the company argued, would result in greater safety for passengers. Also, there is a decreased functional ability, difficult to diagnose, that occurs with increasing age. Since each driver is responsible for the safety of many passengers, having younger drivers decreases the overall risk to passengers. Greyhound submitted statistical data backing up its claims.

Confronted with the claims and statistics, the court agreed with the bus company: "Greyhound has amply demonstrated that its maximum hiring age policy is founded upon a good faith judgment concerning the safety needs of its passengers and others. It has established that its hiring policy is not the result of an arbitrary belief lacking in objective reasons or rationale."

Thus, from this case it appears that an employer may refuse to hire someone because of age if there is a "rational basis" for setting the hiring age-limit. In this case, the basis was the safety of passengers. In general, a rational basis must be reasonably necessary to the effective maintenance of the employer's business. The mere convenience or preference of the employer is not enough.

Some of you may be wondering how the cases of the test pilot and the bus driver can be reconciled. We believe the answer must be found in the fact that the bus driver was fighting an age limit against *hiring* while the test pilot was fighting an arbitrary *firing*. If you assume an employer has a rational basis for concluding that, as a general rule, older workers cannot perform a particular job as well as younger ones, it would be impractical to require the employer to test *every job applicant* to determine if he is an exception to the general rule. However, once a person has been *hired* it *is* reasonable to require the employer to justify a firing or demotion based on age. And the justification must rely on the particular qualifications and abilities of the person being discharged. In other words, does this particular employee have a diminished ability to do his job as a result of being older?

For most of you the BFOQ will pose no serious problems. You are not test pilots or applicants for bus driver positions. In general, the BFOQ issue will arise only when the work you do requires a high degree of physical stamina or quick reflexes. And even in these cases the employer has a heavy burden establishing that age is valid grounds to discriminate.

If you are turned down for a job because the prospective employer considers age a BFOQ, we suggest you consider filing a complaint (the procedure is discussed later in this chapter). You have nothing to lose, and the agency you file the complaint with will be able to tell you whether age is a BFOQ for the job you were applying for.

If you are being retired, transferred, or demoted because your employer believes age is a BFOQ, remember the case of the test pilot. Unless your job requires greater manual skill, quicker reflexes, and better timing than being a test pilot does, you should be in good shape.

Power Play Pointer. Your employer tells you: "You're too old to do this job anymore." Try responding with: "I don't believe age is a *bona fide occupational qualification.*" The term *bona fide occupational qualification* is known to almost every lawyer (and most employers) who is involved in employment decisions. Its use shows that you are at least familiar with your rights. If your employer sticks to his guns and argues that "people your age" clearly can't perform as well as younger people, we suggest you be prepared to refer to *Houghton* v. *McDonnell Douglas.* The Houghton case gives you the opportunity to say: "Look, if age isn't a *bona fide occupational qualification* for a test pilot, how can it be for me?" In most cases that should end the discussion, with you holding the upper hand.

Proving Age Discrimination

There is a big difference between what you know and what you can prove. There is an even bigger difference between what you suspect and what you can prove. In order to make out a case of age discrimination, you need some evidence. How much? Enough to convince a court.

The court in the case of *Carpenter* v. *Continental Trailways* described the amount of evidence needed to make out a case: "After considering all the evidence and observing all the witnesses, the Court is convinced and finds the preponderance of the believable evidence demonstrates that age was a determinative factor in defendant's decision to force plaintiff to retire at age sixty-one. Therefore, defendant violated the Age Discrimination in Employment Act of 1967." Thus, you must present "believable evidence." The court in the Carpenter case shed some light on what this kind of evidence is: "A finding that age was used as one of the determinative factors . . . may be inferred from the totality of the circumstances." Thus, circumstantial evidence will be considered in court. Your job is to have enough evidence, circumstantial if necessary, to convince someone that age was a factor considered when making an employment decision affecting you.

Power Play Pointer. Keep a record of everything that occurs that might tend to show a case of age discrimination. If your employer says: "You're getting a little old for this job," write it down. If there was a witness, note who it was. If other older employees are being eased out, note who they were, how old they were, and how old the people who replaced them were. If you get a compliment for your job, write it down. Do not trust your memory. Make a record of anything that might help you later on.

The evidence you are able to amass will become part of your case should you go to court. But whom are you trying to convince? In the past, the answer was a judge; you had no right to a jury trial. However, in 1978 the law was changed to permit jury trials. This change is most important, since juries tend to be sympathetic to the "little guy," especially when the guy is graying at the temples. We all get old, and the jury members know it.

Power Play Pointer. There is nothing quite so threatening to an employer as a jury. There are more employees than there are employers, which means the jury will probably be your peers, not his. Confronting your employer with the prospect of a jury trial is a strong power play. It should not be used unless you feel it is necessary. However, if in the course of your power play it becomes clear that your employer is trying to impress you with the fact that his battery of lawyers can handle you, you may wish to raise the specter of a jury trial. For example, if your employer says: "Well, why don't we just let the lawyers and the judge work it out," you might respond with: "If necessary, I'll leave it up to a jury of my peers." If he questions your right to a jury trial, remind him that the law was changed recently and you do have the right.

The final part of any antidiscrimination law is the sanction. What are your rights if you are the victim of age discrimination? The answer is that you may have the right to any or all of the following: (1) back pay, (2) damages, (3) an order reinstating you to your old job, and (4) attorney's fees.

Back Pay

Under the law, you have the right to receive any wages you would have earned had you not been subjected to age discrimination. In most cases, any wages you earned during this period (for example, if you get another job) are deducted. As one court decided: "Back pay is measured by the difference between the salary an employee would have received but for a violation of the Act and the salary actually received from other employment less unemployment benefits. The relevant period for measuring back pay begins with the time of the loss of employment as a result of the violation and ends when the affected employee accepts or declines reinstatement."

Damages

In addition to back pay, the law permits the awarding of damages. There are two types of damages that may be awarded: (1) liquidated damages and (2) damages for pain and suffering.

Liquidated damages are specifically authorized by the law to, as one court put it, "provide compensation for the more obscure items of damage resulting from the retention of the employee's pay by his employer." The amount of these damages is the equivalent of any back pay that is awarded. Thus, for example, if you were entitled to $10,000 in back pay, you could claim an additional amount of $10,000 as liquidated damages. A court would award liquidated damages only if it felt the employer had discriminated against you "willfully." Presumably, if the discrimination was inadvertent you would not be entitled to these damages.

Whether or not you are entitled to damages for the

pain and suffering you underwent as a result of the discrimination is an issue that is still unresolved as this book goes to press. The courts simply cannot agree. For purposes of a power play, however, you can assume you are entitled to such an award. You may not be, but your employer and his attorney cannot be sure.

In one recent case, an employee who proved his case of age discrimination claimed damages for pain and suffering. The employee's wife claimed that her husband's "discharge adversely affected their marital relationship and created pressures which curtailed their social activities and vacation plans. The [employee] also testified that the discharge resulted in emotional strain, causing loss of sleep." The employee asked for $50,000 in damages. He was awarded $7,500. (In this case, the damages might have been higher were it not for the fact that the court had already awarded back pay and liquidated damages totaling almost $150,000!).

Power Play Pointer. The prospect of damages for pain and suffering combined with the fact that a jury might determine just how high the damages are is a potent motivating force to get your employer in line. The trick here is to convince your employer that the longer he plays around with you, the higher the damages will be. "This age discrimination has been causing me severe mental and physical distress. My wife is having severe emotional problems because of my difficulties. The damages increase each day. God forbid something serious should happen, because under the law, you might be held responsible. Check with your lawyer."

Reinstatement

In addition to receiving back pay and damages, the law gives courts authority to order an employer to reinstate an employee. Very few courts have dealt with the reinstatement process. However, those that have indicated that it means placing an employee back in the same job he held prior to being discharged or demoted.

Power Play Pointer. Perhaps the best way to convince an employer of the futility of discriminating against you is to point out your right to reinstatement. If your employer seems to be ready to pay a lawyer to get you off the payroll, you might remind him that "under the *Age Discrimination in Employment Act,* when I win my case you're going to have to *reinstate* me. It's part of the equitable relief I'm entitled to."

Attorney's Fees

The law specifically gives you the right to collect your attorney's fees if you win your age-discrimination case. In one case, which we will discuss below, the fees awarded totaled $14,700! Obviously, having to pay your attorney can add a hefty penalty to your employer's losses should you win your case.

Power Play Pointer. You have met face to face with your employer and it has become clear that he thinks you are bluffing. He doesn't think you have enough money to hire an attorney to compete with the hotshot lawyers the company has on retainer. At such a point, you could slip in this observation: "If we have to go to court I'll have no trouble finding a lawyer, since if I win you will have to pay his *fees.*" There are, in fact, many lawyers who will handle your case while agreeing in advance that they will take a fee only if they win your case for you. They rely on your right to collect attorney's fees. So if you are a little short of cash and you find you do need a lawyer, look for one who is willing to take your case with the understanding that he will get paid his full fee only if he wins and the court awards attorney's fees.

The case of *Coates* v. *National Cash Register Company* is a good example of all the different types of remedies available under the law and serves as a good review of the information in this chapter so far. George Coates was 50 years of age when he was fired by the National Cash Register Co. (NRC). He had spent twenty-two years with the company.

George was one of the older field engineers for NCR in the Danville office. New equipment was always being developed by NCR, and retraining programs were needed to keep field engineers up-to-date. George was well trained on mechanical machines but was not up-to-date on the new wave of electronic machines.

NCR asked the younger workers in the Danville office to participate in training programs on the electronic machines. Despite the fact that George had requested such training, he had not received it. Thus, as mechanical machines became more and more obsolete, so did George.

Business got bad for NCR in 1974, and people had to be fired. Despite the fact that George was a good employee, his immediate supervisor decided he would have to be one of those fired, since he lacked the necessary training on electronic machines. After some efforts by NCR to find George another job in the company, he left in 1975. And then he filed a complaint claiming a violation of the Age Discrimination in Employment Act.

The court decided that

NCR's decision to discharge George was not directly based on age, but it was based on the training of George. The evidence clearly established that the relative training levels of NCR employees was directly related to the age of the employees. So by using the training level as the basis of the discharge decision, NCR indirectly discharged George because of his age. Therefore this court holds that the training or lack of training, which ostensibly is an objective and valid criterion for employment decisions, cannot form the basis of an employment decision when that lack of training is created by age discrimination. The age discrimination which invalidates an employment decision need not be direct or intentional. This court further holds that George was discharged "because of" his "age."

The court having found a case of age discrimination—indirect, but discrimination nonetheless—the next task was deciding on the remedy. George asked for everything: back pay, liquidated damages, damages for pain and suffering, and his attorney's fees. The court awarded back pay and liquidated damages of $21,500, damages for pain and suffering of $15,000, and attorney's fees of $14,700!

What should you do if you are, or suspect you might be, subjected to age discrimination? The answer depends on whether the discrimination has occurred or not. If you only suspect that it might occur, keep records and build a file so you will be prepared if your suspicions come true. If you know you are going to be fired or demoted because of your age, consider using a power play to convince your employer that you are one employee not to be tampered with. However, if the discrimination has happened, *do not sit around before using a power play.* Under the Act, you must file a complaint with the appropriate agency within 180 days after the discrimination occurred. Thus, you cannot afford to wait before deciding what you will do. Indeed, a study recently concluded that almost 30 percent of all cases brought under the Age Discrimination in Employment Act were dismissed because the employee did not file his complaint in a timely manner.

In order to file a complaint you should get in touch either with a lawyer or with your local office of the Wage and Hour Division of the Department of Labor.

Codeword Glossary

Age Discrimination in Employment Act   A federal law, found in section 621 of volume 29 of the United States Code, that prohibits discrimination against older workers.

attorney's fee   Your right to have your employer pay your attorney's fees if you win your case.

back pay   Authorized by section 626 of the Age Discrimination in Employment Act. You have the right to collect the wages you would have received had you not been the victim of discrimination.

bona fide occupational qualification (BFOQ)   A legitimate grounds on which an employer can discriminate on the basis of age.

Carpenter v. *Continental Trailways*   A federal court case found in volume 446 of the Federal Supplement at page 70.

Coates v. *National Cash Register Company*   A federal court case found in volume 433 of the Federal Supplement at page 655.

damages   Authorized by section 626 of the Age Discrimination in Employment Act. You have the right to collect money from your employer to compensate you for any injury caused to you by his discrimination.

Hodgson v. *Greyhound Lines, Inc.*   A federal court case found in volume 499 of the Federal Reporter, Second Series, at page 859.

Houghton v. *McDonnell Douglas Corporation*   A federal

court case found in volume 553 of the Federal Reporter, Second Series, at page 561.

jury trial Your new right to have a jury decide whether you have been the victim of discrimination; found in section 626 of the Age Discrimination in Employment Act as amended in 1978.

reinstatement Authorized by section 626 of the Age Discrimination in Employment Act. If you are fired as a result of age discrimination you have the right to be returned to your job.

8

Leasing a New Car

Like many consumers, you may be considering leasing a new car, rather than buying one. Statistics show the increasing popularity of long-term auto leases. According to the National Automobile Dealers Association, about 300,000 newly manufactured cars were leased to consumers in 1965. By 1970 that annual figure had more than doubled. During 1974, over one million new cars were leased to consumers. Detroit's soothsayers project that 80 percent of the growth in auto leasing through 1980 will occur in leases to individuals.

While long-term auto leasing does provide consumers with some advantages—such as manageable monthly payments—it has also proven to be a major source of headaches. Over the years, many consumers who leased cars never really knew what they were getting into, because all the terms of the leasing arrangement were not spelled out in advance. Hidden charges and added costs were constantly popping up. By the time they surfaced, the consumer had already signed a lease and was locked into paying.

The biggest potential trap of all in auto leasing is the notorious *balloon payment,* which comes with so-called open-end leases. There are basically two kinds of long-term auto leases: *closed-end leases* and *open-end leases* (open-end leases are sometimes called *finance leases*). On a closed-end lease, you are obligated to make a fixed number of rental payments: for example, 24 monthly payments of $159 each. When the lease term ends and you return the car, you don't owe anything more. There is *no* balloon payment lurking at the end of a closed-end lease.

But there usually is such a payment when an open-end lease terminates, and it has been a real shocker to many unsuspecting consumers. You see, an open-end lease makes you accountable to the dealer for the resale value of the car when the lease ends. That end-of-lease value is only estimated by the dealer when you originally sign the lease. For example, the end-of-lease value of a car might be estimated at $4,000—but if you return the car after, say, two years of rental use and its resale value is only $3,200, then *you're responsible for making up the difference.* In other words, you get stuck with a balloon payment (over and above all your regular rental payments) of $800.

Considering the unwelcome possibility of such a lead balloon, you may wonder why anyone would choose an open-end lease over one that is closed-end. The answer is simple: rental payments are usually considerably lower on an open-end lease. That's because you, not the dealer, bear the full risk of depreciation during an open-end lease. Since you're the one left holding the bag—or balloon—at the end of the lease, the dealer can afford to offer you lower rental payments during the lease. Chiefly because of these lower rates, the open-end lease is by far the most prevalent form of long-term auto lease today.

Regrettably, there has always been an incentive for dealers to be deliberately overoptimistic when estimating a car's resale value on an open-end lease. By projecting an unrealistically high resale value, the dealer is in a position to offer rental payments that are artificially low; he knows he'll make up the difference later on in a fat balloon payment. Of course, the consumer lacks the expertise necessary to second-guess the dealer's end-of-lease estimate. Accepting that estimate as gospel, and lured by the low rental, the consumer signs the lease. Unwittingly, he commits himself to pay a disproportionately large balloon payment at the end of the lease.

Now a new federal law gives you a needle to burst the dealer's balloon. The Consumer Leasing Act went into effect on March 23, 1978. It covers leases on automobiles that will be used primarily for personal or family purposes (commercial leases aren't covered). The lease must be for a period of over four months. And the consumer's total financial obligation under the lease can't exceed $25,000.

The new Act is designed to benefit you in two ways: first, to let you know everything you ever wanted to know about a car lease *before you sign one;* and second, to let you deflate big balloon payments. The first goal is accomplished by requiring a dealer to disclose to you all the vital figures and terms you need to know in order to decide whether you should sign the lease. (No more hidden charges and unexpected "extras"!) *All of these disclosures must be made together, in writing, clearly and conspicuously, before you sign the lease.* (No more fine print or blank spaces "to be filled in later.")

Basically, there are twenty disclosures that you're legally entitled to under the Consumer Leasing Act. They are listed below. All of them must be made prior to an open-end lease; every item except numbers 10 through 13 must be disclosed on a closed-end lease. As you will see, these twenty disclosures require complete candor and tremendous attention to detail on the part of the dealer. Failure to make even a minor disclosure is a technical violation of the Act that can make the dealer liable to you for a substantial penalty. That's important to bear in mind as you study the list, because you may be able to use the dealer's violation(s) as the basis for a power play later on—as we will see.

1. *Lessor and Lessee.* The auto dealer is the lessor; you are the lessee. Both of you must be identified by name on the lease.

2. *Identification of Auto.* There should be a brief description of the auto to be leased: e.g., make, model, year, body style, vehicle identification number, special accessories.

3. *Initial Payment.* The lease must disclose the total dollar amount of any initial payment that the lessee makes when entering into the lease. Furthermore, the various components of this initial payment must be separately identified, although they don't have to be itemized in terms of dollar amounts. For example, the lessee might make a *down payment*, which reduces the value of the leased vehicle to be amortized over the term of the lease. There might be a *trade-in allowance* for the lessee's old car. Often an *advance monthly payment* is required; if, for instance, the last month's rental payment is collected at the inception of the lease, then "Advance Monthly Payment of the Last Month's Rent" ought to be written down. Other components in the initial payment might include delivery charges, registration fees, and a refundable security deposit.

4. *Lease Term.* The term of the lease period must be stated: for example, "24 months" or "April 1, 1979, through April 1, 1981."

5. *Periodic Payments.* A lessor must disclose the number, amount, and due dates (or payment periods) of the payments scheduled to be made under the lease. For example, the disclosure might read: "The first monthly pay-

ment of $100 is due on May 4, 1979; 23 subsequent payments of $100 due on the 4th day of each month thereafter."

6. *Total Periodic Payments.* This item is the sum of all periodic payments (including any advance payment) to be made over the term of the lease.

7. *Total of Official Charges.* When renting a car, you may have to pay certain official charges, such as license fees, registration fees, certificate of title fees, and taxes. The sum of all such charges must be disclosed.

8. *Total of Other Charges.* Any other charges, such as maintenance, which you will have to pay the lessor must be separately identified and itemized as to their total amount and then added up for one grand total.

9. *Insurance.* The types and amounts of insurance coverage must be disclosed—as well as their total premium cost if they are provided by the lessor.

10. *Estimated Value of Auto at End of Lease.* The lessor must state a reasonable, good-faith estimate of the auto's resale value at the end of the lease term. This figure must be clearly identified as an estimate. The estimate will be critical in determining what, if any, balloon payment you will have to make at the end of the lease.

11. *Total Lease Obligation.* This dollar figure represents basically what the lease will cost the consumer. It is the sum of three other items already disclosed to the consumer: first, any initial down payment or trade-in allowance (item 3 above); second, the total amount of the basic periodic payments (item 6); and third, the estimated value of the auto at the end of the lease (item 10).

12. *Initial Value of Automobile.* The lessor must disclose how much the auto is worth at the start of the lease.

13. *Differential.* This dollar figure is simply the difference between items 11 and 12; it is arrived at by sub-

tracting the initial value of the auto from the total lease obligation.

14. *Standards for Wear and Use.* The lessor is permitted, but not required, to set reasonable standards for evaluating wear and use on the auto. If he sets such standards, they must be disclosed; they will be applied when determining whether a leased car has been subjected to unreasonable or excessive wear or use.

15. *Maintenance.* Who is responsible for servicing the car: the lessor? the lessee? both? The Consumer Leasing Act leaves that up to the parties to the lease. Whatever maintenance responsibilities are agreed on must be spelled out clearly in the lease.

16. *Express Warranties.* The lease must disclose all express warranties made on the car (by either the manufacturer or the lessor) that protect the lessee. A brief reference to the standard manufacturer's warranty would suffice.

17. *Early Termination and Default.* This item contains the conditions under which the lessee may terminate the lease prior to the end of the lease term. There may be a charge for such early termination. If so, it must be listed here, or the method for its computation must be explained.

This item should also contain the grounds on which the lessor may terminate the lease prior to the end of the lease term: for example, default by the lessee in making periodic payments when due. The amount of any default charges, or the method for computing them, must be listed.

18. *Security Interest.* In order to be assured that the lessee will perform his obligations under the lease, the lessor may take a security interest in some of the lessee's property. Then, if the lessee doesn't live up to the lease, the lessor can take legal action to enforce his security interest in the property. Any security interests taken by the lessor must be dis-

closed in the lease, along with an identification of the property covered.

19. *Late Payments.* If the lessor assesses a charge for lateness in making periodic payments, the amount of the charge, or the method for computing it, must be disclosed.

20. *Option to Purchase.* The lease must disclose whether the lessee is afforded an option to purchase the auto and, if so, at what time. Assuming the option may be exercised at the end of the lease term, the purchase price must be disclosed. If the option can be exercised during the lease term, then the lease must disclose either the purchase price or the method by which it will be computed.

Considering how much data must be disclosed to you and in what detail, there are bound to be some omissions or errors. While they may seem relatively insignificant, they are, nonetheless, technical violations of the Consumer Leasing Act. (Remember, one of the chief purposes of this Act is, in Congress's words, "to assure meaningful disclosure of the terms of leases" so that a consumer can comparison-shop and choose the best rental deal.) And the Act treats all violations seriously. Under the "civil liability" section of the Act, a dealer who fails to satisfy all of the disclosure requirements may be held liable to you for:

1. any actual damage you suffer (e.g., unexpected expense you incur because certain costs were not properly disclosed to you); plus

2. a statutory penalty in the amount of 25 percent of the total monthly payments under the lease (this penalty shall not be less than $100, nor more than $1000); plus

3. your attorney's fees and court costs incurred in winning any judgment against the lessor.

You can sue a dealer—should it ever become necessary —in any federal or state court—including your local small claims court, assuming your claim falls within the right dollar limit (see Appendix A). If a lessor should sue you to collect a balloon payment, you would be able to file a *counterclaim* against him for violation of the disclosure provisions of the Act. As we will see shortly, the mere threat of such an expensive counterclaim can be useful in any power play against a greedy lessor.

Besides being a valuable cost-disclosure law, the Consumer Leasing Act also seeks to eradicate the evil of excessive balloon payments. Specific limitations on these payments are imposed. In order to put these limitations in the proper context, you should know that the Act encourages private out-of-court settlements between lessor and lessee whenever a balloon payment is in dispute. The Act authorizes you to make a "mutually agreeable final adjustment" with the lessor regarding any balloon payment demanded of you. That's the legal equivalent of *Let's Make a Deal,* so get set for a power play.

The first of the Act's limitations on balloon payments is a general one: it's illegal for a lessor to deliberately overestimate what the resale value of the car will be at the end of the lease. According to the Act, this estimate (item 10 in the disclosure checklist) must be a "reasonable approximation of the anticipated actual fair market value of the property on lease expiration."

For example, all available auto-industry price indicators might point to a resale value of $4,400 for a car that is going to be leased for three years. If, despite this reasonable forecast, a lessor blithely estimated the resale value at $5,000, he would almost certainly be violating the Act.

The second limitation on balloon payments relates to the actual resale price on the car at the end of the lease. You don't have to submit blindly to whatever resale price the lessor dreams up. (Remember, the less he claims the car is actually worth, the bigger your balloon payment will be.)

The Consumer Leasing Act gives you the right to insist on an outside appraisal of the car's fair market value. You have the right to select an independent third party (e.g., an auto mechanic or appraiser) who will render his professional opinion as to how much the car could be sold for. Whoever you choose must be acceptable to the lessor, and you will have to bear the cost of the appraisal (it'll be way less than the balloon payment you face). *The result of this independent appraisal is absolutely final and binding on both you and the lessor.*

The third limitation on balloon payments is a direct one, which is bound to save consumers money. Under the Consumer Leasing Act, a balloon payment is generally limited to *no more than three times your average monthly payment under the lease.* Thus, if your monthly payment is $100, the balloon payment, if any, shouldn't exceed $300.

Suppose the balloon payment turns out to more than three times your monthly payment? For example, it's six times your $100 monthly payment, or $600. Then a legal presumption arises: the lessor's original estimate of the car's resale value was unreasonable and not made in good faith. In order to overcome this legal presumption and stand a chance of collecting the excess $300, the lessor will have to sue you. In court he will have to prove—no mean feat— that despite the large discrepancy between the car's resale value as originally estimated and as it actually turned out (resulting in a $600 balloon payment), still, the original estimate was somehow reasonable and made in good faith. This burden of proof is a difficult one for the lessor to bear. He may not even want to attempt it, considering the legal expenses he will have to incur.

Added to the lessor's difficulties is the fact that the Act requires him to pay *your legal fees,* too! That's right: whether the lessor *wins or loses* his lawsuit against you, he winds up footing your lawyer's fees. (Only in one circumstance will you have to pay your own attorney's fees: if the lessor can prove in court that you exceeded reasonable standards set in the lease for ordinary wear and tear on the car—disclosure item 14 in the checklist—and that, as a result of your abuse, the car was either damaged or so run-down that its resale value fell unexpectedly low. Such a burden of proof is difficult to carry—and the lessor knows it—unless you really did a number on the car, such as driving it in a demolition derby!)

The Federal Trade Commission is the agency that enforces the Consumer Leasing Act as it applies to most lessors. While the FTC won't act as your private lawyer, it may investigate your complaint about a specific lessor, especially if other consumers have also complained. (The regional offices of the FTC are listed in Appendix E.) Since no businessperson enjoys the prospect of the federal government snooping around his files, you'll discover that the name of the Federal Trade Commission can be a potent codeword in any power play with a lessor.

Power Play Pointer. Any power play you're likely to get into will arise because of the lessor's demand for an outrageous balloon payment. Be prepared for such a showdown by consulting another dealer or an auto mechanic to get some idea of whether the lessor's estimated resale figure and current resale figure seem to meet industry guidelines. If his figures are out of line, you'll be able to catch him off guard.

The most important preparatory step is to go over your lease with a fine-tooth comb, searching for any violation of the Act's disclosure requirements. (Any lawyer worth his salt would do just that.) You are bound to find something —anything—missing or erroneous. For example, the various components in the initial payment (disclosure item 3) may not have been separately identified; or the estimated resale value (item 10) may not have been properly labeled as an estimate; or the late-payment charge (item 19) may have been omitted altogether. If this all sounds like nit-picking to you, you're right. (Nit-picking is what lawyers do for a living.) But it will pay off, because every nit you pick opens the lessor up to a potentially expensive claim that he has violated the Act.

Is this nit-picking realistic? No one can be sure, because the Act is so new. However, money damages have been awarded to consumers for minor violations of other laws very similar to the Consumer Leasing Act. For example, the federal Truth In Lending Law requires certain itemized disclosures when you buy a car on credit. In a 1974 federal case, a woman successfully sued a Dodge dealer who had listed a $15 charge for "tag, title, and fees" without separately itemizing each one of these three charges. The woman was awarded the maximum statutory penalty of $1,000 plus $3,000 in attorney's fees! So nit-pick away— you're bound to come up with some useful legal ammunition.

Now let's apply all your savvy to a hypothetical situation. You leased a car for 24 months at $100 per month. The estimated resale price stated in the lease was $4,600. But when you returned the car the lessor claimed it could be sold for only $4,000. You face a balloon payment of $600—six times your monthly payment. You are confident that you gave the car no more than ordinary wear and tear.

You might start by raising a smokescreen—that is, without committing yourself, create some doubts in the lessor's mind just to see how accommodating he seems to be. For example, tell the lessor you've spoken to other dealers (or mechanics) who think the lessor's resale figures (both estimated and actual) are out of line. You might suggest to the lessor, "I'm giving serious thought to having an outside *independent appraisal* made of the car's actual resale value. As you may know, that appraisal would be legally binding on us both." See if that unwelcome prospect shakes the lessor's confidence and opens him up to a settlement—which is your ultimate goal.

If you don't seem to be making headway, get down to brass tacks: "Look, this balloon payment is six times my monthly payment. The *Consumer Leasing Act* presumes that anything over three times is unreasonable, unless you can prove otherwise in court. Can we knock off three hundred dollars right now, or do you plan to waste your time and money in court?"

If the lessor vows he'll drag you into court, don't get nervous. Just ask with genuine disbelief, "You mean you're going to pick up my *attorney's fees,* too—just on the chance of getting another three hundred dollars?" Be prepared for him to accuse you of having abused the car, thereby relieving him of the obligation to pay your legal fees. You can dispute this accusation and press him to the point where he admits that settling with you for, say, $300 (instead of the entire $600 balloon payment) beats paying his own lawyer to go to court for the other $300.

But there may be an even better power play if your earlier nit-picking was fruitful. Look the lessor in the eye and say calmly: "By the way, if you insist on taking me to court for this balloon payment, I want you to know that I'm going to make my own *counterclaim.* You've violated the *Consumer Leasing Act,* because you forgot to list the certificate of title fee on this lease. So I'm going to *counterclaim* against you for the *maximum statutory penalty*— that's twenty-five percent of my total monthly payments (which comes to six hundred dollars), plus, of course, my *attorney's fees.* I bet you'll come out of court owing *me* money!"

Now you've got the lessor over a barrel. If the lessor

consults his lawyer, he'll discover that, yes, there is indeed a very good chance that you could win the statutory penalty and attorney's fees. (Note that you're entitled to your attorney's fees on the counterclaim, even if lessor can prove that you abused the car.) The lessor can't be at all sure of proving his own claim, let alone defeating your counterclaim. That old soft spot over legal liability and legal expense is wide open. If you feel confident enough about your position, you might press hard for a "mutually agreeable final adjustment" in which the balloon payment is wiped out completely—zero dollars. Even if you settle for, say, a $100 balloon payment, treat yourself to a night on the town—you've just won your first $500 case.

Codeword Glossary

attorney's fees Under the Consumer Leasing Act, if you win a judgment against the lessor for violation of the Act, he may be held liable for your attorney's fees. Also, he will probably have to pay your attorney's fees if he sues you to collect an excessive balloon payment.

Consumer Leasing Act The federal statute that requires detailed prerental disclosures by auto lessors and severely limits the size of balloon payments. This Act can be found in section 1667 of title 15 of the United States Code.

counterclaim The legal procedure by which you assert your claim for violation of the Act against the lessor if he sues you to collect a balloon payment.

Federal Trade Commission The main agency charged with enforcing the Consumer Leasing Act.

independent appraisal An evaluation of the car's actual fair market value at the end of the lease, performed by an outside party, which is legally binding on both the lessor and the lessee.

maximum statutory penalty Twenty-five percent of the total monthly payments under the lease (not less than $100 nor more than $1000) is the penalty for violation of the disclosure requirements under the Act.

9 Up Against the Bill Collector

All of the power plays we've been learning about so far are rooted in the law. There is another brand of power play that relies on twisting, stretching, and sometimes stomping on the law. At this sort of no-holds-barred power play, the bill collector is a superstar. If a bill collector ever gets on your trail, you're going to have to play like a pro in order to overpower him fair and square.

Bill collectors are prepared to go to extremes to collect on a debt, because they operate on a commission basis— fifty cents of every dollar collected normally goes to the bill collector. So the incentive is there to squeeze something —anything—out of the consumer. The bill collector is more interested in getting a buck than in listening to excuses, no matter how legitimate you may think they are.

Daisy Wright of Missouri discovered how brazen a bill collector can be. Daisy and her husband disputed the amount of money they owed on some new furniture. Nevertheless, a bill collector hounded her for the money, showing up repeatedly at Mary's Café in Springfield, where Daisy

166

worked as a waitress. While Daisy tried to wait on customers, the bill collector followed her around the café, berating her loudly: "Your day's arrived"; "You *will* talk to me"; "Something is going to be done here while I am here—I think you're deadbeats—I don't think you intended to pay for the furniture when you got it."

Other tricks of the trade include incessant phone calls, embarrassing postcards, and special delivery letters dispatched around midnight and guaranteed to awaken you. One bill collector threatened an elderly widow with having her husband's body exhumed and his casket repossessed unless she paid his overdue funeral bill!

Perhaps the Bill Collector's Browbeating Award should go to an agent of Federated Credit Corporation in Massachusetts. He kept after Richard Maller of Maine, chiefly through an incessant stream of abusive long-distance phone calls. Here's part of just one out of four calls that poor Maller received in a single evening:

MALLER. What's your name? Who do you work for?

AGENT: Oh, you gotta be kidding.

MALLER: No, I ain't kidding.

AGENT: You got a cement block in between your ears. Who the hell do you think I work for?

MALLER: Would you mind telling me?

AGENT: I work for the Federated Credit Corporation. Okay? Write it down so you can write it in to your lawyer and maybe we can talk sense into your lawyer.

MALLER: Well, I hope you can, buddy.

AGENT: You haven't even got a dime to pay a lawyer. Who the hell are you kidding?

MALLER: I don't need a dime. I can go to Legal Aid.

AGENT: Legal Aid. Well, maybe they'll pay your bills for you, too.

MALLER: I have a wife that's under psychiatric treatment and has been that way for three years, and if you make her any worse, buddy, you *are* in trouble.

AGENT: When are you gonna pay the bill?

MALLER: If you put her over the brink, you will have had it, and believe me, I know this.

AGENT: Don't give me that baloney. You owe us the money and when are you gonna mail it?

MALLER: Do you understand what I said?

AGENT: Nobody will listen to you. I wanta know when I'm gonna get my money.

MALLER: She was under psychiatric treatment and if you want to talk to the psychiatrist. . . .

AGENT: You're the one that needs a psychiatrist. . . . Listen, when are you gonna mail the money?

Finally Richard Maller hung up in disgust.

Neither he nor Daisy Wright nor the elderly widow was a deadbeat—that is, someone who willfully refuses to pay a just debt. Contrary to popular belief, only a minuscule percentage (less than 5 percent) of the people whom bill collectors chase are deadbeats. "The vast majority of consumers who obtain credit," reported a Senate banking committee in 1977, "fully intend to repay their debts. When default occurs, it is nearly always due to an unforeseen event such as unemployment, overextension, serious illness, or marital difficulties or divorce." While such beleaguered consumers are of course bound to pay what they owe, they are also entitled to have their homes, jobs, and peace of mind insulated from the invasions of privacy typical of too many bill collectors.

Until 1978 there was little meaningful legislation protecting consumers from debt-collection abuse. Not all states had laws regulating debt collection, and those laws that did exist lacked teeth. Because of the dearth of protection at the state level and the evidence of widespread abuses, Congress enacted the Fair Debt Collection Practices Act, which became effective on March 20, 1978.

The Act regulates collection methods on all basic consumer indebtedness—whether it arises out of a purchase, a loan, a contract for services, insurance, etc. Knowing the practices outlawed by the Act, as well as the new rights given to consumers, you'll be prepared to meet a bill collector's show of force with some legal power of your own. The confrontations you have with a bill collector are most likely to occur via his favorite weapon—the telephone.

Power Play Pointer. If your first contact with a bill collector is an unexpected telephone call, keep cool. Don't let the conversation descend into prolonged bickering, the way Richard Maller did. Instead, be businesslike and to the point; that way the bill collector will not even be tempted to browbeat you.

If, for instance, the bill collector starts off abruptly pressuring you for money without an introduction, interrupt him firmly: "Pardon me, but would you please identify yourself? Who are you? Whom do you work for? Why are you calling me? You must know it's against federal law to make anonymous calls like this." That should make the bill collector back off a little; anyone who has enough presence of mind to say what you've just said probably won't succumb to harassment. So you're one step ahead.

Once a bill collector has contacted you, the immediate question is, do you really owe the money? If you do and you know it, don't beat around the bush. Let the bill collector know you're making a determined effort to meet your financial obligations. Try to arrange a schedule of payments that you can keep up with. If you unjustifiably take refuge behind every legal protection at your disposal, you may wind up exploiting your rights at your own expense. (Your credit rating can suffer, and you may get entangled in an otherwise avoidable lawsuit.)

What if it's immediately apparent to you that you don't owe the money; or what if you're not sure; or what if you dispute the amount claimed by the bill collector? Then you should exercise your legal right to have the debt *verified*. Prior to the Fair Debt Collection Practices Act, if a consumer disputed the validity of a debt, he had no right to demand that the bill collector produce some written proof that the debt was in fact genuine and accurate. As a result, the bill collector might go right on badgering the consumer for payment, despite denials or explanations by the consumer. This sort of senseless harassment need no longer be tolerated.

Under the Act, the consumer has the right to verification of any debt, whether he disputes it entirely or just in part. The Act sets up a timetable for verification: within 5 days after initial contact with the consumer regarding collection, the bill collector must send the consumer written notification containing: (1) the amount of the debt; (2) the name of the creditor to whom the debt is owed; and (3) a statement that unless the consumer, within 30 days after receipt of the notification, disputes the validity of the debt (in whole or in part), the bill collector will assume that the debt is valid.

Within this 30-day period, the consumer has a right to notify the bill collector that he disputes part or all of the debt; notification must be made *in writing*. In the case of such a dispute, the bill collector is obligated to verify the debt and report back to the consumer by mail with the verification. *During the period it takes for verification, the bill collector must cease all efforts to collect any portion of the debt that is disputed.*

Power Play Pointer. It's up to you to assert your right to verification. If the bill collector's error in contacting you is apparent, clue him in promptly. Over the phone, for example, you might simply explain: "I'm sorry, but you must have the wrong T. Smith. That's my name, but I've never had a charge account with the store you're representing." If there's some less apparent explanation, offer that to the bill collector. For instance, "That bill you've got is for the wrong amount; I've been disputing it with the store for months, and it still isn't cleared up."

Don't expect to get off the hook that easily, however. The bill collector may figure he can argue you down in the hope that you'll pay up just to get rid of him. Should he try to steamroll you, cut him off firmly, as is your right: "Look, there's no point in our wasting time arguing over this thing. I insist on *verification* of this debt, which you must give me under the *Fair Debt Collection Practices Act.* I will write you a letter today requesting verification, and until I receive that verification you have no authority to bother me further about this debt. I trust that's clear?"

As soon as you get off the phone, write the bill collector a formal request for verification. (Remember, you have only 30 days in which to act.) Here's a sample letter you can adapt to suit your particular case:

[Insert date of mailing]

> *[Your name*
> *Mailing address*
> *City, state, zip code]*

[Bill collector's name
Company name
Mailing address
City, state, zip code]

*Re: Verification of Debt under Fair Debt Collection
Practices Act*

Dear [bill collector's name]:
    Pursuant to the federal Fair Debt Collection
Practices Act (title 15 of the United States Code,
section 1692), I request written verification of the
alleged debt you described to me in our telephone
conversation [substitute "your letter" if appropriate] of
[Insert date].
    As I understand it, you are claiming that I owe
[Insert amount] to [Insert name of creditor, if known]
for [Relate whatever is known about the origin and
subject matter of the debt].
    I dispute the validity of this debt. [Briefly explain
whether you dispute it in whole or in part and on what
grounds. For example:] The color television set which I
charged at the XYZ Department Store malfunctioned
within two weeks after it was delivered. Despite
repeated attempts, XYZ's service personnel were
unable to repair the set. At my request, they removed
the set and promised to replace it with a new one. To
date I have still not received that replacement. Until I
do receive that new working set, I have asked XYZ to
credit my account for the full purchase price, which
they have apparently failed to do. Therefore, I do not
owe the amount of the purchase price which you claim;
I owe nothing.
    Please recheck this alleged debt with [Insert name
of creditor] and obtain a written verification of it. Mail
that verification to me at the above address.
    I understand that until you have mailed
verification of the debt to me, the Fair Debt Collection
Practices Act requires you to cease collection of the
debt [Substitute "collection of the disputed portion of

the debt" if you are disputing only part of the debt],
and I shall expect your compliance.
Sincerely,

[Signature]
_____
[Your name]
cc: [Insert name of creditor]

As the "cc" at the foot of the letter indicates, you
will send a carbon copy of your letter to the creditor whom
the bill collector represents. (You may want to include a
brief cover letter to the creditor, identifying yourself—e.g.,
by charge account number—and urging prompt resolution
of your dispute with the creditor.) If your dispute is bona
fide, the creditor—unlike the bill collector—has a vested
interest in preserving his ongoing business relationship with
you. Rather than alienate you even further, the creditor
may hasten to clear matters up and get the bill collector
off your back.

Whether or not the bill collector ever succeeds in
verifying the debt, he may decide to keep after you. (Consumers have been known to pay debts they never incurred,
just to get a bill collector off their back.) If you start
getting victimized, it will come in handy to know what
collection techniques are prohibited by the Fair Debt Collection Practices Act. Here is a laundry list of dirty tricks
prohibited by the Act:

Badmouthing Behind Your Back. A favorite pressure
device of bill collectors has been to embarrass a consumer
by leaking news of his financial distress to friends, relatives,
coworkers, the boss, etc. This tactic is illegal. Under the
Act, the bill collector can generally contact only the consumer, the creditor, and attorneys involved in the case.

Tracking Down the Consumer. While a bill collector

is permitted to discover your whereabouts by contacting other people, he can't overstep certain bounds. All he can do is seek to confirm information about your residence, home telephone number, and place of employment; these are the only three items that the bill collector can ask about. He cannot mention that you owe any debt; nor can he even identify his employer (e.g., City Collection Company), unless he's asked to do so.

Harassing Phone Calls and Visits. It's against the law for a bill collector to contact you at any unusual time or place that is inconvenient for you. The Act even goes so far as to warn bill collectors to assume that the convenient time for communicating with a consumer is *after 8:00 A.M. and before 9:00 P.M.* Making anonymous phone calls is prohibited. It's even against the law to make a telephone ring repeatedly just to annoy someone.

Profane or Abusive Language. Both are prohibited, whether spoken or written.

Violence. Whether threatened or actually used to harm any person or property, violence is illegal.

Embarrassing Ads. A bill collector must not advertise a debt for sale in order to coerce payment. Another nasty trick is the publication of so-called shame lists—that is, publishing the names of consumers who allegedly refuse to pay debts. This sort of public humiliation violates the Act.

Trumped-up Credentials. Bill collectors are masters of disguise. No trick is too devious if it will bring the consumer within the bill collector's grasp. For example, bill collectors have posed as public-opinion pollsters, delivery boys, even casting directors hunting for television performers. Such dissembling is illegal.

The bill collector must not use any business name other than his company's true name. Indeed, a bill collector may not even be able to use his *own* business name on his business envelopes. While a bill collector can put his return address on envelopes sent to you, he can put his business name on only if it doesn't indicate that he is in the debt-collection business. Thus, printing "XYZ Collection Agency" on an envelope would be forbidden. Even using symbols is forbidden. (A Midwestern collection agency used to print on its envelopes an illustration of a lightning bolt about to strike some poor man. This sort of lurid symbolism is out now.)

A bill collector must not falsely represent that he works for a *credit bureau*. (Credit bureaus are not debt-collection agencies. Instead, they compile credit histories on individuals and provide credit ratings to stores, banks, etc. A bill collector can't deceive you into thinking he works for a bureau that could adversely affect your credit rating.)

A bill collector is forbidden to trick you into thinking he is affiliated with, or vouched for by, some government agency.

Phony Legal Documents. Watch out for official-looking letters designed to scare you into thinking the G-men or some hard-nosed courtroom lawyers are breathing down your neck. Bill collectors love to doctor up letters and forms to make them look as though they have the sanction of the law behind them. This ploy is now illegal. It's also illegal for a bill collector to imply that he is an attorney, so watch out for bill collectors who write to you on a legal letterhead.

Phony Legal Threats. The Act prohibits bill collectors from threatening to take any action that cannot legally be taken or that is not really intended to be taken. For example, a bill collector might try to deceive you into thinking that you could be arrested or your property could be seized for failure to pay a debt.

Phony Smear Threats. A bill collector must not threaten to give anyone credit information about you that is known—or should be known—to be false. For example, it would be a violation of the Act if a bill collector told you that unless you paid up he was going to spread false information about you at a credit bureau.

Postcards. It's against the law to communicate with a consumer about a debt via a postcard.

Collect Calls. It's against the law for a bill collector to make anyone incur expense for some communication (typically, a collect telephone call) by concealing the true purpose of that communication (e.g., by pretending to be a sick relative).

Postdated Checks. Beware of bill collectors who try to lure you into writing them a postdated check just to get them off your back for a while. The bill collector may be planning to betray you by then turning around and threatening to have you prosecuted for knowingly issuing rubber checks. The Act prohibits this nasty practice.

It is illegal for a bill collector to accept a check of yours postdated by more than five days, unless he gives you advance notification in writing of his intention to deposit your check; you're entitled to receive this notification not more than ten nor less than three business days prior to deposit of the check. (Given this advance warning, you still have the option of directing your bank to stop payment on the check before it can be deposited.)

In no case may a bill collector threaten to deposit any postdated check prior to the date on the check.

Collection Fees. Too often bill collectors tack on unauthorized fees, charges, and expenses to the basic amount owed by the consumer. This practice proceeds on the cynical theory of "you might as well ask people to chip in toward your business expenses because they just may be foolish enough to give it to you." The Act makes this money-grabbing tactic illegal, so don't fall for it.

Power Play Pointer. As you can see, your legal armory is filled with weapons. They can be used defensively (to ward off an aggressive bill collector) or offensively (as we'll see, a bill collector can be sued for violating the Act). For practical purposes, you simply ought to be prepared to hit the bill collector hard with your knowledge of the Act's prohibitions whenever he engages in dirty tricks. In all probability, your confrontations with a bill collector will transpire over the phone, which bill collectors use constantly.

If, for example, a bill collector calls you after 9:00 P.M., or while you're at work or anywhere else that's inconvenient, tell him firmly that you consider his call a gross imposition and a violation of the Act. Warn him not to repeat it.

Suppose you're disputing the accuracy of the debt, but the bill collector nevertheless threatens to report your indebtedness to a credit bureau. Inform him sternly that he's playing with legal dynamite, because it's a violation of the Act to spread false information.

If a bill collector threatens to sue you for, say, some piddling amount (e.g., $12.95), press him hard on his intentions: "You can't be serious. You don't really intend to go to all the time and expense of going to court over thirteen bucks! Don't you know it's a violation of the *Fair Debt Collection Practices Act* to threaten legal action that you don't really intend to take?"

Of course, if a bill collector ever gets abusive, cut him short. "I don't have to listen to your foul talk. It happens to violate federal law. You'd better clean up your act if you want the right to talk with me." Hang up!

There's another sure-fire power play you can pull on any bill collector who keeps harassing you with repeated phone calls. One important condition for continuing telephone service is that any subscriber (such as a bill collector) refrain from making calls "in a manner reasonably to be expected to frighten, abuse, torment, or harass another." This restriction is contained in the *telephone companies' tariffs,* which are regulations filed with the Public Service Commission in your state and with the Federal Communications Commission (FCC) in Washington. (These agencies regulate the phone companies.) A telephone company is obligated to suspend phone service to any of its subscribers who violate the tariff. The FCC or your state Public Service Commission will oversee proper enforcement of the tariff by the phone company. (Indeed, the FCC has made a special point of warning telephone companies about their duty to police harassing calls by bill collectors—in FCC Public Notice 70-609, issued on June 10, 1970.)

Are you beginning to see the makings of a very heavy power play? The next time a bill collector harasses or frightens you over the phone, just say calmly: "I hope you realize that what you're doing violates *telephone company tariffs.* If you persist in harassing me, I'm going to report you to the *Federal Communications Commission.* They will direct the telephone company to suspend your phone service." There's a set of codewords that should unnerve the brassiest bill collector! The telephone is the bill collector's lifeline; cut it off and he might as well close up shop. By needling the bill collector with these codewords, you're letting him know that you know how to get at his soft spot.

Suppose the bill collector has thick skin (most do). Your codewords stall him off for a while, but then he's back again, telephoning, sending letters, etc. You've got still another potent legal weapon. The Fair Debt Collection Practices Act gives you the right to cut off further communications with even the most dogged bill collector. All you have to do is notify the bill collector *in writing* that you refuse to pay the bill in question, or, simply, that the bill collector should cease further communications with you. The bill collector must then stop contacting you except:

—to advise you that further contacts are, in fact, being discontinued; or

—to notify you that certain specified remedies (e.g., a lawsuit), which are ordinarily invoked by the bill collector or creditor, may be invoked in this instance (notice this is not a license for idle threats; the remedies mentioned by the bill collector must be ones which are "ordinarily invoked," not merely threatened); or

—to notify you that the bill collector or creditor intends to invoke a specified remedy (here, again, there must be an actual intention to carry out the remedy specified; no bluffing is allowed).

Once the bill collector has completed his final communication with you, that's it: *no more calls, letters, or contacts with you are permitted.* The bill collector must either resort to whatever remedies the law provides or forget about collecting. Assuming a bill collector does give serious thought to suing you, he's going to have to get by without one of his favorite legal tricks—the default judgment. In the past, bill collectors routinely denied consumers their day in court by cleverly filing lawsuits in courts so far away or inconvenient that the consumers were unable to appear. When a consumer failed to show up, the bill collector won an easy judgment by default, which could then be enforced against the consumer. To combat this abuse, the Act requires that a bill collector who sues a consumer must file suit in either the judicial district where the consumer resides or where the consumer signed the underlying contract on which he allegedly owes money; if the suit is against real estate owned by the consumer, it must be filed in the judicial district where the property is located.

Power Play Pointer. Before you notify the bill collector to stop all further communications, you should be convinced that there is nothing left to be gained through continued communication. Because you're really telling him now to put up or shut up. If he heeds your message, he has to decide whether his claim is worth the time and expense of litigation or whether he should drop the whole thing.

Here's an appropriately intimidating notice that you can type up and mail to the bill collector. (As always, send it via certified mail, return receipt requested, and keep a copy for yourself).

NOTICE

Re alleged debt of [Insert your name]
[Bill collector's name   [Insert date of mailing]
Company name
Mailing address
City, state, zip code]

NOTICE TO CEASE COMMUNICATIONS

PLEASE TAKE NOTICE: Pursuant to the Fair Debt Collection Practices Act, title 15 United States Code, section 1692, you are hereby directed to cease further communication, through whatever medium, with the undersigned, regarding the above-mentioned debt.

YOUR FAILURE TO COMPLY with this notice may lead to civil liability and/or administrative penalties under said Act.

[Signature]
_____
[Your name
Your mailing address
City, state, zip code]

By now you may feel as though you've clubbed the bill collector into senseless submission. Don't start getting too sympathetic. Remember, a bill collector won't always play by the rules, even though you clearly know them all. Therefore, it's good to know that you have two ultimate power plays left: you can call in the feds or you can sue.

Calling in the feds may be enough to scare away a bill collector, even if the feds never actually intervene. Official enforcement of the Fair Debt Collection Practices Act was delegated by Congress to the Federal Trade Commission (FTC). Although the FTC doesn't ordinarily take any formal action on an individual complaint, the commission may at least investigate and thereby intimidate the bill collector.

More important, you, the individual consumer, have the power to enforce the Act on your own, without having to wait for any government bureaucracy to crank up its gears. Under the Act, if you have been abused by a bill collector or your rights have been denied, you can sue him for money damages. Raising this prospect should make even the most callous of bill collectors nervous, because he stands to lose a potentially large sum of money. First, you may be awarded your *actual damages,* that is, the losses caused by the bill collector's misconduct. For example, you may have lost earnings on your job because of the bill collector's badmouthing of you. Your credit rating may have fallen. Even the nervousness, lack of sleep, and mental distress you suffer because of the bill collector's tactics are losses for which you can be compensated in court. Actual damages can easily add up to thousands of dollars.

Second, you may be awarded *punitive damages.* Also known as *sting money,* punitive damages are awarded purely as a means of punishing violators of the Act and making an example of them. In setting the amount of punitive damages (the maximum is $1,000), the judge will appraise the bill collector's violations in terms of their nature, frequency, and persistence—that is, their basic nastiness.

(It should be noted that punitive damages can be enormous if a *class action* is brought against the bill collector—that is, a lawsuit brought on behalf of a group of consumers who have been damaged by the bill collector's violations. The judge can award the class punitive damages of up to $500,000 or 1 percent of the bill collector's net worth—whichever sum is less.)

Third—and here's a wonderful additional gift—as part of any judgment in your favor, you can be awarded court costs and your *attorney's fees*. In other words, the bill collector gets stuck with your legal bill. This particular provision makes it likelier that if you have a promising case, you will have no trouble finding an attorney.

Power Play Pointer. Try using the threat of an FTC investigation to give the bill collector pause for thought. "By the way," you might interject casually, "you ought to know that I'm petitioning the *Federal Trade Commission* to investigate your business for violations of the *Fair Debt Collection Practices Act.*" Your codewords will raise a prospect that no bill collector wishes to contemplate: namely, federal bureaucrats snooping around and asking embarrassing legal questions. Who knows what dirt they would dig up in addition to your case?!

To actually invoke the FTC's authority, simply write a straightforward complaint letter to the regional director of the FTC for your area (see Appendix E). Give the bill collector's name and address, and set forth why you think he's violated the Act. Be sure to send a copy of your letter to the bill collector and the creditor, to put a little more pressure on them.

If you seriously believe that a bill collector has acted outrageously and unjustifiably, you should seriously consider suing him for violating the Act. Suit can be brought in either federal or state court. Assuming you're within the right dollar limits, you can even sue in small claims court, thereby avoiding having to hire a lawyer (see Appendix A). But remember that the Act authorizes an award of legal fees to you, so you may be better off consulting a lawyer, especially if you believe you have suffered considerable damage.

Power Play Pointer. Make no bones about your lawsuit fever if you're having a showdown with the bill collector: "You know, I'm not sure I'm going to wait for the FTC to teach you a lesson. I think I'm going to sue you myself. You've caused me considerable damage, and your misconduct should result in *one thousand dollars in punitive damages.* I may even have my lawyer look into the possibility of a *class action* against your company for *five hundred thousand dollars.*"

If the bill collector pooh-poohs the fact that you're going to go out and spend money on a lawyer, let him know where he's wrong: "Oh, I'm not going to pay for my lawyer —you are! I'm entitled to an award of my *attorney's fees* from you. So I'll just hire the best, thank you!"

Your codewords will have needled the bill collector in a soft spot common to many: potential financial liability. Here it's not only damages—actual and punitive—plus attorney's fees, but also the threat of a class action. For any bill collector who's played dirty pool with many consumers, the fear of a class action has to be very real and very unsettling. Who wants to risk a big chunk of his business over one little account—especially one that the bill collector was probably unsure of to start with? Chances are you'll have finally succeeded in getting rid of the bill collector, without having to see a lawyer or sue.

Codeword Glossary

actual damages   Lost earnings, mental distress, and other losses caused by a bill collector, which can be compensated for in a lawsuit under the Fair Debt Collection Practices Act.

attorney's fees   In any judgment you win under the Act, your attorney's fees can be included.

class action   A group lawsuit authorized by the Act, it can result in punitive damages of up to $500,000.

Fair Debt Collection Practices Act   This federal law strictly regulates unfair tactics by bill collectors and gives consumers the right to have a debt verified and not to be harassed. The law can be found in section 1692 of title 15 of the United States Code.

Federal Communications Commission (FCC)   The federal agency that regulates telephone companies and the enforcement of their tariffs.

Federal Trade Commission (FTC)   The federal agency that enforces the Fair Debt Collection Practices Act.

punitive damages   A penalty of up to $1,000 that can be added to any judgment won against a bill collector under the Act.

telephone company tariff   The company rule that prohibits phone subscribers from making harassing calls (penalty: suspension of phone service).

verification   The mandatory procedure by which a bill collector must verify any disputed debt and suspend all collection efforts until the procedure has been completed.

10

The
Credit Rights
of Women

Credit Discrimination Against Women

For years women seeking credit have been discriminated against by banks, finance companies, credit card issuers, and stores. Women were stereotyped by creditors as childbearers (potential if not yet actual), whose earnings were viewed as little more than play money. A married woman's credit-worthiness was arbitarily merged with her husband's, and she found it virtually impossible to establish an independent financial identity. While such anonymity may have been tolerable during marriage, it created acute problems later on if a wife was divorced or widowed and left on her own.

The discrimination practiced against women was often so arbitrary as to be grimly amusing. Consider the California woman with sound financial credentials who married an ex-convict whose credit standing was zilch. The woman applied for a credit card in her own name. Based on her credit-worthiness, not his, the card was granted to her—but in his name!

A young woman named Jorie Luteloff married and became Jorie Luteloff Friedman. "Shortly after my marriage," she testified in 1972 before a national blue-ribbon commission, "I wrote all the stores where I had charge accounts and requested new credit cards with my new name and address. That's all that had changed—my name and address. Otherwise, I maintained the same status—the same job, the same salary, and, presumably, the same credit rating. The response of the stores was swift. One store closed my account immediately. All of them sent me application forms that asked for my husband's name, my husband's bank, my husband's employer. There was no longer any interest in me, my job, my bank, or my ability to pay my own bills."

In 1973 a New York couple, the Carrolls, were refused a mortgage by two banks in Queens because Mr. Carroll's income of $12,500 was not considered sufficient. Mrs. Carroll's $4,000 salary was not even counted. She was informed that her salary would be counted only if she was more than thirty-eight years old or if she could produce sworn proof that she had had a hysterectomy.

The Department of Human Rights in St. Paul, Minnesota, conducted an experiment that graphically demonstrated how men and women were judged by different standards in the credit marketplace. A man and a woman with identical qualifications applied to local banks for a $600 loan to finance a used car. Each applicant was twenty-four years old, earning $12,000 as a research analyst, and married to a full-time student; both applicants sought the loan without having to supply the bank with the signature of the other spouse. Eleven of the banks visited by the female applicant required that she get her husband's signature before they would make the loan. When the same eleven banks—plus two more that had made no commitment to the female applicant—were visited by the male applicant, only one of the thirteen insisted on his spouse's signature; six said they preferred both signatures but would make an exception for him; and six said that, as a married man, he could obtain the loan without his wife's signature.

In 1973, after extensive study, Congress reported on the variety of discriminatory acts regularly practiced by creditors on the basis of a woman's sex or marital status:

1. Holding women and men to different standards in determining credit-worthiness—for example, different minimum salary levels, lengths of employment, or lengths of residence.

2. Requiring a newly married woman whose credit-worthiness has otherwise remained the same to reapply for credit as a new applicant.

3. Refusing to extend credit to a married woman in her own name, even though she would be deemed credit-worthy if unmarried.

4. Refusing to count a wife's income when a married couple applies for credit. This practice includes arbitrarily *discounting* a wife's income—that is, counting it at only a fraction (e.g., half) of its actual worth.

5. Refusing to extend credit to a newly separated or divorced woman solely because of her change in marital status.

6. Refusing to consider alimony and child support as a valid source of income even though the source is subject to verification.

7. Applying stricter standards in the case of married applicants where the wife rather than the husband is the primary family supporter.

8. Requesting or using information about birth control practices in evaluating a credit application.

9. Requesting or using information concerning the credit-worthiness of a husband where an otherwise credit-worthy wife applies for credit as an individual.

10. Refusing to issue separate accounts to a husband and wife when each would be creditworthy if unmarried.

11. Considering as "dependents" wives who are employed and not actually dependent on the husband-applicant.

12. Using credit scoring tests that allot different amounts of points to credit applicants depending on their sex or marital status.

13. Altering a wife's credit rating on the basis of her husband's credit rating.

The Equal Credit Opportunity Act and Regulation B

Faced with such a clear pattern of discrimination against women, Congress enacted the Equal Credit Opportunity Act (ECOA), which went into effect in 1975. In a nutshell, the ECOA outlaws discriminatory credit practices, whether they are based on a person's sex, marital status, race, color, religion, national origin, age, or because the person's income is derived from any public assistance program (e.g., Social Security, unemployment compensation, food stamps, Aid to Families with Dependent Children). Among the more important safeguards afforded women under the new law are these:

—In general, a creditor cannot inquire about the marital status of any person applying for credit.

—Receipt of alimony or child support doesn't have to be revealed to a creditor.

—A creditor can't inquire about an applicant's intention or capacity to bear children, nor can he make any negative assumptions about who is likely to bear children and what effect this will have on the potential mother's earning capacity.

—A creditor must give full consideration to a woman's

income, even if it is derived from part-time employment (or alimony, if she chooses to reveal it).

—A creditor must provide an applicant with specific reasons for his decision, usually within 30 days.

—A married woman can choose to have her own separate credit account, and under her maiden name, if she wishes.

—A woman's credit account cannot be closed, nor may she be forced to reapply for it, merely because of a change in her marital status or name.

—For violations of the new law, a creditor can be sued by a credit applicant for any damage suffered plus up to $10,000 in penalties plus attorney's fees and court costs.

Enactment of the ECOA was a giant step forward in the legal battle against discrimination. Passing a new law, however, doesn't always cure the underlying ill. As with many recent consumer-protection laws, the effectiveness of the ECOA depends in large part on informed citizens resisting violations of the law as they occur. To date this kind of alert self-help has not been widespread among female credit applicants. Women's organizations and feminist attorneys still encounter horror stories involving women unaware of their ECOA rights who continue to be victimized by creditors. As recently as December, 1977 (after almost three years of the ECOA), *The New York Times* reported the plight of a young female writer who walked into a New York City bank with her fiancé in search of a mortgage; she was shocked when the bank officer said he couldn't take her income into account because she was of "childbearing age."

If you are a woman about to seek some form of credit —be it a credit card, charge account, overdraft checking, installment sales contract, personal loan, mortgage, etc.— you should forearm yourself with a knowledge of your

ECOA rights. The same advice holds true even if you already enjoy considerable credit privileges; you don't want to lose what you've gained just because of a change in your marital status or some other irrelevant event.

Let's start from scratch, examining your total credit picture and seeing how you can make the law your ally. We'll be looking chiefly at the impact of the ECOA, as well as a complex body of law known cryptically as *Regulation B*. Regulation B is actually a series of detailed regulations issued by the Federal Reserve Board (FRB) to implement the ECOA. In Regulation B, the FRB carried out Congress's intentions by fleshing out the skeleton created in the ECOA. Although all creditors may not be aware of every legal responsibility spelled out in Regulation B, they are acutely aware of the Regulation's demanding attention to detail and the fact that infractions can lead to substantial penalties. (As you can probably guess already, Regulation B is going to emerge as a potent codeword to drop liberally in any confrontation with an obstinate creditor.)

At the outset, you should recognize that the ECOA does not guarantee you the *right* to get credit. All the Act promises, as its name implies, is an *equal opportunity* with other credit applicants, regardless of your sex, marital status, race, etc. You cannot be discriminated against on any illegal basis, but you may very well be discriminated against, and justifiably so, on rational bases involving ordinary credit criteria. Such rational bases might include, for example, the excessive financial obligations you've already undertaken, or the lack of sufficient credit references. In this sense, even legitimate credit decisions are discriminatory by nature: they discriminate between persons who are predictably sound credit risks and those who are not. The trick is to distinguish between legal and illegal acts of discrimination, and to resist the latter vigorously.

Although there is no pat formula for getting credit, there are seven basic guidelines you can follow, using your legal know-how, which will make credit both quicker to come by and easier to maintain:

1. Set your sights on "credit-worthiness."
2. Establish a credit history in your own name.
3. Check up on your credit history.
4. Open checking and savings accounts.
5. Start with small credit transactions.
6. Know your equal credit opportunity rights.
7. Enforce your equal credit opportunity rights.

Let's examine each of these guidelines more closely.

Set Your Sights on "Credit-worthiness"

When you seek credit, the basic point you must establish is your *credit-worthiness.* The person across the desk from you will be asking himself two key questions about you: (1) Are you *able* to pay back the indebtedness you wish to incur? (2) Are you *willing* to make this repayment? If the answer to both questions is yes, you will be considered credit-worthy.

The first question is largely a matter of dollars and cents. Your ability to repay depends on the size and reliability of your financial resources. The most significant factor is usually your earning power—measured by the amount of your salary and the length of time that you've been earning it. Other assets can also be important, such as income-producing investments, although they are not necessarily as reliable as a good steady salary. (As we'll see later on, receipt of alimony can be established as a reliable source of income.)

The answer to the second question about your willingness to repay depends upon your *credit history.* If you have ever gotten credit in the past, chances are you already have a credit history. It is a record of the circumstances under which you have received and repaid—or failed to repay—credit.

Who is the keeper of your credit history? There is an enormous nationwide industry devoted to this task. It consists of hundreds of companies known as credit reporting agencies or, more popularly, *credit bureaus*. Based on data supplied by creditors and sometimes dug up by investigators, a credit bureau compiles individual credit histories, keeps them on file, and updates them regularly. Your credit history might record such data as:

—loans taken out and any instances of tardiness in meeting the repayment schedules;

—charge accounts at stores and any delinquency in paying bills on time;

—civil judgments rendered against you (if you are bound to pay money damages as the result of a lawsuit, you will obviously be less able to pay off any new indebtedness);

—bankruptcy (if you've been adjudged bankrupt, your credit history will haunt you for years);

—unsatisfactory payment of debts (for instance, some creditor had to sic a lawyer or bill collector on you in order to make you finally pay up).

Whenever you apply for credit, the creditor will routinely contact a credit bureau and request a report on your credit history. Your willingness to repay any newly incurred debt will be inferred from the history of how well you've satisfied financial obligations in the past. If your credit history is sparse, or, worse still, if the credit bureau reports that it has no file on you at all, you may have difficulty establishing your willingness to repay debt—and, hence, ultimately your credit-worthiness.

An insufficient or nonexistent credit history was a problem that plagued a married or formerly married woman prior to the ECOA—not because she had failed to get credit in the past or had misused it, but because traditionally it had been extended to her on the basis of her husband's credit-worthiness, and probably in his name, too. The creditors who had extended such credit routinely reported its history to credit bureaus *in the husband's name alone*—thus perpetuating the vicious circle in which a woman without a credit history would be denied credit, but couldn't build a credit history without first getting and using credit. As a result, a married woman acquired no financial identity of her own.

Indeed, a single woman with a solid credit history stood a good chance—as we saw earlier—of losing it on marriage. All her accounts would be changed to her husband's name and then reported in this manner to credit bureaus. If the woman was later divorced or widowed, she would emerge from the marriage without a credit history of her own.

Fortunately, Regulation B gives a married woman the right to insist on her own financial identity. This is an important step for her to take toward establishment of her individual credit-worthiness.

Establish a Credit History in Your Own Name

A married woman now has the right to build her own credit history, separate from her husband's, in whatever name she has chosen for herself. As a married or formerly married woman, you can no longer be compelled to use your married name on any credit account. Regulation B gives you the right to choose the name you will use, whether you are opening a new account or maintaining one already in existence.

Under Regulation B, you can notify a creditor that you wish your account to be designated by your birth-given first name and a surname that is:

1. your birth-given surname; or
2. your spouse's surname; or
3. a combination of the two.

Thus, if you were born Jane Fremont and married Samuel Jessup, you could designate any one of the following names for your credit account: Jane Fremont, Jane Jessup, or Jane Fremont-Jessup.

If the account is an individual one under your name, its history will be reported as such by the creditor to the credit bureau. But what about an account that you open with your husband? Under Regulation B, creditors who maintain accounts with married couples must make sure that the wife as well as the husband builds a credit history. First, the creditor must determine whether the account is a joint account or an open-end account that both spouses are permitted to use. With a *joint account,* both husband and wife obligate themselves to be liable for repaying any indebtedness. An *open-end account* that both spouses can use is an ongoing extension of credit, like a revolving charge account in a department store, that one spouse establishes in his or her name (usually his!) but that the other spouse can use, say, to charge purchases or take out repeated loans.

Assuming an account is one of these two types, the creditor can no longer automatically report credit information on the account in the name of just one spouse (traditionally the husband). Instead, the creditor must take steps that will redound to the benefit of both spouses. Exactly what these steps are depends on when the account was established; the key date is June 1, 1977.

For an account established *on or after June 1, 1977,* a creditor who supplies information to a credit bureau must do so in both spouses' names so that the bureau, in turn, can report that information to its clients in the name of either spouse. If the creditor responds directly to an inquiry about one of the spouses (e.g., an inquiry from another creditor), the information must be supplied in the name of that spouse.

For an account established *before June 1, 1977,* and still in existence on that date, the creditor who supplies information was supposed to follow one of two procedures. IIe could have voluntarily taken the same steps prescribed above for accounts established after June 1, 1977. Or, prior to October 1, 1977, he could have mailed a special notice to married couples with accounts. Entitled "Credit History for Married Persons," this notice (designed by the Federal Reserve Board) was supposed to have been signed and returned to the creditor if the recipients wanted credit information on the account reported in the wife's name as well as the husband's.

Over 300 million of these notices were sent out by creditors (chiefly because resorting to the notice saved creditors the effort of checking back through all of their then-current accounts to determine on their own how credit information should be reported). Unfortunately, only a very small fraction of the notices were signed and returned, leaving creditors to keep reporting information on pre-June 1, 1977, accounts as they always had—that is, in the name of the husband alone.

Power Play Pointer. You may very well be one of those who didn't return the notice. Perhaps it intimidated you; maybe you just didn't want to get mixed up in more seeming red tape; you may even have discarded the notice as junk mail. That was shortsighted, especially if the notice referred to an account that you still maintain, because you are not building an individual credit history based on that account.

Fortunately, it's not too late for you to change the way information is reported on accounts you maintain with your husband. Regulation B gives you the right to request that any creditor report information in your name as well as in your husband's. *The creditor must comply with your request within 90 days.*

How do you exercise this right? Simply type out the following request form, sign it, and send it to creditors with whom you and your husband maintain an account that was opened before June 1, 1977.

REQUEST
CREDIT HISTORY FOR MARRIED PERSONS

Pursuant to the Equal Credit Opportunity Act, title 15 United States Code, section 1691, and Regulation B, title 12 Code of Federal Regulations, section 202, I request that you report all credit information on this account in both our names:

_____

Account number

[*Your first name*]	[*Middle name*]	[*Last name*]

[*Your husband's first name*]	[*Middle name*]	[*Last name*]

_____

[*Street address, including apartment number*]

[*City*]	[*State*]	[*Zip code*]

Kindly comply with this request within the 90-day period allowed by Regulation B.

Thank you,

_____

[*Signature of either spouse*]

Signing and submitting this request form does not in any way alter your legal liability or your spouse's on the account. Still, it's not inconceivable that husbands and wives may disagree over making the request. An insecure husband may feel that the stability of his marriage will be threatened if his wife starts building her own credit history. While we don't propose an interspousal power play, we do think a wife should know that legally she does *not* need her husband's signature on the request form in order to make it valid. Her signature alone will suffice.

Check Up on Your Credit History

Before you apply for credit, it's a good idea to check what's on file under your name at the local credit bureau. That way you'll preview data that will be reported to creditors whom you approach later on.

You have the right to discover the contents of your credit history at the credit bureau. This right arises not out of the ECOA, but another important federal law, the Fair Credit Reporting Act (FCRA). You will be invoking your rights under one law—the FCRA—to help you get your rights under another—the ECOA.

How do you exercise your right to discovery? First, find out which credit bureau keeps a file on you. Go to the credit officer at a department store or bank you patronize. Ask which credit bureau his store (or bank) sends reports to.

Armed with the name, you can look up the bureau's address and telephone number in the Yellow Pages of the telephone directory under such headings as "Credit Rating Agencies" or "Consumer Reporting Agencies." Call the bureau and inquire whether they have any special application form for consumers who request a credit report on themselves. If so, get the form, fill it out, and submit it.

Power Play Pointer. If there is no application form, simply write a letter to the bureau, identifying yourself and requesting: "Please clearly and accurately disclose to me: (1) the nature and substance of all information contained in your files on me; (2) the sources of that information; and (3) the names of recipients of any credit report you have made on me within the past six months." (If this sounds a bit legalistic to you, you're right—it's a paraphrase of your discovery rights under the FCRA, and you can rest assured the credit bureau will recognize the legal force behind your codewords.)

Be aware that the credit bureau can legitimately make a "reasonable charge" (e.g., several dollars) for providing you with the report. A sample credit report, like the one you may receive, is reproduced on page 199. Examine your report carefully. If you don't understand any of the data recorded on the report, call or visit the credit bureau and ask for an explanation.

Check the report to make sure that creditors have complied with your credit history request and are in fact reporting credit information in your name. (Remember, they have 90 days in which to comply.) If any creditor does not appear to be complying, renew your request to him, and remind him that Regulation B requires prompt compliance.

Suppose you conclude that some of the information in your credit report is erroneous or incomplete. For example, there's a record of your owing $89.95 on a department store charge account. You know that you actually returned the $89.95 merchandise for credit. What can you do? Protest! Under the FCRA, you have the right to insist that the bureau reinvestigate any item in your file which you believe is inaccurate or incomplete. (It's certainly worth trying to clear up your file before it becomes the basis for a report to a creditor.) Following the bureau's reinvestigation, if the

TRW *CREDIT DATA*

```
┌                      ┐        P.O. BOX 5450
   JOHN Q CONSUMER               ORANGE CA 92667
   989 BLUE STREET               (714) 991-6000
   BURBANK CA 91502              (213) 254-9153
└                      ┘
                                 DATE   APRIL 3, 1978
```

Dear Consumer:

In response to your recent request, we are providing this transcript of the credit information maintained by TRW Credit Data under the name and address(es) you have submitted.

IF you disagree with any of the information shown below:

Please PRINT your comments next to the item(s) in the "CONSUMER COMMENTS" column, then SIGN on the reverse side and return this form in the enclosed envelope. Additional information regarding these items may be supplied in the "ADDITIONAL COMMENTS" area on the reverse side.

NOTE: Please read the reverse side for additional "INSTRUCTIONS" and for "DEFINITIONS" of some of the terminology used below.

PAGE 1

	CONSUMER COMMENTS *(IF ANY)*
EMPLOYMENT: AJAX HARDWARE 2035 BROADWAY LOS ANGELES 90019 --REPORTED ON 1/78 --BY OCEAN BANK	
(POS) OPEN ACCT REPORTED IN 12/77 BY MOUNTAIN BANK-- RECREATIONAL MERCHANDISE CONTRACT--ORIGINAL AMOUNT $5300-- FOR 48 MONTHS--ACCT OPENED IN 11/77--ACCT #29144508119-- AS OF 2/15/78 THE ACCOUNT BALANCE WAS $6120--ACCOUNT ASSOCIATION-1-INDIVIDUAL	
INQUIRY BY OCEAN BANK IN 1/78	
ACCT WAS PAST DUE 30 DAYS/NOW CURRENT REPORTED IN 9/75 BY HILLSIDE BANK--CREDIT CARD--CREDIT LIMIT $300--REVOLVING TERMS--ACCT OPENED IN 1/75--ACCT #40812391013986--AS OF 2/28/78 THE ACCOUNT BALANCE WAS $206--ACCOUNT ASSOCIATION- 1-INDIVIDUAL	
INQUIRY BY HILLSIDE BANK IN 3/78	
(POS) OPEN TO CHARGE REPORTED IN 3/76 BY HEMLOCKS--CHARGE ACCT--CREDIT LIMIT OR HIGHEST AMOUNT $600--REVOLVING CHARGE-- ACCT OPENED IN 2/76--ACCT #98643973201146--AS OF 2/25/78 THE ACCOUNT BALANCE WAS $437	
PAID ACCT REPORTED IN 10/77 BY WISTERIA FINANCE LOANS-- INSTALLMENT CONTRACT--ORIGINAL AMOUNT $500--FOR 12 MONTHS-- ACCT OPENED IN 9/76--ACCT #41061924023	
(NEG) ACCOUNT PAST DUE 90 DAYS REPORTED IN 3/78 BY TRANSATLANTIC CREDIT CORP--CHARGE ACCT--CREDIT LIMIT OR HIGHEST AMOUNT $700--REVOLVING CHARGE--ACCT OPENED OVER 5 YEARS AGO--ACCT #209946234573	
(POS) OPEN ACCT REPORTED IN 1974 BY WHITE CAP SAVINGS & LOAN--REAL ESTATE MORTGAGE--ORIGINAL AMOUNT $60000-- FOR 30 YEARS--ACCT OPENED IN 1974--ACCT #361940238-- ACCOUNT ASSOCIATION-2-JOINT-ACCOUNT-CONTRACTUAL RESPONSIBILITY	
JUDGMENT SATISFIED OR PAID 12/5/74--BURBANK MUNICIPAL CT/ BURBANK--AMOUNT $200--CASE #63401--PLAINTIFF/MELROSE TIRE	
THANKS FOR THE OPPORTUNITY TO SERVE YOU	

Any item(s) you have marked will be investigated by contacting the source of the information. We will notify you, by mail, of the results of this investigation and changes, if any, made to the file. If for any reason we have not contacted you within three weeks, please call us at the number listed above, collect, if out of your toll free area.   OVER

CD-101 G-79   FILE

Reproduced by permission of TRW Credit Data, a division of TRW Inc.

information you disputed is indeed found to be inaccurate, or if it can no longer be verified, the FCRA requires that the bureau delete the information from your file.

Power Play Pointer. What if the reinvestigation fails to clear up your dispute with the bureau? Then you have the further right under the FCRA to submit a brief statement of your own for inclusion in your file; in this statement (which probably shouldn't be more than one hundred words) you can explain why you dispute the bureau's data. This statement may redound to your benefit later on. Whenever the bureau makes a report on you to a creditor, it must note that you dispute a particular item in your credit history. Moreover, the bureau must attach your statement or an accurate codification or summary of it so future creditors will be on notice of your self-defense.

Open Checking and Savings Accounts

If you don't already have checking and savings accounts *in your own name,* open them before you seek credit. The name you designate on these accounts should be the same one you will use when you later apply for credit (and the same one you may already have used when requesting separate credit reports from creditors who maintain accounts with both you and your husband). It's important to use the same name consistently; otherwise, your credit history may get split up under different names in different files. The checking and savings accounts you open in your own name give you an individual financial identity, which you will use when you seek credit.

Don't be concerned if your opening balance in the savings account is not a sizable sum. Neither the opening balance nor, for that matter, the overall size of your account is as important as the regularity with which you make deposits. Suppose you open the account with $100 and deposit $100 every month. With each deposit—assuming it is not later depleted by withdrawals—you are demonstrating your ability to meet your regular expenses and still be able to set aside savings. Such systematic savings show greater financial self-control than opening a savings account with $1,000 and regularly withdrawing money to meet current expenses. Ideally, you should try to save each month somewhere between 5 and 10 percent of your monthly wages (before taxes).

Start with Small Credit Transactions

You don't build a solid credit history overnight. It takes time and steady attention. Generally speaking, your best bet is to start with modest credit arrangements which are well within your means to repay on schedule.

Don't expect to start off with a $50,000 mortgage loan; unless your salary is substantial, you're simply not going to qualify. Instead, start with something that's easier to obtain: for example, a charge account at a department store or a bank credit card (such as Master Charge or Visa). Such accounts allow you to defer payment for purchases without incurring costly interest charges—that is, assuming you pay your bills within the period set by the creditor. Also ask your bank about other credit accounts they may offer, such as a line of credit on your checking account. (The line of credit allows you to write checks for more than your balance, up to a certain predesignated limit, say, $1,000. What you are doing is taking out a personal loan for the amount of the overdraft, and you pay interest on this loan.)

If you've built up a good balance in your savings account, you might consider borrowing against it. In other words, you take out a personal loan from the bank. The sum you borrow is covered by your savings, which you won't be able to draw on until you've repaid the loan. In the meantime, however, you'll keep earning interest on your savings; to some extent, this will offset the interest you must pay on the loan. Such loans are called *passbook loans;* ask your banker how you can qualify. Paying back such a loan on time is one of the best ways to strengthen your credit history and make it easier to get the next (larger) loan.

Know Your Equal Credit Opportunity Rights

Earlier we highlighted the legal protection afforded by the ECOA. Now let's take a closer look at your rights, so you won't be victimized as you enter the world of credit transactions.

Applying for Credit

We can begin at the application stage. Whenever you apply for credit—be it a line of credit, a charge account, car financing, a mortgage, etc.—you can expect to be asked many questions. They may be in an application form, or you may have a personal interview. Creditors are of course entitled to gather information that will help them decide whether you're credit-worthy. They have no right, however, to seek information that could only be used to discriminate against you. To deny creditors access to such information, the ECOA and Regulation B prohibit or severely restrict certain inquiries that might facilitate discrimination.

No Discouraging Words. We begin with a general prohibition against discouraging credit applicants on a discriminatory basis. "A creditor shall not make any oral or written statement," Regulation B provides, "in advertising or otherwise, to applicants or prospective applicants that would discourage on a prohibited basis a reasonable person from making or pursuing an application."

There are four important aspects to this rule. First, it covers both written and oral statements. The former might occur in an advertisement, a letter, a brochure, etc. The latter might occur over the telephone or during a visit to the creditor's office.

Second, the rule applies to *prospective* applicants as well as those who have already applied. It is as illegal for a creditor to discourage you from initially making an application as it is for him to discourage you from pursuing that application once made.

Third, the creditor mustn't discourage you on any *prohibited basis;* that would include sex, marital status, race, color, religion, national origin, age, public assistance income, or the exercise of your consumer credit rights.

Fourth, only statements that would discourage a *reasonable* person from applying for credit are forbidden. Not every little slip of the tongue that might give pause to the overly sensitive will violate Regulation B. Still, you should give yourself the benefit of the doubt and refuse to stand for any discouragement that strikes you as discriminatory.

Sex. Regulation B prohibits a creditor from requesting the sex (male or female) of any applicant. All terms in an application form must be neutral as to sex.

Mr., Mrs., Miss, Ms. An applicant may not be required to designate a courtesy title (such as "Mr.," "Mrs.," "Miss," or "Ms.") on an application form. Courtesy titles may be requested, but only if the applicant is first advised that compliance is purely optional.

Race, Color, Religion, or National Origin. A creditor must not inquire about your race, color, religion, or national origin when you apply for credit; nor can he ask this information about any other person (e.g., your spouse, your employer) in connection with the credit transaction.

Marital Status. A creditor must not ask about your marital status if you're applying for credit on an *individual unsecured basis.* (*Individual* means credit issued in your name alone; *unsecured* means you're not pledging any property or other collateral that you will forfeit to the creditor should you fail to repay him.) For example, you apply for a personal loan or your own credit card, relying solely on your salary; the creditor cannot ask any questions about your marital status.

(There is an exception to this rule if you happen to live in a *community-property state*—that is, Arizona, California, Idaho, Louisiana, Nevada, New Mexico, Texas, or Washington. In these eight states, both partners to a marriage can claim equal ownership of all property acquired during a marriage. There the creditor may ask you about your marital status, because he needs to check on your spouse's finances in order to make sure that your joint assets will cover your new credit obligations.)

If you're applying for a joint account, a creditor can ask you about your marital status. He can inquire whether you're married, unmarried, or separated. The term *unmarried* covers never-married, divorced, and widowed persons, so if you're a divorcee you can legitimately identify yourself as unmarried without also having to reveal that you were divorced.

Indirect Marital-Status Inquiries. The general prohibition against inquiries into marital status does not prevent a creditor from requesting relevant financial data that may indirectly disclose your marital status. For example, a creditor is permitted to ask about:

—your liability, if any, to pay alimony, child support, or separate maintenance;

—the source of the income you plan to use for repaying any credit (this may disclose that you're relying on your spouse's income);

—the nature of the ownership of any assets you rely on as a basis for repayment (your answer may disclose your spouse's interest in those assets);

—the name and address on any credit account on which you may be liable, as well as any other name in which you have previously received credit (revealing, perhaps, accounts you maintain or used to maintain under a married name);

—whether any financial obligation you report involves a co-obligor, that is, someone who shares the responsibility with you (that person might be your spouse).

Your Spouse or Former Spouse. As a general rule, you cannot be asked for information about your spouse. There are five exceptional situations involving your spouse, in which you can be asked about him:

1. You are applying for an open-end credit account that your spouse will be able to use with you. (An open-end account, it will be recalled, is an ongoing extension of credit, such as a revolving charge account at a department store.)

2. You are applying for a joint account with your spouse, under which you are both liable for repayment.

3. You are relying on your spouse's income to repay the credit extended.

4. You reside in a community-property state.

5. You rely on alimony, child support, or separate-maintenance payments from a spouse or former spouse to repay the credit extended. (Here the creditor might have to ask about your former spouse.)

Alimony, Child Support, Separate Maintenance. You don't have to reveal income from any of these sources, unless, of course, you want to rely on this income to establish your ability to repay. Suppose you receive only a small amount of alimony and are relying solely on your regular wages when you apply for credit. You can simply report nothing in the way of alimony. (We will see later on that if you do want the creditor to take account of alimony, child support, or separate maintenance, he must do so.)

Birth Control, Childbearing, Dependents. Regulation B prohibits creditors from prying into intimate details of your family life. It is illegal for a creditor to ask you about your (1) birth control practices, (2) intentions concerning the bearing or rearing of children, or (3) capability to bear children. Indirectly, a creditor may elicit information about your children, because he is allowed to ask about the number and ages of your dependents and about any dependent-related financial obligations or expenditures. These questions, however, must be asked, if at all, of *all* applicants, regardless of their sex or marital status; thus, married women cannot legally be singled out for this type of inquiry.

Application Forms. Now that we've reviewed some of the do's and don'ts of information gathering, it may be helpful to consider what a written application form looks like. (Incidentally, a creditor is not required to use written forms; oral transactions are perfectly legal.) To guide creditors who use written applications, the Federal Reserve Board has devised several model application forms. One such form (designed for open-end unsecured credit applications) appears on pages 208–209. Reading this form will give you a good idea of what to expect on a credit application. (Of course, you can always ask a creditor for a copy of his application form to study.)

Creditors don't have to adopt the Board's model. And if they do, they can change it in any way that doesn't violate the restrictions on information gathering.

Power Play Pointer. During the application process, it's up to you to use the ECOA as a shield, warding off improper (and in some cases possibly offensive) inquiries from a creditor. Admittedly, you're in a fairly delicate position: on the one hand, you want to obtain credit; at the same time, you don't want to be victimized by discrimination. Therefore, when safeguarding your rights, tread lightly, using a mixture of tact, firmness, and, where appropriate, humor; that way, you can stand up for your rights without also alienating the creditor.

For example, you go into a bank and ask for a personal-loan application. The officer suggests that it might be a lot easier if you returned the next day with your husband so that he can sign the application. Don't explode and accuse the officer of violating Regulation B by discouraging your application—which, of course, he is doing. Instead, try to brush aside this relatively minor hurdle and get on with applying. You might say: "Oh, there's no need to waste my husband's time. I'm the one who wants the loan, and my financial resources are the only ones I'm relying on. Is this bank different from others that don't discourage applications from married women?" By merely hinting at possible discrimination, you've probably prodded the banker enough to make him stop playing games. (It's often effective to hint at brighter prospects at other banks. Remember, banks are moneylenders that compete with one another to sell their product—money—for as good a return as they can get—interest. So they need customers, like yourself, just as any other seller does.)

If a creditor, after writing down your name, asks, "Is that 'Miss' or 'Mrs.'?" gloss over his violation of the law as smoothly as possible: "I don't use any titles at all, actually. Just 'Janet Jones' suits me fine. All that information is optional anyway, isn't it?" Once again, without actually mentioning the law, you're hinting at it unmistakably through your rhetorical question.

In certain egregious circumstances, you should feel free to make your indignation known. Suppose some Ne-

CREDIT APPLICATION

IMPORTANT: Read these Directions before completing this Application.

Check
Appropriate
Box

☐ If you are applying for an individual account in your own name and are relying on your own income or assets and not the income or assets of another person as the basis for repayment of the credit requested, complete only Sections A and D.

☐ If you are applying for a joint account or an account that you and another person will use, complete all Sections, providing information in B about the joint applicant or user.

☐ If you are applying for an individual account, but are relying on income from alimony, child support, or separate maintenance or on the income or assets of another person as the basis for repayment of the credit requested, complete all Sections to the extent possible, providing information in B about the person on whose alimony, support, or maintenance payments or income or assets you are relying.

SECTION A—INFORMATION REGARDING APPLICANT

Full Name (Last, First, Middle): .... **Birthdate:** / /

Present Street Address: .... **Years there:** ....

City: .... State: .... Zip: .... Telephone: ....

Social Security No.: .... Driver's License No.: ....

Previous Street Address: .... **Years there:** ....

City: .... State: .... Zip: ....

Present Employer: .... Years there: .... Telephone: ....

Position or title: .... Name of supervisor: ....

Employer's Address: ....

Previous Employer: .... **Years there:** ......

Previous Employer's Address: ....

Present net salary or commission: $ .... per .... No. Dependents: .... Ages: ....

Alimony, child support, or separate maintenance income need not be revealed if you do not wish to have it considered as a basis for repaying this obligation.

Alimony, child support, separate maintenance received under: court order ☐ written agreement ☐ oral understanding ☐

Other income: $ .... per .... Source(s) of other income: ....

Is any income listed in this Section likely to be reduced in the next two years?
☐ Yes (Explain in detail on a separate sheet.) No ☐

Have you ever received credit from us? .... When? .... Office: ....

Checking Account No.: .... Institution and Branch: ....

Savings Account No.: .... Institution and Branch: ....

Name of nearest relative
not living with you: .... Telephone: ....

Relationship: .... Address: ....

SECTION B—INFORMATION REGARDING JOINT APPLICANT, USER, OR OTHER PARTY (Use separate sheets if necessary.)

Full Name (Last, First, Middle): .... **Birthdate:** / /

Relationship to Applicant (if any): ....

Present Street Address: .... **Years there:** ....

City: .... State: .... Zip: .... Telephone: ....

Social Security No.: .... Driver's License No.: ....

Present Employer: .... Years there: .... Telephone: ....

Position or title: .... Name of supervisor: ....

Employer's Address: ....

Previous Employer: .... **Years there:** ......

Previous Employer's Address: ....

Present net salary or commission: $ .... per .... No. Dependents: .... Ages: ....

Alimony, child support, or separate maintenance income need not be revealed if you do not wish to have it considered as a basis for repaying this obligation.

Alimony, child support, separate maintenance received under: court order ☐ written agreement ☐ oral understanding ☐

Other income: $ .... per .... Source(s) of other income: ....

Is any income listed in this Section likely to be reduced in the next two years?
☐ Yes (Explain in detail on a separate sheet.) ☐ No

Checking Account No.: .... Institution and Branch: ....

Savings Account No.: .... Institution and Branch: ....

Name of nearest relative not living
with Joint Applicant, User, or Other Party: .... Telephone: ....

Relationship: .... Address: ....

SECTION C—MARITAL STATUS
(Do not complete if this is an application for an individual account.)

Applicant: ☐ Married   ☐ Separated   ☐ Unmarried (including single, divorced, and widowed)
Other Party: ☐ Married   ☐ Separated   ☐ Unmarried (including single, divorced, and widowed)

SECTION D—ASSET AND DEBT INFORMATION (If Section B has been completed, this Section should be completed giving information about both the Applicant and Joint Applicant, User, or Other Person. Please mark Applicant-related information with an "A." If Section B was not completed, only give information about the Applicant in this Section.)

ASSETS OWNED (Use separate sheet if necessary.)

Description of Assets	Value	Subject to Debt? Yes/No	Name(s) of Owner(s)
Cash	$		
Automobiles (Make, Model, Year)			
Cash Value of Life Insurance (Issuer, Face Value)			
Real Estate (Location, Date Acquired)			
Marketable Securities (Issuer, Type, No. of Shares)			
Other (List)			
Total Assets	$		

OUTSTANDING DEBTS (Include charge accounts, instalment contracts, credit cards, rent, mortgages, etc. Use separate sheet if necessary.)

Creditor	Type of Debt or Acct. No.	Name in Which Acct. Carried	Original Debt	Present Balance	Monthly Payments	Past Due? Yes/No
1. (Landlord or Mortgage Holder)	☐ Rent Payment ☐ Mortgage		$ (Omit rent)	$ (Omit rent)	$	
2.						
3.						
4.						
5.						
6.						
Total Debts			$	$	$	

(Credit References) | | | | Date Paid

1.	$	
2.		

Are you a co-maker, endorser, or guarantor on any loan or contract?	Yes ☐ No ☐	If "yes" for whom? To whom?
Are there any unsatisfied judgments against you?	Yes ☐ No ☐ Amount $	If "yes" to whom owed?
Have you been declared bankrupt in the last 14 years?	Yes ☐ No ☐ If "yes" where?	Year

Other Obligations—(E.g., liability to pay alimony, child support, separate maintenance. Use separate sheet if necessary.)

Everything that I have stated in this application is correct to the best of my knowledge. I understand that you will retain this application whether or not it is approved. You are authorized to check my credit and employment history and to answer questions about your credit experience with me.

Applicant's Signature	Date	Other Signature (Where Applicable)	Date

anderthal creditor asks whether you're planning on settling down and having babies. "Just what are you driving at," you could retort sharply, "that I'll just drop everything— my salary, my career—and take up mothering? That sort of thinking is a bit old-fashioned. Anyway, it happens to violate the *Equal Credit Opportunity Act,* and I'm surprised that you would even raise it." You might sober him up further to his irresponsibility by adding, "Do the officers of this bank know that you make such illegal inquiries of women applicants?" There's no point in pussyfooting around when somebody brazenly oversteps the boundaries set by the law—not to mention common decency.

The Credit Decision

After the application stage of the credit process comes the evaluation and decision-making stage. The creditor will consider what he's learned about you and determine whether you're credit-worthy. Here, too, Regulation B lays down some specific requirements: certain kinds of information cannot be ignored by creditors, while other information is strictly off limits and must never be considered.

Sex and Marital Status. The cardinal sin under the ECOA is for a creditor to deny you credit based on the fact that you're a woman or because of your marital status (i.e., whether you're single, married, divorced, separated, or widowed).

Childbearing Prospects. You will recall that prior to ECOA many young women had a hard time securing credit because of assumptions made about their potential for motherhood. Creditors often assumed that every young woman would eventually settle down, raise a family, and in the process suffer a drop in earnings. While this theory may have proven true in *some* cases, it was certainly untrue for *every* individual. The result was credit discrimination against women, who were unfairly stereotyped as little more than future childbearers.

Such stereotyping is illegal under Regulation B. In evaluating an applicant's credit-worthiness, a creditor cannot employ any assumptions or aggregate statistics about the likelihood that any particular group (e.g., young women) will bear or rear children and experience a loss in earnings.

Woman's Income. In general, a creditor cannot refuse to consider any woman's income just because of her sex or marital status. A woman's income must be taken into account whether she is applying for credit herself or is married to a credit applicant.

Discounting a Woman's Income. Regulation B specifically prohibits the discriminatory practice of discounting a woman's income—that is, valuing it at less than its actual worth. Prior to the ECOA, when a husband applied for credit and relied in part on his wife's income, it was not uncommon for the creditor to discount her income by as much as 50 percent; in other words, her income would be counted at only half its actual dollar value. Such a practice is now illegal.

Part-time Employment. Suppose you're a homemaker who works part-time as a substitute teacher. Can a creditor disregard the income you earn because it's derived from part-time work? Absolutely not. The creditor must consider income from part-time employment, although he is free to evaluate it in terms of both amount and probable continuance.

Alimony, Child Support, and Separate Maintenance. We saw earlier that you don't have to reveal income from these sources if you don't want to. But what if you do? Must the creditor consider it in assessing your ability to repay any credit that may be extended to you? Yes, absolutely. The creditor must consider all such payments as income *to the extent that they are likely to be consistently made.*

And how will the creditor determine the likelihood of consistent payments? Regulation B suggests some of the factors that a creditor may consider:

—whether the payments are required to be made under a written agreement (e.g., separation agreement) or court decree;

—the length of time that the payments have been received;

—the regularity with which payments have been made;

—whether there are any legal procedures available to compel payment;

—the credit-worthiness of the person making the payments.

If factors like these indicate a regular source of income, the creditor must consider it as such and not arbitrarily devalue it. Failure to do so would discriminate illegally against separated and divorced women.

Age. A creditor can't discriminate against you because of your age. One practice in particular outlawed by Regulation B is the use of a *credit scoring system* by which elderly applicants automatically lose points because of their age. A credit scoring system is a numerical point system used to predict an applicant's credit-worthiness. Points are awarded or withheld depending on several characteristics supposed to be indicative of credit-worthiness: e.g., years at the same job and residence, ownership of a car, savings account. Under Regulation B no applicant over sixty-two years old can lose points just because of his or her age.

Your age may be considered by a creditor if it bears some logical relationship to the determination of credit-worthiness. For example, a creditor might consider your occupation and the amount of time left before you retire in order to determine whether your income (including any retirement income) will be sufficient to enable you to repay whatever credit may be extended to you.

A creditor may also consider whether any security you offer to assure repayment will be adequate if the duration of the credit extension will exceed your life expectancy. For example, if you're elderly, you might not qualify for a 5 percent down, 30-year mortgage; the duration of the loan exceeds your life expectancy, and the cost to the creditor of realizing on your mortgaged property might be greater than your equity interest in the property. On the other hand, you might well qualify for a loan with a larger down payment and a shorter term. And you should have no trouble qualifying for, say, a $10,000 home-improvement loan that is secured by a $50,000 homesite.

Telephone Listing. Regulation B prohibits a creditor from taking into account whether or not you have a telephone *listed in your name.* A creditor may consider only whether a telephone exists in your residence, regardless of whose name it's listed in.

Citizenship. A creditor may consider whether an applicant is a permanent resident of the United States. The applicant's immigration status may also be considered.

Credit History. We saw earlier how important a solid credit history can be in determining your willingness to repay debt. We also saw how a married woman can build her own credit history based on joint accounts she shares with her husband or open-end accounts with him that she is permitted to use. Regulation B specifically requires creditors to take into consideration any available credit history on these joint and open-end accounts. If the credit history is not available from a credit bureau, make sure you bring it to the creditor's attention, or else ask him to contact the other creditor directly in order to obtain the credit history that you want considered.

Suppose you and your husband both signed on a bank loan but it was subsequently recorded only in your husband's name. Bring the creditor a copy of the original loan contract, which bears your signature as well as your husband's. The creditor must consider the credit history of this transaction in evaluating your individual credit-worthiness.

Regulation B also requires a creditor to consider any available credit history on accounts in the name of your spouse or *former spouse,* if you can demonstrate that the record of these accounts accurately reflects your own credit-worthiness. Say your ex-husband had a charge account at the ABC Department Store. While married to him, you charged purchases for yourself and your family on his account. Then you actually contributed to the payment of bills that ABC sent your ex. Even though the account was your ex's, a creditor must consider any evidence you present to document your participation in the account.

A creditor must also consider any clarification or correction you wish to make concerning your credit history. For instance, you can straighten out errors or omissions that may be in a report from the credit bureau. Let's say you once signed your husband's application for an airline credit card, at his request. He used the card solely for business, and you never saw any of the bills. Because his company was slow in reimbursing him for travel expenses, the credit account developed a record of delinquent payments, which was picked up and recorded by the local credit bureau. Don't let this derogatory credit information be used against you when you apply for credit in your own name. If you explain the facts to the creditor, he must consider them when evaluating your credit-worthiness.

Notification of Decision

The evaluation stage of the credit process culminates with the creditor's decision to grant you credit, or deny it, or perhaps offer you something different from what you had originally requested. When will you learn about the decision? And if it is negative, how much will you learn about the creditor's reasons? Both questions are answered by the ECOA and Regulation B.

Time for Notification. Let's start optimistically, by assuming that your application for credit is granted. Regulation B says you must be notified of this decision within 30 days after the creditor has received your completed application. (An application is legally "completed" once the creditor has received all the information he needs and ordinarily considers when evaluating applications like yours, for the type and amount of credit you're seeking. Thus, if the creditor needed to consider a credit bureau report, your application would not be deemed "completed" until he had received the report.)

If you're denied credit, when must you be notified? Within the same 30-day period after your application has been completed. This 30-day deadline also applies when your application is incomplete. If the incompleteness arises from gaps that you could fill (e.g., by supplying missing data), the creditor must make a reasonable effort to alert you to this fact, and he must allow you a reasonable opportunity to complete your application. After this effort fails, the creditor has 30 days in which to notify you of his adverse decision.

Suppose that instead of just denying the type and amount of credit you sought, the creditor makes a counteroffer—that is, credit in a substantially different amount and on substantially different terms. For example, you seek a line of credit totaling $700, but the creditor offers a credit line with a ceiling of only $400. Or you apply for a mortgage loan of $50,000 at an 8½ percent interest for a term of thirty years, but the creditor offers a loan of $35,000 at 9½ percent for a term of only twenty years.

Let's assume you find the counteroffer unacceptable. You must be notified of whatever action the creditor then decides to take—e.g., withdrawal of the counteroffer and rejection of your application. This notification must come within 90 days after the counteroffer, if within this time you haven't accepted or used the credit offered.

Form of Notification. Once again, let's begin on the sunny side: your application for credit is granted. Don't expect heartfelt congratulations and a dozen roses. Regulation B doesn't even require written notification of the creditor's approval, although as a matter of practice you may very well receive a letter. Approval may be conveyed orally, in writing, or simply by extending the credit—for instance, sending you the credit card or money you requested.

So much for the sunny side. Now what happens if your credit application is turned down; what will you be told about the reason for this action? "Nothing at all" was the answer that prevailed among creditors prior to the ECOA. "With few exceptions," the United States Senate Banking Committee reported in 1976, "creditors have refused to do anything more than notify rejected applicants of the fact of the rejection. Only rarely do creditors give even a cursory explanation of the reasons why. The creditors' apparent rationale has been that since they had no legal obligation to explain their action they would not venture the effort or the potential embarrassment of doing so."

But now the ECOA requires creditors to give *specific reasons* to applicants who are denied credit. Congress believed that this notification requirement was essential in order to fully implement the antidiscriminatory purpose of the ECOA. If a creditor knows he must explain his decision, he will be discouraged from relying on improper grounds.

This requirement—one of the most significant changes wrought by ECOA—also fulfills a practical consumer need. According to the Senate Banking Committee:

> *Rejected credit applicants will now be able to learn where and how their credit status is deficient and this information should have a pervasive and valuable educational benefit. Instead of being told only that they do not meet a particular creditor's standards, consumers particularly should benefit from knowing, for example, that the reason for the denial is their short residence in the area, or their recent change of employment, or their already over-extended financial situation. In those cases where the creditor may have acted on misinformation or inadequate information, the statement of reasons gives the applicant a chance to rectify the mistake.*

Regulation B provides the fine print, spelling out how creditors are to comply with ECOA notification requirements. Basically, the notification must meet five formal requirements:

1. *Written Notification.* In general, you must be given written notification of any negative decision. (Oral notification is permissible only in the case of certain small creditors —specifically, creditors who did not receive more than 150 applications during the calendar year immediately preceding the calendar year in which you are to receive notification.)

2. *Statement of Action Taken.* You must be informed of the nature of the adverse action that has been taken by the creditor: for example, your application for a loan has

been rejected, or your request for an increase in your line of credit from $500 to $1,000 has been turned down.

3. *Specific Reasons.* As we saw earlier, one of the most significant innovations wrought by ECOA is the requirement that creditors explain their adverse decisions to credit applicants. A creditor must give you a *specific statement of his principal reasons* for the adverse action. Where appropriate, for instance, you must be informed that you haven't been employed long enough, or your income level is too low, or your credit references were insufficient, or you're already overextended financially because of your outstanding obligations.

The statement of reasons will not suffice if, say, the creditor merely alludes in highly generalized terms to "internal standards" or "internal policies" as the reason for his action. Nor can a creditor offer the vague excuse that you failed to achieve a satisfactory qualifying score on the credit scoring system used by the creditor. While that score may be the ultimate reason for rejection, it is really only a conclusion. After all, many factors are figured into a typical credit scoring system (e.g., years at the same residence, age of your car, credit bureau report). Those factors that actually detracted from your overall score are the principal reasons why a negative decision resulted.

In a 1977 case, *Carroll* v. *Exxon Company,* the oil company violated the ECOA notice requirements by failing to provide a credit applicant with adequate reasons for her rejection. Kathleen Carroll, a single working woman, had applied for an Exxon credit card. In denying her a card, Exxon sent a letter stating only that a credit bureau contacted by the oil company was able to offer no definitive information regarding Carroll's credit-worthiness. She sued Exxon for failing to provide adequate reasons for the denial of credit. According to the court's findings, Exxon had relied on several important reasons besides the credit bureau report: e.g., Carroll didn't have a major credit card; she didn't list a savings account on her application; and she had been employed for only one year. The failure to notify Carroll of these reasons violated the ECOA and Regulation B.

The creditor may formulate his own statement of reasons, which can be written out in letter form or presented in checklist format. Another alternative is to use the sample form drawn up by the Federal Reserve Board (see pages 219–221); that form employs a checklist and fill-in-the-blanks format.

4. *Legal Warning.* The notification must inform you of the fundamental protection against discrimination afforded by the ECOA (see the boilerplate notice at the end of the sample form on page 221).

Model ECOA Notification Form

STATEMENT OF CREDIT DENIAL, TERMINATION, OR CHANGE

DATE _____

Applicant's Name: _____

Applicant's Address: _____

_____

Description of Account, Transaction, or Requested Credit:

_____

Description of Adverse Action Taken:

_____

_____

PRINCIPAL REASON(S) FOR ADVERSE ACTION CONCERNING CREDIT

____ Credit application incomplete
____ Insufficient credit references

___ Unable to verify credit references
___ Temporary or irregular employment
___ Unable to verify employment
___ Length of employment
___ Insufficient income
___ Excessive obligations
___ Unable to verify income
___ Inadequate collateral
___ Too short a period of residence
___ Temporary residence
___ Unable to verify residence
___ No credit file
___ Insufficient credit file
___ Delinquent credit obligations
___ Garnishment, attachment, foreclosure, repossession, or suit
___ Bankruptcy
___ We do not grant credit to any applicant on the terms and conditions you request.
___ Other, specify: _____

_____

DISCLOSURE OF USE OF INFORMATION OBTAINED FROM AN OUTSIDE SOURCE

___ Disclosure inapplicable
___ Information obtained in a report from a consumer reporting agency
Name: _____

_____

Street address: _____

_____

Telephone number: _____

—— Information obtained from an outside source other than a consumer reporting agency. Under the Fair Credit Reporting Act, you have the right to make a written request, within 60 days of receipt of this notice, for disclosure of the nature of the adverse information.

Creditor's name: _____

Creditor's address: _____

_____

Creditor's telephone number: _____

Equal Credit Opportunity Act Notice

The Federal Equal Credit Opportunity Act prohibits creditors from discriminating against credit applicants on the basis of race, color, religion, national origin, sex, marital status, age (provided that the applicant has the capacity to enter into a binding contract); because all or part of the applicant's income derives from any public assistance program; or because the applicant has in good faith exercised any right under the Consumer Credit Protection Act.* The Federal agency that administers compliance with this law concerning this creditor is [here creditor to supply name and address of the appropriate agency from Appendix F].

5. *Enforcement Agency.* You must be supplied with the name and address of the federal agency that oversees compliance with ECOA, by the creditor with whom you're dealing (see the very end of the sample form).

Under Regulation B, there is an alternative method of notification, which differs in several respects from the one just outlined. Instead of stating reasons for adverse ac-

* [The Consumer Credit Protection Act is an omnibus title for the body of federal law that includes such laws as the Equal Credit Opportunity Act and the Fair Credit Reporting Act.]

tion in the written notification, the creditor can just state in the notification that the applicant has a right to receive such reasons if he makes the proper request. This disclosure must contain the name, address, and telephone number of the person or office from which the statement of reasons can be obtained. The applicant then has 60 days from the date of notification to request a statement of reasons, and the creditor then has 30 days in which to fill that request. The statement of reasons may be given orally, but the applicant has the right to demand written confirmation. This confirmation must be supplied within 30 days after the demand is made.

Maintaining Your Credit

Thus far we've been looking at your rights when you apply for credit. Now let's assume the application process is over and you've been granted credit and wish to maintain it. What continuing protection do you have against discrimination?

Use of Your Own Name. As we saw earlier, you have the right to maintain a credit account in your own name. You cannot be compelled to use your married name if you don't want to.

Signature of Your Spouse. Before the ECOA, when credit was extended to a woman, her signature was not enough to satisfy creditors anxious about repayment. For added assurance, creditors regularly insisted upon a cosignature—usually that of the woman's husband or father—binding someone else besides the woman to make repayment. In one ludicrous case, a working woman in her forties who was the head of a household wanted to buy a house for herself and her children; she could not get a mortgage without the signature of her seventy-year-old father, who was living on a pension.

The ECOA and Regulation B outlaw this form of discrimination. Now when you qualify for credit on your own, your signature alone will suffice. For example, you apply for a personal loan. You qualify on the basis of your salary level and length of employment. The creditor cannot insist that your spouse or any other person sign the credit documents along with you. (Of course, if you qualify for joint credit with another applicant who will be jointly responsible with you for repayment, the creditor can insist on having the joint applicant's signature as well as yours.)

There are some exceptional circumstances under which cosignature may be required, even though you qualify for credit in your own right. For example:

Guarantor Needed. Suppose your salary doesn't qualify you for the credit you seek. According to the creditor's standards, you need a backup—someone who will guarantee repayment by making himself personally liable should you default. This person is a guarantor—a financial guardian angel. In such a situation, the guarantor's cosignature could legitimately be required. There is no requirement, however, that the guarantor be your spouse or parent.

Property as Security for Credit. Suppose you offer property as security for repayment but you are not free to dispose of that property on your own, because someone else shares ownership in that property. For example, as security for repayment of a personal loan to you, you offer a new car that you own jointly with your husband. His cosignature may be legitimately required by the creditor to assure that, if necessary, the car will be available as a source of repayment.

Community Property. If you live in a community-property state, a creditor may generally insist on your spouse's cosignature.

Change in Marital Status, Retirement. We've already seen how credit-worthy women often lost their charge cards and lines of credit as soon as they married. Their accounts would be suddenly canceled, and they would be told to reapply in their husband's name. The same sort of rude awakening awaited elderly people when they retired from work.

Regulation B prohibits this form of discrimination against anyone who maintains an open-end credit account. (Such an account, you will remember, is an ongoing extension of credit, like a revolving charge account or a line of credit, that allows you to charge repeated purchases or obtain repeated loans.) With regard to any open-end account you may have, a creditor cannot close the account, require you to reapply for the account, or change the terms of the account on the basis of any of the following events:

—you reach a certain age;

—you retire; or

—you change your name or marital status.

No adverse action can be taken against you so long as there is no evidence of your inability or unwillingness to repay the credit extended to you.

There is only one circumstance in which a change in marital status might justify your having to reapply for an account. Assume you have an account that was originally based on your spouse's income, because yours was insufficient. If you are separated or divorced, the creditor can insist that you reapply for the account.

Notification of Changes in Your Account. We saw earlier the notification requirements when a creditor rejects a credit application. Much the same requirements apply when any adverse action is taken against one of your existing accounts. For example, you request an increase in the amount of credit already available to you (say, from a $500 line of credit to a $1,000 line) but you're turned down. Or a creditor changes the terms of your account unfavorably (and the action doesn't affect most of the other accounts in your category). Or perhaps the creditor just closes your account. In the case of such adverse actions, you must be notified within 30 days after the action occurs.

In form and substance, the notification must fulfill the same requirements that govern notification when an application for credit is rejected. Thus, the notification must be in writing, state the action taken, and give specific reasons for the action, etc.

Enforce Your Equal Credit Opportunity Rights

When it comes to getting your rights from creditors, the ECOA gives you some powerful legal leverage. Several different federal agencies have authority to police violations of the Act. Which one you should complain to depends on the category of creditor you're dealing with (e.g., retail store, bank). Whenever you are denied credit, you will recall, the creditor is supposed to notify you of the right agency to contact. In case the creditor forgets, we have provided a directory to the proper agencies in Appendix F.

Understand that none of these agencies will represent you or take your case, so to speak, the way an attorney would. They will use your complaint, however, and others they receive to single out violation-prone creditors for investigation and possible administrative action. (At least one of these agencies, the Comtroller of the Currency, which oversees nationally chartered banks, presently investigates every complaint it receives.) No creditor wants to be put to the time, expense, and hassle of the bureaucratic red tape that inevitably accompanies a government inquiry. Indeed, not too long ago one major oil company was issuing its credit card to any rejected applicant who complained about credit discrimination to the Federal Trade Commission. So calling in the feds, or just intimating that you will, can bring strong pressure to bear on a creditor who's discriminating against you.

Fortunately, though, you're not beholden to Big Government to reach out from Washington and vindicate your rights. The ECOA arms you with some awesome firepower of your own, namely, a very expensive (for the creditor) lawsuit. Under the *civil liability* section of the ECOA, you can sue a creditor for any violation of your credit rights. The creditor may be held liable for:

—*actual damages* (that is, any loss you incur because you were denied credit); plus

—*punitive damages* of up to $10,000 (punitive damages are awarded to punish a creditor and give fair warning to others who might consider acting as he did); plus

—*attorney's fees* and court costs (these will be added to any judgment awarded to you).

If a *class action* is brought against a creditor by consumers who have grievances similar to yours, the punitive damage award can be staggering—as much as $500,000 or 1 percent of the creditor's net worth (whichever sum is less). Clearly the ECOA creates a dollars-and-cents soft spot in any creditor.

Power Play Pointers. Power plays using the ECOA are most likely to occur after you've been denied credit and you suspect discrimination. Sometimes a violation of the law will be clear to you, and you should mince no words in taking the creditor to task.

To take a blatant example, suppose some obtuse credit manager at a local department store insists that you can't open a charge account in your maiden name. "The store requires," he states flatly, "that you open this account in your husband's surname. It's an old store policy."

"Too old!" you could respond. "The store's policy

doesn't coincide with the federal government's. I have a perfect legal right under the *Equal Credit Opportunity Act* to open this account in my maiden name. So I'll thank you to get in step with the law or get a lawyer, because I'd be more than happy to sue you for ten thousand dollars in *punitive damages*, plus my *attorney's fees.*" That set of code-words will send a cold wind whistling up the credit manager's kilt; he'll think twice before he sticks to some archaic policy and plunges the store into expensive legal trouble.

Or suppose a bank officer insists that your husband cosign on a personal loan for which you've just qualified on your own. "Would I need a cosigner if I were single?" you might inquire innocently.

"Oh no," the insensitive officer replies, "the bank just needs this because you're married."

"You can't be serious," you could shoot back. "I can't believe the bank is still discriminating against married women. Surely you're familiar with the *Equal Credit Opportunity Act* and *Regulation B*. What you're demanding of me violates these federal laws. Either we clear this up now or your attorney will wind up talking to my attorney." Once again, the chilling blast of your codewords will alert the creditor to the gravity of the faux pas he's making.

What if all those charge accounts you enjoyed while single get canceled as soon as you marry, and you're requested to reapply in your husband's name? The violation here is so fundamental, you should probably bypass the bumbling credit department and contact the president of the company directly. Inform him bluntly that there's been an unfortunate violation of federal law that you'd like to clear up with him, rather than embarrass the store in federal court. Make him an offer he can't refuse: you won't take any legal action on the store's infraction if your charge account is reinstated within 72 hours. Generally speaking, you'll discover that few creditors are foolhardy enough to pursue a course of obvious discrimination after you've caught them with their pants (they all wear pants!) down.

Be alert for discrimination that is not as obvious as the instances mentioned thus far. Violations of the ECOA can lurk beneath seemingly innocent actions. If you're denied credit and the reason given to you doesn't make sense, or you just don't understand it, by all means go back to the creditor and request an explanation. Not infrequently, in the course of that explanation the creditor will reveal— whether intentionally or not—a discriminatory basis for his action.

Let's say your application for a loan is turned down and the only reason given on the notice you receive from the creditor is "insufficient credit references." That conclusion doesn't jibe with the references you gave to the creditor, so you make an appointment to see him. The creditor explains that you lacked a major credit card or a department store charge account; therefore, your references were insufficient.

"What about my oil company card? and the charge account at ABC Department Store?" you might ask incredulously. "Surely they must meet your standards "

"Oh, I can't really consider those," replies the creditor unabashedly. "They're just accounts that you're allowed to use with your husband. They're really his accounts."

An alarm should go off in your head: v-i-o-l-a-t-i-o-n! You know that Regulation B requires the creditor to consider precisely the kinds of accounts that he has disregarded. Thus, contrary to what the creditor said, you did have a major credit card—and a charge account to boot! Before getting hard-nosed, try as politely as possible to bring the creditor in line with the law. "Well, I think maybe you're following a practice that antedates the *Equal Credit Opportunity Act.* Under *Regulation B,* aren't you bound to give consideration to any accounts that I use along with my husband? Looking at this from the legal viewpoint, my credit references would seem to be perfectly sufficient."

Allow a few moments for your codewords to sink in. It's not every day that creditors get the ECOA and Regulation B thrown at them. Don't be surprised if the creditor shuffles some papers—or his feet—and suggests, after some hemming and hawing, that your application will have to be "rechecked." Fine. Don't push things. You'll have time enough to raise the possibility of litigation should the creditor adhere to his initial position.

Suppose the reason given for the rejection of your application is "insufficient income." You're puzzled, because the total income you reported was rather substantial. You're also suspicious, because that total income comprised not only your salary but also alimony and child support. When you return to question the creditor about his reasoning, you say: "I don't understand how my income could have been insufficient. There's my regular salary. If that's not enough by itself, certainly, when it's added to the alimony and child support I reported, I must qualify for credit."

"What you probably don't realize," the creditor responds, "is that I can't count that alimony at face value."

You hang right in there. "But why not? After all, I've been receiving that alimony regularly for three years under a divorce decree."

"Yes, but it's still just alimony—not salary. At best it's worth maybe fifty percent of face value—"

V-i-o-l-a-t-i-o-n! the alarm should sound off again. You know that Regulation B requires creditors to consider regular alimony and child support payments just like any other steady source of income. Had your alimony been calculated at face value, your income might well have been sufficient.

Once again, before making a federal case out of the creditor's violation, see if you can induce him to go straight: "The guidelines you're following strike me as awfully discriminatory toward divorced women. It's my understanding that the *Federal Reserve Board* prohibited creditors from discounting alimony and child support. Isn't that what *Regulation B* is all about?"

The glaze you see in the creditor's eyes shows he's been slightly stunned by your codewords. There you are innocently enough spouting off about the bane of the creditor's existence—Regulation B! You can rest assured that your case is far from closed.

With any luck, after you leave the creditor will take advantage of the breathing space you've left him, reconsider the mistake he knows he's made, and decide it's more prudent to follow the law and grant you the credit that was initially denied. But what happens if the creditor turns out to be made of sterner—and more reckless—stuff than you had imagined? Your codewords rocked him back on his heels briefly, but after due consideration, he decides to stand pat. It's time to escalate.

Check in Appendix F for the federal agency charged with policing the creditor you're dealing with. Contact the creditor again and tell him in no uncertain terms that you now believe he has discriminated against you in violation of the ECOA and Regulation B. Let him know that you are "drafting a formal complaint" that you expect to "file with the agency" within ten days.

If the creditor remains unmoved, carry out your threat. Write a straightforward complaint letter to the agency. Outline the facts in your case, state the reason given to you for denial of credit, and explain why you suspect the creditor may have discriminated against you illegally. In this last regard, try to demonstrate why no reason you can think of

—other than a discriminatory one—accounts for the creditor's action. (Attach copies, not originals, of any documents that will assist the agency in appraising your complaint.) Be sure to send a copy of your complaint letter to the creditor; the prospect of a federal investigation may just give him the right prod to make amends.

If you still don't get satisfaction, you might try one last power play before taking legal action. Instead of meeting the creditor head-on again, take an end run around him directly to the legal department of his company. The lawyers you will be addressing there are more likely to appreciate the gravity of what you have to say, and they may just sway the creditor to see things your way.

You can adopt the following model letter to accommodate the facts in your particular case:

[Insert date of mailing]

> *[Your name*
> *Mailing address*
> *City, state, zip code]*

Legal Department
[Name of Creditor's Company
Mailing address
City, state, zip code]

Re: Violation of the Equal Credit Opportunity Act
    and Regulation B

Dear Counsel [or the attorney's name if you know it]:
    I believe that your company has denied me credit on a discriminatory basis, which is prohibited by the federal laws mentioned above.
    Under applicable federal law [Relate the legal principle you are relying on—for example:] "it is illegal

*for a creditor to arbitrarily discount alimony when it is
a consistent source of the applicant's income."*

*Your company has violated the law because
[Briefly recount the facts that substantiate a violation.
For example:], despite my evidence of consistent
alimony payments, Mr. Smith refused to consider these
payments at face value. He told me they could be
counted at only 50 percent of their face value.*

*Unless this matter has been cleared up to my
satisfaction no later than [Allow two weeks], I intend
to seek legal counsel and commence a civil proceeding
against you for violating the Equal Credit Opportunity
Act and Regulation B. Since your refusal to abide by
the law has been unrelenting, I shall seek the full
amount of punitive damages—$10,000. I shall also
instruct counsel, whose fees I expect you will be
ordered to pay, to consider the advisability of filing a
class action against you, seeking damages in the
amount of $500,000 or one percent of your net worth.*

> *Sincerely,*

_____

[Signature]

Now you've ticked off all the heavy codewords guaranteed to press on a sensitive legal nerve: e.g., *discrimination, civil proceeding, punitive damages,* and *class action.* Any lawyer who reads your letter will quickly see that you know the law and mean serious business. If he thinks your claim has some merit and could wind up costing the company money, he may advise the creditor you dealt with to resolve the matter amicably. You can bet that if the creditor "hears from legal" you stand a good chance of hearing from the creditor—this time with good news.

In the event that all your power plays meet with is solid resistance, then you'll have to reassess your case. Do you still think it's a pretty clear case of discrimination? If so, see a lawyer to determine whether you should carry out your threat to sue the creditor.

Codeword Glossary

actual damages Any loss you incur because of a discriminatory denial of credit, which can be compensated for in a lawsuit under the Equal Credit Opportunity Act.

attorney's fees In any judgment you win against a creditor under the ECOA, your attorney's fees can be included.

class action A group lawsuit brought by consumers against a creditor, which can result in a punitive damage award (under the ECOA) of up to $500,000 or 1 percent of the creditor's net worth—whichever sum is less.

Equal Credit Opportunity Act (ECOA) The federal statute that prohibits discrimination in any aspect of a credit transaction, whether based on sex, marital status, race, national origin, religion, age, or receipt of public assistance. This law can be found in section 1691 of title 15 of the United States Code.

Fair Credit Reporting Act (FCRA) The federal statute that gives you the right to inspect and correct your file at a credit bureau. This law can be found in section 1681 of title 15 of the United States Code.

Federal Reserve Board (FRB) The federal agency that promulgated Regulation B to implement the ECOA.

Federal Trade Commission (FTC) The federal agency that enforces the ECOA against most non-bank creditors. (See Appendix F for the FTC's exact jurisdiction, as well as the other federal agencies that enforce the ECOA.)

punitive damages A penalty of up to $10,000 that can be added to any judgment won against a creditor for violations of the ECOA.

Regulation B Promulgated by the Federal Reserve Board,

this complex set of rules implements the basic provisions of the ECOA and has the full force of law. Regulation B can be found in section 202 of title 12 of the Code of Federal Regulations (the basic compilation of all federal regulations).

II

Overpowering Your Landlord

The second most passionate relationship in life is that between landlord and tenant. If you rent an apartment, you no doubt regard it as your home. The landlord, on the other hand, views your home as his business. Therefore, confrontations are almost inevitable. Let's examine three areas of conflict between many landlords and tenants: first, eviction threats leveled against tenants who try to get their living conditions upgraded; second, unauthorized intrusions by a landlord into a tenant's apartment; third, illegal attempts by a landlord to keep a tenant's security deposit. In each of these situations a power play can bring your landlord into line.

Getting Repairs without Getting Evicted

Virtually every state and good-sized city in this country has a housing code. These codes, enacted by state or local governments, set minimum standards for safe, clean, and comfortable apartment living. Generally, a landlord is bound to keep his apartment building in good repair; to clean the halls and keep them well lit; to supply adequate heat and hot water; and to maintain the plumbing and electrical systems.

Wherever a housing code exists, some government agency—usually called the Housing Department or the Office of Code Enforcement—is responsible for enforcing the code. Typical enforcement techniques include sending out inspectors to check on tenant complaints about violations of the code; issuance of summonses notifying landlords that they are violating the code and ordering them to take corrective steps; and imposition of fines or other sanctions when landlords don't comply.

Many states and localities also empower tenants to take direct action when they are being deprived of essential building services. For example, tenants may have the right to withhold rent payments; to make their own repairs and deduct the expense from the rent; to organize all the tenants and initiate a buildingwide rent strike. The available legal remedies vary widely from state to state, and especially from city to city. To make sure of exactly what rights you have, you should contact your city's housing enforcement agency; they can best explain what the local regulations provide.

The overriding problem we would like to address is not the variety of rights and remedies at your disposal, but one universal obstacle to asserting them. Put simply, tenants are afraid of their landlord; they fear that he will throw them out if they dare to complain or, heaven forbid, join a tenants' union to demand better living conditions.

The law has a fitting epithet to describe the punishment that tenants fear: *retaliatory eviction*. " 'Retaliatory eviction,' " one judge recently explained, "is the nomenclature that has developed to define the action of a landlord who evicts his tenant because of the tenant's reporting of housing code violations to the public authorities. It might have been called anything; 'vengeful eviction' or, simply, 'getting even.' Essentially, it comes down to the control over the property which the landlord claims to reserve to himself not only to let and relet, but to immunize himself from the disclosure of housing violations."

Retaliatory eviction is illegal. Judges across the country have concluded that a landlord seeking revenge should not be allowed to avail himself of the court system to secure an eviction. This judicial viewpoint was expressed well by federal Judge J. Skelly Wright in *Edwards* v. *Habib,* the landmark 1968 case that outlawed retaliatory evictions in Washington, D.C.:

> *While a landlord may evict for any legal reason . . . he is not, we hold, free to evict in retaliation for the tenant's report of housing code violations to the authorities. . . . For reasons of public policy, such an eviction cannot be permitted.*
>
> *The housing and sanitary codes . . . indicate a strong and pervasive congressional concern to secure for the city's [tenants] decent, or at least safe and sanitary, places to live. Effective implementation and enforcement of the codes obviously depend in part on private initiative in reporting of violations. . . . For fiscal year 1966 nearly a third of the cases handled by the [Washington, D.C., housing department] arose from private complaints. To permit retaliatory evictions, then, would clearly frustrate the effectiveness of the housing code as a means of upgrading the quality of housing in Washington.*
>
> *In light of the appalling condition and shortage of housing in Washington, the expense of moving, the inequality of bargaining power between tenant and landlord, and the social and economic importance of*

*assuring at least minimum standards in housing
conditions, we do not hesitate to declare that
retaliatory eviction cannot be tolerated. There can be
no doubt that the [tenant], even though his home be
marred by housing code violations, will pause long
before he complains of them, if he fears eviction
as a consequence. Hence an eviction under the
circumstances of this case would not only punish the
[tenant] for making a complaint . . . but also would
stand as a warning to others that they dare not be so
bold, a result which from the authorization of the
housing code, we think Congress affirmatively sought
to avoid.*

The reasoning in *Edwards* v. *Habib* has been followed by many other judges who did not wish to be used by landlords as an instrument for circumventing state and local housing codes. Sometimes judges have evidenced a practical concern for the budget crunch faced by many cities: "Unfortunately," one New York judge remarked, "no municipality in these times is blessed with sufficient resources . . . to hire enough building inspectors. . . . It must depend upon citizen cooperation." In other words, tenants should be encouraged to act as "private building inspectors," reporting potential code violations that might otherwise be overlooked by understaffed housing agencies.

Besides public policy, there is another powerful reason why judges are reluctant to lend their weight to attempts at retaliatory eviction: the First Amendment to the United States Constitution guarantees your right to free speech; it also assures "the right of the people peaceably to assemble, and to petition the Government for a redress of grievances." You may have always associated these Constitutional rights with soapbox orators, labor union organizers, and political action groups that "march on the Capitol." As a tenant, however, every time you complain about housing conditions, or participate in a tenants' meeting, or make a protest to a governmental housing agency, you are also exercising your Constitutional rights to free speech, assembly, and petition. To the extent that retaliation inhibits your activism—or has what judges call a "chilling effect" on your exercise of First Amendment rights—it may be declared unconstitutional.

In the 1972 New York case, *Church* v. *Allen Meadows Apartments,* the court ruled: "The tenants have been active and vocal in a tenants' association which has been seeking correctives for what it feels were housing . . . code violations. . . . There is no doubt that the landlord's decision not to renew the lease was motivated solely by these activities of the tenants. Any proceeding for eviction so motivated and retaliatory is unconstitutional in that it seeks to . . . penalize a person for exercising his constitutional rights of free speech."

The 1970s have seen a flurry of legislative activity across the country. State after state has enacted laws prohibiting retaliatory evictions. Currently, twenty-six jurisdictions, including the District of Columbia, have adopted such retaliatory eviction laws: Alaska, Arizona, California, Connecticut, Delaware, District of Columbia, Hawaii, Illinois, Kentucky, Maine, Maryland, Massachusetts, Michigan, Minnesota, Nebraska, New Hampshire, New Jersey, New Mexico, New York, Ohio, Oregon, Pennsylvania, Rhode Island, Tennessee, Virginia, and Washington. Wisconsin, too, has adopted the same basic rule prevailing in these states through a ruling by its highest court—thus bringing the total number of jurisdictions to twenty-seven. (Legal citations to the laws in these twenty-seven jurisdictions appear in Appendix G.)

The laws in these states differ somewhat, but they all shield legitimate tenant activities from landlord retaliation. Basically, there are three forms of activity that are protected: (1) filing a complaint with the governmental agency that oversees enforcement of the housing code; (2) complaining directly to the landlord; and (3) organizing or participating in a tenants' group.

A tenant who engages in such activity is generally protected against three kinds of retaliation on the part of the landlord: (1) threatening or seeking eviction; (2) increasing the rent; and (3) decreasing the services (e.g., turning down the heat, cutting off the electricity). These forms of retaliation are prohibited.

Generally speaking, a tenant can avail himself of the new laws against retaliatory eviction either by (1) suing the landlord for money damages—to compensate the tenant for any expense, loss, or suffering; or by (2) defending against an eviction action and getting it dismissed on the grounds that it is retaliatory. In certain instances, a tenant cannot take advantage of the new laws: for example, if he caused the housing condition that he is complaining about, or if his complaint is not being made in good faith.

Some state laws help the tenant to prove in court that his landlord was motivated by vengeance. These laws create a presumption favorable to the tenant: if the landlord's retaliatory action occurred soon after the tenant engaged in some protected activity—e.g., an attempted eviction three months after the tenant complained to housing authorities—then the judge will presume that the landlord was seeking revenge. (This presumption shifts the burden of proof to the landlord, who must struggle to prove that in fact he harbored no retaliatory intent.) The time span between the acts of the tenant and the landlord that gives rise to this helpful presumption varies from state to state: it's 90 days in some states (Delaware, Michigan, Minnesota, New Hampshire, and Washington), 6 months in others (Arizona, Maine, Massachusetts, and Oregon), and 1 year in Kentucky.

Although the laws protect a tenant from being evicted out of vengeance, they don't insure that he'll be able to stay in the apartment forever, merely by continuously crying "Retaliation!" Once the housing violation has been corrected and there are no longer any grounds for believing that the landlord is motivated by some retaliatory intent, the tenant can be evicted *so long as proper legal grounds exist for eviction.* Such grounds might include expiration of the tenant's lease, or perhaps a serious violation of that lease—such as damaging the apartment or creating a nuisance. Whatever the reason for the eviction, it must be *legitimate*—not just some phony camouflage for continuing retaliation.

Power Play Pointer. Is your apartment building going downhill—no repairs, inadequate heat, and deteriorating services? Perhaps it's time your building got organized with a tenants' union that knows what the local housing regulations provide and how they can be enforced. The landlord is more likely to upgrade the building if organized pressure is brought to bear. What's more, there's strength in numbers—the landlord can't very well retaliate against the whole building!

But assume the worst. Suppose he starts threatening reprisals because you've joined the tenants' union or made complaints on your own. For example, the landlord knocks on your door and tells you, "There'll be no more tenant meetings in this building." Don't be cowed. Ask the landlord why. If he can't come up with a good excuse (and don't be duped by the old line that tenant meetings are a fire hazard), tell him that you know tenants have a perfect legal right to assemble peaceably: "In fact, they have a Constitutional right under the *First Amendment.*"

If a landlord tells you to stop making complaints to the housing agency, tell him that you don't intend to pay rent for an apartment that's filled with violations of the housing code. "It's my right as a tenant to see that the code is enforced. I'd prefer that you fix my place without my having to complain. But when you ignore my complaints I have no alternative but to petition the government. That's my Constitutional right."

Don't be surprised if your landlord turns out not to be a fan of Constitutional law. He may rapidly tire of playing Justice Holmes to your Justice Brandeis, in which case he's apt to respond: "The hell with the damn Constitution"— most unHolmesian—"either you cut out this troublemaking or I'm gonna evict ya!"

Fight his fire with some fire of your own: "*Retaliatory eviction* happens to be illegal in this state. There's a state law against it. If you try to evict me, the court will throw the case out." If the landlord thinks you're bluffing, hit him with the legal citation for your state's retaliatory eviction law (see Appendix G). That will show him you're not just some civil rights egghead sounding off about vague Constitutional rights.

Follow up your confrontation with a dated confirming letter to the landlord. In it you might say something polite, like: "I was surprised today to hear you threaten me with eviction if I did not refrain from making complaints to the city housing agency. Your intentions seem unduly harsh. I made those complaints only because you failed to respond when I first complained to you. I do hope that you will make a more constructive response in the future so that I won't have to complain elsewhere." Send the letter via certified mail, return receipt requested, and keep a copy for yourself.

Does this confirming letter mean you're backing down from your doorway power play? Not at all. Like a smart lawyer, you're simply taking out a little insurance policy. Your letter is useful evidence that on a certain date the landlord threatened to evict you because of legitimate conduct on your part. In short, you're starting to build up a handy legal defense against possible future retaliation by the landlord.

Of course, just how far you push your rights depends largely on you and how bad your housing conditions are. Ultimately, a landlord bent on evicting you can probably accomplish it if he stifles his own desire for vengeance long enough. That grim eventuality may lead you to stifle yourself, in the hopes that you can hang on to your apartment a bit longer. Understand, however, that even if you choose this safe route, there's no guarantee that the landlord will renew your lease anyway. He can usually rerent your apartment to whomever he pleases (unless you're protected by some form of rent control), and he may just take advantage of your docility by cutting back on services—not out of vengeance, but out of plain old greed. From this viewpoint, you may be more or less forced to stand up for your rights, rather than suffer silently with substandard housing. If you do decide to stand up, you now know that you have some legal support should the landlord huff and puff and try to blow you down.

Codeword Glossary

Edwards v. *Habib*   A 1968 federal case found in volume 397 of the Federal Reporter, Second Series, at page 687; the leading court case outlawing retaliatory eviction.

First Amendment   Contained in the Bill of Rights to the United States Constitution; it guarantees you the Constitutional rights to free speech and peaceable assembly, and to petition the government for help.

housing code   Check with your local housing department for the precise title of the housing code that sets minimum housing standards in your city.

housing department   Check in your telephone directory under "City Government" for the precise title of the governmental agency that enforces the housing code in your city.

retaliatory eviction law   General codeword for the law in twenty-six states plus Washington, D.C., that prohibits landlords from retaliating against tenants who exercise their rights. (See Appendix G for the legal citations to use when referring to your state's law.)

Your Right to Privacy

What do you say to a nosy landlord? You know the type. He's always paying you surprise visits. At 8:00 A.M. on a Sunday morning, or right in the middle of your Friday-night cocktail party, comes a knock on the door: "This is the landlord. I gotta inspect something in your apartment. Open up, will ya?"

Well, will ya? More important, do you have to? Generally speaking, the answer is no. Even though you live in an apartment, you're still protected by the ancient legal maxim *domus sua cuique est tutissimum refugium* (a man's home is his castle). Of course, your three-and-a-half-room castle happens to be inside the landlord's castle, so he has an understandable interest in the condition of your castle, at least insofar as it affects other parts of his castle. But that interest may be indulged only with due regard for your privacy and convenience.

You may not realize it, but your lease already protects your privacy against unwarranted intrusions. Buried in the legal gobbledygook is a clause rather pompously labeled the *covenant of quiet enjoyment*. It reads something like this: "Landlord covenants that Tenant, on paying the rent and performing the covenants herein, shall peaceably and quietly have, hold, and enjoy the demised premises for the term herein mentioned." Freely translated, this legalese says: if you pay the rent and observe the rest of your obligations under the lease, you may enjoy the apartment in peace, without any disturbance from the landlord. This gentle-sounding covenant may conjure up the image of a tenant with pipe and slippers, beaming at the blissful tranquility of apartment living. Legally speaking, however, the covenant has a much more narrowly defined function: it guarantees your exclusive right to possess and occupy the apartment, without wrongful intrusions by any outsider—including the landlord!

If the landlord makes an unauthorized entry into your apartment, he violates the covenant and in doing so commits a *trespass* on your property. That's right—the landlord is actually a trespasser, and you can sue him for money damages if he harms any of your belongings or acts violently. It's even possible to sue for the mental distress that the landlord's intrusion caused you. In a 1959 Louisiana case, the landlord entered the tenant's apartment without permission. Despite the fact that a few weeks remained on the tenant's lease, the landlord began to fix up the apartment for the next tenant. The neighbors got the impression that the old tenant was being unceremoniously evicted. Claiming he had been humiliated by the landlord's intrusion, the old tenant sued and collected $150 to soothe his pride.

Besides the covenant of quiet enjoyment, your lease probably also contains a clause defining certain limited circumstances under which you agree to admit the landlord: for example, to make repairs; to show the building to prospective purchasers. Invariably the clause says that in these circumstances you will not unreasonably refuse entry to the landlord. The key factor here is *reasonableness*. You mustn't arbitrarily deny the landlord access to your apartment. If there's an emergency, like a leak flooding the apartment below you, or a buildingwide power failure, you could not reasonably refuse to let the landlord in. In any genuine emergency the landlord has the right to enter despite your objections.

On the other hand, in nonemergency situations it would be reasonable for you to turn the landlord away from your door if he showed up, unannounced, at some ungodly hour. Reasonableness dictates that, whenever practicable, the landlord give you advance notice and show up during normal business hours—say, 9:00 A.M. to 5:00 P.M. If the landlord—or, for that matter, any of his employees, like the superintendent—enters your apartment without permission, or without any reasonable justification, he will be trespassing on your private property.

Tenants in eighteen states are protected by special *apartment access laws* against unauthorized intrusions by the landlord or his employees. The states are: Alaska, Arizona, California, Connecticut, Delaware, Florida, Hawaii, Kansas, Kentucky, Nebraska, New Mexico, New York, Ohio, Oregon, Tennessee, Virginia, Washington and Wisconsin. (Legal citations for the apartment access law in each of these states appear in Appendix H.) In general, these laws spell out a limited set of circumstances under which a landlord may enter your apartment. While there are some differences among the eighteen laws, they provide many similar safeguards:

Entry for Legitimate Purpose Only. You cannot unreasonably refuse to admit the landlord (or his employee) if he has a legitimate purpose for entering. Legally acceptable purposes would include: inspection of the apartment in order to detect flaws; making necessary repairs or alterations; supplying necessary services; exhibiting the apartment to actual or prospective purchasers of the building or future tenants. (Ohio's law also allows for entry to "deliver parcels which are too large for the tenant's mail facilities.") Notice that all these purposes bear some logical relationship to the care and running of the building. Under no circumstances do the apartment access laws give your landlord license to drop by anytime he wants to chat or to snoop on you and your guests. Whenever the landlord lacks a legitimate purpose for entry, it would not be unreasonable for you to refuse to let him in.

Emergency. Don't start getting huffy over the covenant of quiet enjoyment if there's an emergency that the landlord must attend to. In that situation the landlord can enter your apartment even without your consent. Tennessee's apartment access law provides a good definition of an emergency: "Emergency means a sudden, generally unexpected occurrence or set of circumstances demanding immediate action." The Kansas law says, "The landlord may enter the dwelling unit without consent of the tenant in case of an extreme hazard involving potential loss of life or severe property damage."

Advance Notification. Assuming no emergency exists and the landlord has a legitimate purpose for entering your apartment, what factors determine whether the reception you give him is reasonable? One key factor is advance notification: Did the landlord warn you beforehand that he would be showing up? Almost all the apartment access laws require advance notification, although exactly how much varies from state to state.

Some states say you're entitled to 24 hours' advance notification: Alaska, California, Nebraska, New York (24 hours before an inspection, 7 days before repair work), and Oregon. Five states allow you 2 days' fair warning: Arizona, Delaware, Hawaii, Kentucky, and Washington. Still other states just provide for "reasonable" advance notice: Connecticut, Kansas, Virginia, and Wisconsin.

Time of Entry. The other key factor for determining reasonableness is the timing of the landlord's entry. Here common sense should prevail. Clearly, it's unreasonable for a handyman to show up for repair work at 7:00 A.M. or 10:30 P.M., and you would be justified in saying that it was too early or too late for a visit. Delaware explicitly provides that, "Insofar as it is practicable to do so, the landlord . . . shall enter only between 8:00 A.M. and 9:00 P.M., after announcing his presence and being admitted. . . ." Ordinarily, New York City tenants don't have to admit the landlord except on weekdays from 9:00 A.M. to 5:00 P.M.; weekends and holidays are off limits. (Remember, of course, that in case of an emergency the landlord can enter at any time.)

Harassment. All of the apartment access laws provide that the landlord's limited right of entry must not be abused. The landlord is prohibited from using his entry privileges to harass the tenant.

Power Play Pointer. We go back to where we began— the surprise knock at your door: "Will ya let me in?" asks the landlord. You may be half asleep or half dressed or half drunk or half a dozen other things. But you should still be alert enough to know that your privacy can't be invaded on the landlord's whim.

Find out what the landlord's purpose is: "Why do you want to come in?" If the landlord says he wants to ask you about another tenant, or discuss a rent raise, or warn you against joining the tenants' organization, etc., you will know immediately that he has no legitimate purpose for entering your apartment. "Well, that's nice," you may respond, "but I have no interest in discussing that now, thanks." If the landlord persists, tell him you're under no obligation to let him in "except for legitimate building-related purposes." (You know what they are.)

Suppose, however, that the landlord gives you one of those legitimate purposes: "I gotta check to see if all your storm windows were installed okay by the handyman." Just because there's a legitimate purpose for letting the landlord in doesn't mean you have to; he may still be imposing on you in a manner that is legally unreasonable. In that case (unless you don't mind the imposition), tell the landlord to go away and come again some other day.

For example: "Why didn't you give me *advance notification* that you were coming around? You can't just barge in here unannounced. I happen to have company, and I'd prefer that you make a later appointment with me."

Or you might point out: "Do you realize it's seven o'clock in the morning? I have no obligation to let you in now, and I'll thank you never to bother me at this hour again!"

Don't be surprised if your landlord rebukes you with "You can't treat me this way. I own this building. I got a right to come into your apartment anytime I want."

"You may own the building," your reply would go, "but so long as I'm renting this apartment the law gives *me* the exclusive right to possession. My right is superior to any outsider's—including yours!" (If you think your landlord speaks fluent Latin, you might add: *"Domus sua cuique est tutissimum refugium!"* However, these particular codewords are not recommended in Brooklyn or tough sections of Chicago.)

By now your landlord should be getting the point: that you don't intend to be unreasonably disturbed. Don't press your luck, though, and alienate him entirely, because you still have to get along with him. Suggest some other, more convenient time when you will be more than happy to let him in. That should settle the matter.

If it doesn't and the landlord persists, or if he makes a practice of showing up under unreasonable circumstances, let him know that you view his would-be intrusions as more than a mere inconvenience: "Whether you know it or not, I have the legal right to enjoy this apartment undisturbed by these intrusions of yours. That's what the *covenant of quiet enjoyment* in my lease says. It happens to be *trespassing* if you barge in on me. It's also against the *apartment access law* in this state for you to harass me all the time. If you force me to, I'll sue you for money damages for the annoyance you're causing me." (By all means hit the landlord with the legal citation for the apartment access law in your state.)

After the verbal barrage, even the most insensitive landlord should get the message that the law hangs a "No Trespassing" sign on your apartment door.

Codeword Glossary

advance notification   Generally required before the landlord's attempted entry will be deemed reasonable.

apartment access law   General codeword for the law in eighteen states that limits a landlord's right of entry (see Appendix H for the legal citations to use when referring to your state's law).

covenant of quiet enjoyment   The binding promise that the landlord makes in your lease, assuring you the exclusive right to possession of your apartment during your lease term.

trespass   An unauthorized intrusion by the landlord onto property that you alone have the right to possess and occupy (i.e., your apartment).

Getting Your Security Deposit Back

For years landlords have had a nice little racket going. When you rent an apartment, the landlord collects a security deposit. You're supposed to get it back at the end of your lease if you're a good tenant. But if you're bad and damage the apartment or leave it a mess, deductions are made from your deposit. Too often, however, even when you've been good, the landlord claims deductions for phony undocumented damages, or he just stalls you off until you forget about getting a refund. No wonder your down payment is called a security deposit—it provides security for the landlord's old age!

Fortunately, there are some tough new state laws guaranteed to make any greedy landlord feel insecure. Thirty-four states have enacted laws that give you real legal leverage when dealing with a landlord who won't refund your deposit. The states are: Alaska, Arizona, California, Colorado, Connecticut, Delaware, Florida, Georgia, Hawaii, Idaho, Illinois, Iowa, Kansas, Kentucky, Louisiana, Maine, Maryland, Massachusetts, Michigan, Minnesota, Montana, New Jersey, New Mexico, New York, North Carolina, North Dakota, Ohio, Oklahoma, Oregon, Pennsylvania, South Dakota, Tennessee, Texas, and Washington. (Appendix I contains detailed information on each of these laws as well as their legal citations.)

While there are some differences in how security deposit laws operate from state to state, they generally provide these basic safeguards:

Maximum Security Deposit. Over half of the thirty-four states limit the amount of money a landlord can demand as a security deposit. Usually, one or two months' rent is the maximum (see Appendix I.) In Maryland, if your landlord takes an excessive deposit, you can take him to court and win three times the excess, plus your attorney's fees.

Interest. Over one third of the states require landlords to pay tenants interest on their security deposits (see Appendix I).

Use of the Deposit. The landlord can't spend your security deposit on a new furnace, or overdue property taxes, or a weekend in Atlantic City. Security deposits may be used for only a limited range of expenditures that are legitimately related to your apartment. Chief among these is unpaid rent. If you skipped out still owing rent, your security deposit can be applied against what you owe.

Legitimate repair costs incurred by the landlord to fix up your apartment may be deducted from your deposit. However, money spent to correct the effects of ordinary wear and tear is not a legitimate expense. A typical definition of *ordinary wear and tear* occurs in the Idaho security deposit statute: "that deterioration which occurs based upon the use for which the rental unit is intended and without negligence, carelessness, accident, or misuse or abuse of the premises or contents by the tenant or members of his household, or their invitees or guests."

Let's translate this legalese into some meaningful examples. If you leave behind some nail holes where your pictures once hung, that's ordinary wear and tear. After all, hanging pictures is a normal incident of apartment living; it's reasonably to be expected. On the other hand, if you left some gaping holes in the wall where you carelessly ripped out bookshelves, then there's little doubt that you've exceeded the bounds of ordinary wear and tear.

A refrigerator that gradually succumbs to old age and stops defrosting is a victim of ordinary wear and tear, but if you went at the freezer compartment with an ice pick and punctured the coils, you've abused the landlord's property, and you can kiss part of your security deposit goodbye.

Cleaning expenses can be another legitimate deduction. If you don't leave the apartment in as clean a condition as you found it (or as your lease directs) and the landlord has to hire a cleaning crew, you may lose part of your security deposit. On the other hand, the landlord can't go on a "Mr. Clean" orgy at your expense, performing a major sanitation blitz and then sticking you with the bill. Thus, if the floors were not freshly sanded and varnished when you moved into the apartment, the landlord can't charge you for having such a major cleaning performed when you leave—unless you used the apartment as an art studio and dribbled paint all over the floor.

Itemized Accounting. In thirty-one of the thirty-four states, the law requires the landlord to give you an itemized accounting *in writing* of any expenses he claims as deductions from your security deposit. You are entitled to know how much money the landlord is deducting and on exactly what items (e.g., $47 carpenter's bill, $16.95 for purchase of a new medicine cabinet, $75 in unpaid rent). That way you will be in a position to challenge any expenditures that you know are unjustified or overpriced. The deadline for submitting this itemized statement generally coincides with the deadline for making refunds.

Refunds. No longer can a landlord take his own sweet time returning your security deposit. Virtually all thirty-four states require prompt refunds—roughly speaking, within 14 to 30 days after your tenancy ends (see Appendix I).

Power Play Pointer. The best time to take steps toward recouping your security deposit is not when you're leaving the apartment but, ironically, when you first move in. Go over the apartment with a fine-tooth comb, looking for any existing defects: e.g., broken windows, missing soap dish, loose tiles, collapsing shelves, nonfunctioning air conditioner. Write all these defects down and have the landlord sign your list. (While you're at it, get him to agree to fix all these things!) (Under the security deposit laws in five states —Georgia, Kentucky, Maryland, Michigan, and Montana —this kind of prerental inventory must be performed at the start of tenancy; failure to do so may deprive the landlord of his right to deduct anything from the security deposit after the tenancy ends.) With your checklist completed and signed, you'll have documentary evidence at the end of your lease that certain defects were already there in the beginning. By checking your list against any end-of-lease damages claimed by the landlord in his itemized accounting, you can protect yourself from having to pay for your predecessor's destructiveness.

A week or so before you move out, telephone the landlord. Give him your new mailing address, so he'll know where to send the check for your security deposit. Ask him politely how soon you can expect a refund. If he's at all evasive, or if you know him to be generally uncooperative, casually mention, "It's my understanding that the *state security deposit law* requires refunds within X days." (You will find the right number for X listed under your state in Appendix I.) This "friendly" little use of codewords will signal that you don't intend to put up with any funny business or procrastination.

If you haven't heard from the landlord within one week after your tenancy ends, call him again. (Check Appendix I first to see exactly how many days the landlord has for rendering his itemized accounting.) Ask whether the landlord has yet inspected the apartment. Remind him that he has only a certain number of days left in which to refund either all of your money or part of it accompanied by an itemized accounting. Should your landlord question where you came up with this timetable, by all means give him the legal citation for the security deposit law in your state (Appendix I). That should spur him on a bit.

In thirteen states (Colorado, Delaware, Florida, Hawaii, Iowa, Maine, Maryland, Michigan, Montana, Pennsylvania, South Dakota, Tennessee, and Texas) a landlord forfeits his right to retain anything from your security deposit if he fails to give you an itemized accounting before the legal deadline. (That's so even though the landlord may actually have grounds for retaining something.) If you live in one of the lucky thirteen states, needle a lazy landlord with the codeword *forfeiture:* "I hope you realize that you'll *forfeit* any right to my security deposit unless you give me an itemized accounting within *X* days."

The thirty-four security deposit laws are tremendously persuasive when it comes to pressuring a little action out of your landlord. But what if you're up against a real tough nut? Then it'll take more than citing a deadline to make him comply. And even if he does comply on time, suppose he deducts all sorts of trumped-up expenses? You're going to need some heavier legal ammo than just a formal deadline.

Fortunately, you'll get it from almost all of the security deposit laws. They empower you to sue the landlord for money damages if he wrongfully withholds your security deposit, in whole or in part. The overwhelming majority of states allow you to collect more than just the amount of money being wrongfully withheld. For example you can collect *twice* that amount in ten states, *triple* the amount in seven, and *quadruple* the amount in one; what's more, fourteen states give you the right to collect your *attorney's fees* from the landlord as part of your victory (see Appendix I). Clearly, you are in a position to threaten a recalcitrant landlord with an unexpectedly costly lawsuit.

Power Play Pointer. There are basically two situations where you're likely to have a showdown with the landlord. Either he's refusing to make any itemized accounting or refund within the proper time limit, or else he's doctored the accounting with a bunch of false expenses, thereby eating

up your security deposit. In either case you must be prepared to get tough and, if need be, threaten to drag the
landlord into court and sue him for money damages.

For example, the landlord claims he had to pay a
carpenter $72 to repair two doors in the apartment, which
you allegedly damaged. Your first line of attack should
always be to determine the exact nature and cause of the
damage (assuming you don't know what they are). If, after
questioning the landlord, you're satisfied that the damage is
being exaggerated or falls under ordinary wear and tear,
say so. For example: "I didn't damage those doors. They
were sticking for months, and I complained to you about
them, but you didn't fix them. What finally did them in was
not my abuse, but ordinary wear and tear. I'm sure you
realize it's a violation of the *state security deposit law* to
deduct expenses for ordinary wear and tear." Here you're
using *ordinary wear and tear* as a legal sword with which
to hack away at the questionable repair expenses claimed
by the landlord.

Suppose the landlord hangs tough. Then you must
respond in kind. Citing the maximum penalty available in
your state, impress on the landlord that he stands to lose
more than he might imagine—all for just an extra slice of
your security money. Let the landlord know that unless he
settles the matter to your satisfaction within, say, ten more
days, you intend to sue him for everything you can.

For example, if you are an Ohio tenant you could say:
"Either you knock out that phony seventy-two-dollar deduction for ordinary wear and tear or I'm going to sue you
for it." If the landlord pooh-poohs your hiring a lawyer
for a $72 claim, remind him that under Ohio law (see
Appendix I), the landlord gets stuck with paying the tenant's attorney's fees: "By the time I get through beating
you in court, you'll probably pay five times that seventy-two
dollars in *attorney's fees!*" By using codewords *attorney's*

fees you've all of a sudden inflated your threat into something the landlord can't afford to ignore.

If you're a tall Texan, hit your landlord hard: "I just can't believe you're still haggling with me over this security deposit. You are just a hair away from a lawsuit where I'm going to take you for *treble damages* plus a *hundred-dollar penalty* plus my *attorney's fees.*" There's a triple-whammy set of codewords guaranteed to make any landlord cringe —and cooperate.

And blissful indeed is the Hawaiian tenant who can say with icy self-assurance: "Mister, you are an inch away from a *quadruple-damage lawsuit!*"

Needless to say, these are not idle threats you're making. You can sue for the penalties cited in your codewords. As a practical matter, the easiest way for you to sue over a security deposit is to use your local small claims court (see Appendix A). One of the most common cases settled in small claims court is the security deposit suit.

Codeword Glossary

attorney's fees   Fourteen out of thirty-four state security deposit laws let you collect your attorney's fees as part of any judgment you win against the landlord (see Appendix I).

double damages   Ten out of thirty-four state laws let you sue for twice the amount wrongfully withheld by the landlord (see Appendix I).

forfeiture   In thirteen states, a landlord forfeits the right to deduct anything from your security deposit if he fails to give you an itemized accounting on time.

itemized accounting   The written breakdown of deductions from your security deposit that thirty-one state laws require your landlord to give to you along with a refund (see Appendix I).

quadruple damages Hawaiians only!

state security deposit law General codeword for the law in thirty-four states requiring landlords to make prompt refunds of security deposits. (See Appendix I for the technical legal codewords to use when referring to your state's law.)

treble damages Seven out of thirty-four state laws let you sue for triple the amount wrongfully withheld by the landlord.

12

Nasty People

How to Handle a Vandal

"Kids will be kids." You usually hear this excuse following a prank by some vandal who is hiding behind his parents' indifference. For example, when the neighbor's kid spray-paints his name on your front door, you can expect your neighbor to console you with "Kids will be kids." A lot of good it will do you! It certainly won't fix your door. But you can fix your neighbor, because legally you don't have to put up with his nasty kids.

Some children pose a real danger to people and property. The child who throws firecrackers at other children; the boy who throws "water bombs" out of a fourteenth-floor window; the girl who likes to "borrow" Daddy's car for a spin around the supermarket parking lot—these children are not criminals. But their actions *are* dangerous, and when something or someone gets hurt, the fact that a child caused the damage will not ease the loss.

When the actions of some child threatens to eventually injure you, your family, or your property, your first reaction is to speak to the child's parents. Sometimes this approach works, but often it doesn't. (After all, how do you think the child got to be the way he is in the first place?) A parent who hasn't properly disciplined a child over the years is not likely to respond to your polite request.

Does that mean you are at the mercy of any malicious juvenile? We don't think so.

The law does not give children a license to be destructive. (We are talking about *civil* law, not criminal law, which in some states refuses to believe that children can commit criminal acts.) If a child spray-paints your front door, breaks light bulbs on your front porch, lets air out of your tires, punches your son in the nose, or does any other destructive act, he can be sued. With the exception of very young children, youth is not a defense to a civil suit. So the problem of dealing with children is not in suing them. Rather, it's in collecting any judgment. For example, how do you collect an $800 judgment against a ten-year-old? You can't exactly garnishee the kid's allowance.

Our power play will utilize an end run around the judgment-proof child and the parent who throws "Kids will be kids" at you. We will hold the *parents* responsible for the acts of their children. As one court recently put it, "The old adage 'an ounce of prevention is worth a pound of cure,' could be applied in these situations if the responsibility for the prevention is placed on the parents."

Traditionally parents have not been held responsible for the acts of their children. However, the law did make parents responsible for *supervising* their children. If a parent failed to perform this duty and knew, or should have known, that his child would cause damage, then the parent was acting negligently and could be held responsible for this negligence. As one court stated the rule: "With the right to bear and raise children comes the responsibility to see that one's children are properly raised so that the rights of other people are protected."

For example, in one case, *Langford* v. *Shu*, two youngsters had a box labeled "Danger African Mongoose, Live Snake Eater." Actually, there was nothing inside except a spring-loaded "furry object." The boys' mother knew about this practical joke. But the family's housekeeper, Athlyn, did not. She was afraid of snakes, and since she'd been told the mongoose was feeding in the box, she gave the box a wide berth. However, as she inadvertently walked near it, the boys lifted the top and, as a court later described it, "with a whoosh and a screech, a furry object, which Athlyn believed to be an animal, sprang out at her. She jumped back and turned to run. There was so little room on the porch that she hit the lounge and stumbled back into a brick wall of the house. . . . Athlyn spent sixty-three days in the hospital . . . and incurred medical bills in the sum of $2,219.88."

Athlyn also incurred the expense of a lawyer and sued the parents of the two boys for the injuries she had received because of the practical joke. In deciding that the parents could be held responsible, the court stated the general rule: "A parent may be liable for the consequences of failure to exercise the power of control which he has over his children, where he knows, or in the exercise of due care should have known, that injury to another is a probable consequence. . . . Failure to restrain the child, it is said, amounts to a sanction of or consent to his acts by the parent. . . . As in all negligence cases, the issue in the last analysis is whether the parent exercised reasonable care under all the circumstances. . . ."

Thus, under traditional common law a parent *can* be held financially responsible for failing to properly supervise his children. However, in each case this responsibility depends on the parent's knowing or having good reason to know that his child may injure someone. This is the critical requirement. As one court said: "Mere knowledge by the parents of the child's mischievous and reckless disposition is not enough to make them liable . . . but their liability arises from the failure to exercise the control which they have over their child, when they know, or in the exercise of due care, should know, that injury to another is a natural and probable consequence, for such failure to act and restrain the child amounts to an approval and sanction of, or consent to, his acts by the parents."

Consider the case of *Singer* v. *Marx*. Young Tim Marx, the son of one of the famous Marx Brothers, Zeppo Marx, was prone to throw rocks at passing people, cars, and just about anything else. Tim's school principal had warned Mrs. Marx about young Tim's dangerous habit. Nothing was done. Finally Tim hit a bull's-eye on a young girl named Denise. Denise sued Tim's parents. The court decided that "it is fairly inferable that Mrs. Marx had notice of Tim's dangerous proclivities and did not administer effective discipline." Mrs. Marx could therefore be sued for the damage caused by Tim. However, there was no evidence that Zeppo, Tim's father, knew of Tim's rock-throwing proclivity. Therefore, Zeppo could not be sued.

A parent's potential liability for his children's malicious acts is unlimited. In one case, a parent negligently entrusted a gun to his child. The child promptly turned around and shot a house guest, who, after a few months to recover, turned around and sued the girl's parents. The recovery was $100,000!

Power Play Pointer. When the parent of a dangerous child throws "Kids will be kids" at you, be prepared to tell the parent that *he* is responsible for his child: "I am serving notice on you that your child is dangerous. If, in the future, your child causes any injury or damage, I will hold *you* personally responsible. Your liability is unlimited. Your child could wipe out all your savings if you don't watch him better."

There is one major problem with invoking the common-law liability that we have just discussed. Most people know when a child is dangerous, but they don't know whether the parent has been remiss in trying to control his child. Unless a parent has failed to adequately supervise his child or has provided his child with a dangerous instrument, there is no liability on his part.

State legislatures have recognized this problem, and over the years forty-seven states have enacted so-called vandalism laws (see Appendix J). These laws typically hold a parent liable for any "wanton," "willful," or "unlawful" acts committed by his child. For example, Connecticut's vandalism law reads: "The parent or parents or guardian of any unemancipated minor or minors, which minor or minors wilfully or maliciously cause damage to any property or injury to any person . . . shall be jointly and severally liable with such minor or minors for such damage or injury in an amount not exceeding fifteen hundred dollars. . . ." Under this law, and the vandalism laws of most other states, liability does not depend on a showing of fault by the parent. Rather, the law holds a parent responsible for *any* intentional malicious act committed by his child.

As is the case with Connecticut's law, most vandalism laws impose restrictions on the right to collect damages. In almost every state there is a limit to the amount of damages that may be collected. In Connecticut the limit is $1,500. However, under most laws, if more than one child is involved in the malicious act, each child's parents can be held liable to the limit of the law. For example, in one Ohio case four minors broke into a house and destroyed property worth $2,000. Under Ohio's vandalism law, the maximum recovery is $250. The owner of the vandalized house sued the parents of each minor for $250 and recovered $1,000.

The laws also generally restrict parental responsibility to acts of children committed while they were under eighteen years of age, though some states provide for a lower age limit also. For example, in New York the law applies only to acts committed by children "over ten and less than eighteen years of age."

Finally, some of the laws permit recovery only for property damage committed by a child; personal injuries are not covered. So, for example, in Missouri, if a child punched your boy in the nose, breaking his glasses and his nose, you could recover only for the value of the glasses. Medical expenses for repairing the nose would not be recoverable.

The chart in Appendix J lists the rules for all forty-seven states with vandalism laws.

Power Play Pointer. If the problem child you are dealing with is not really dangerous, just a menace, try using the vandalism law in your state. Assume, for example, the local vandal spray-paints your front door. You go to the child's parents and ask them to pay for fixing it. You are told, "He's a child. We can't be responsible for everything he does." Just answer: "You not only can be, you are!" Be prepared to refer to your state law, which is listed in Appendix J. For example, you might say: "Look at section 600.2913 of Michigan's Compiled Laws. Don't make me use the law."

Thus, we have two possible sources for our power play. Each remedy has a drawback and a virtue. The common-law approach has the virtue of no limit on the potential recovery, but the drawback is that you must show that the paient knew, or had reason to know, that his child might cause damage or injury, and failed to exercise reasonable supervision to avoid the damage.

The vandalism laws have the virtue of, in general, not requiring you to prove that the parent was negligent in failing to supervise his child, thus eliminating the drawback of the common-law remedy. However, under most vandalism laws the amount of money which can be recovered is limited.

Codeword Glossary

Langford v. Shu   A North Carolina court case found in volume 128 of the South Eastern Reporter, Second Series, at page 210. Parents were liable for the damage caused by their children's practical joke, in the amount of $2,219.88.
Singer v. Marx   A California court case found in volume 301 of the Pacific Reporter, Second Series, at page 440. A parent who is on notice of his child's destructive tendencies is responsible for any damage the child causes.
State vandalism law   General codeword for the law in forty-seven states that hold parents liable for the vandalism committed by their children. (See Appendix J for the legal citations to use when referring to your state's law.)

Public Transportation and Restaurants

We move now from nasty kids to nasty adults. We don't have a power play to deal with every nasty adult you come across. The law simply does not protect you from every unpleasant person. However, there are times when people owe you a duty to be nice. And if these people get nasty, there is something you can do about it.

We will look at two of these situations. The first involves people who run public transportation. The law calls these people *common carriers,* and when you are a passenger on a common carrier you have the right to expect courteous treatment.

The second situation arises when you eat at a restaurant. In the law, restaurant operators are known as *innkeepers,* and innkeepers also have a special duty to be nice to you.

Public Transportation

The law has long recognized that companies that provide public transportation owe a special duty to passengers. The duty is to make sure passengers are transported in a safe and comfortable manner. The law believes that when you buy a ticket to go somewhere, you enter into a contract, and one of the terms of the contract is that the people who are transporting you will be nice to you.

You can see how this special duty operates in the case of *Brown* v. *Fifth Avenue Coach Lines, Inc.* Mrs. Brown took a bus operated by the Fifth Avenue Coach Lines in Manhattan. She wanted to get off at the last stop before the bus crossed over the Fifty-ninth Street Bridge into Queens.

She signaled for the bus to stop, but it didn't. Involuntarily she went to Queens. Unfortunately, she had some out-of-town guests at home, to whom she was planning to serve dinner. She was very upset at the idea of getting home late. When she complained to the bus driver, he became abusive and shouted at her in a "stentorian manner." He finally gave her a transfer to get a return bus to Manhattan. Unfortunately, the transfer was invalid, so Brown had to pay an additional fare to get home.

Brown went to small claims court, arguing she was

entitled to get the additional fare returned to her. She also claimed she had suffered mental distress because the bus driver was so nasty. She wanted damages for the injury caused to her peace of mind.

The court decided Brown could recover the cost of the additional fare. But could she recover for her mental distress? The court decided she could : "[T]he mere absence of physical injuries is not sufficient to prevent liability for damages for the indignity, humiliation and nervous strain caused by insulting and abusive language." The damages assessed against Fifth Avenue Coach were $150 to compensate Brown for her "mortification and humiliation."

Obviously, had some stranger on the street come up to Brown and been nasty, she would not have been able to go to court and collect these damages. But the bus driver was not a stranger. Brown had a relationship with him. When she paid her fare, the driver agreed to take her to her destination in a safe and courteous manner. His breach of that agreement is what allowed Brown to collect damages. And notice that Brown collected $150 even though there was no physical injury to her!

What is missing from the Brown case is a transcript of what the bus driver said. What is abusive language? For the answer, let's look at two other cases. The first is *Haile* v. *New Orleans Railroad and Light Co.* The mode of transportation in this case was a trolley, and the passenger was Ms. Haile. As the trolley was going around a curve, Haile fell down. She didn't hurt herself, and the trolley conductor was not going too fast. She just fell. So far, no problems. However, after she got up the conductor said to her: "You had no business sitting in the front of the car—a big fat woman like you had no business sitting in the front of the car." This language, the court decided, was abusive and Haile collected $500 in damages.

The second example of abusive language is found in

the case of *Southeastern Greyhound Corp* v. *Graham*. In this case, the mode of transportation was once again a bus. Mr. Graham was a passenger on the bus, and he wanted the window open. The bus driver, a Mr. Turnipseed, wanted it shut. An argument ensued, during which Turnipseed told Graham: "You goddamned baldheaded son of a bitch, step over here and I'll settle the whole damn business with you." The court had no problem concluding that this language was abusive and Graham, who turned out to be a Baptist minister, could sue the bus company and a jury would decide how much the damages should be.

Notice that in all of these cases the defendant was the transportation company and not the driver or conductor. Had he or she wanted to, each passenger could have sued the person who was abusive. However, under the law the employer is responsible for the misconduct of his employees. This concept is known as *respondeat superior*. So if you want to sue the transportation company instead of the person who was abusive, you can.

Restaurants

When you eat at a restaurant you are paying for more than the food. You are paying for good service. Under the law, that means that the restaurant owes you a duty not to be abusive. If a restaurant employee is abusive, the restaurant has broken its agreement with you. You can sue the restaurant, or the employee, to collect any damages you suffered.

For example, consider the case of *Wiggs* v. *Courshon*. Mr. Wiggs went to the Caesars Motel in Florida with his family. According to a court which later heard his case, here's what happened. "Knowing of the fondness of the family members for seafood, Joe Wiggs . . . ordered the fisherman's platter. The fisherman's platter normally included shrimps, scallops and fillet of fish. The evidence is undisputed that the waitress went to check to see if all the ingredients for the fisherman's platter were available and it is undisputed that the platters contained shrimps and fish fillet but not scallops when served."

After being served, Mr. Wiggs summoned the waitress to the table with a gesture and inquired as to the missing scallops; the dispute developed and he testified that he told her she had said they could have the seafood platter and if she said otherwise they would have ordered something else. The waitress then exclaimed: "You can't talk to me like that, you black son-of-a-bitch. I will kill you."

This case is a little unusual in that you usually don't have people threatening to kill over a dispute involving missing scallops. However, arguments tend to get heated beyond the simmering point and boil over into this type of abusive language.

Were an argument such as this to occur on a street corner, there is not much Wiggs could do. However, the argument occurred in a restaurant and Wiggs was a patron. The waitress and Caesars Motel owed him a special duty to be courteous. The waitress's outburst violated that duty. The court decided that Wiggs was entitled to $2,500 as damages for the humiliation and mental distress he suffered.

Power Play Pointer. We realize that most of you will not be in a position to prepare yourselves in anticipation of meeting a nasty person. However, we think the cases we have discussed are so memorable many of you will be able to remember the principles involved. You should at least be able to say: "Look, I know the law. I know you owe me a special duty not to be obnoxious. I know that I can sue you and the people who own this restaurant/bus line/railroad. And let's face it—if I sue your employer, chances are you're going to be fired." For those of you who may want to follow through by actually suing (or who like to carry legal citations around with you) we have provided a codeword glossary. And remember that if you decide to sue, you can always use small claims court (see Appendix A).

Codeword Glossary

Brown v. *Fifth Avenue Coach Lines, Inc.* A small claims court case found in volume 185 of the New York Supplement, Second Series, at page 923, in which a passenger collected $150 because the abusive language of the bus driver caused her mental distress.

common carrier A legal term to describe businesses that are involved in public transportation.

Haile v. *New Orleans Railroad and Light Co.* A Louisiana court case found in volume 65 of the Southern Reporter at page 225, in which a trolley passenger who had been verbally abused recovered $500.

innkeeper A legal term to describe restaurateurs.

respondeat superior The legal principle that an employer is accountable for the misconduct of an employee.

Southeastern Greyhound Corp. v. *Graham* A Georgia court case found in volume 26 of the South Eastern Reporter at page 371, in which a bus passenger who had been verbally abused was entitled to sue for his humiliation.

Wiggs v. *Courshon* A federal court case found in volume 355 of the Federal Supplement at page 206, in which an abused restaurant patron recovered $2,500 in damages for humiliation and mental distress.

Appendix A

How to Sue in Small Claims Court

Suing your adversary in small claims court is often an effective way to enforce a power play. As of January, 1977, all but eight states (Arizona, Delaware, Louisiana, Mississippi, South Carolina, Tennessee, Virginia, and West Virginia) had some form of small claims procedure. Small claims court is fast, easy, and cheap to use, and you don't need a lawyer. While the small claims procedure does vary from state to state, here is a general idea of what to expect.

What is small claims court? Don't scour your neighborhood for a little brick courthouse with "Small Claims Court" painted on the door. Small claims court is not a separate courthouse; the term *small claims court* describes an informal procedure held in courtrooms normally reserved for other, more formal types of judicial activity. For example, small claims court cases in Connecticut are heard during special sessions of the state's Court of Common Pleas; in Florida there is a small claims division of the state's County Courts; in still other states small claims cases may

271

be heard in Justice of the Peace Courts or the local Magistrate's Courts.

How do you find small claims court? Ironically, the search for the court in your state may be the biggest obstacle to using it. If you're lucky, there may be a listing in the telephone book for "Small Claims Court." Otherwise, look under the listings for local or state government for what appears to be the lowest-level *trial* court (not *appellate* court). That may turn out to be something called "Justice of Peace Court," "District Court," "Municipal Court," or "County Court." Call the number and ask for the court clerk; he can tell you about small claims procedure. *The clerk will be your best source of up-to-date information on how to use the court.* The clerk can tell you what steps to take in order to file your case.

What can you sue for? In a word, *money.* A small claim is by definition a legal complaint that can be satisfied by the award of money damages. If you're seeking something besides money, you can generally forget about using small claims court. For example, you might want to stop your neighbor from making too much bothersome noise. The legal relief you'd be seeking would not be money but an injunction, and small claims courts can't issue injunctions.

How much can you sue for? Among the states there is considerable variation in the maximum dollar amount you can sue for. Here is a state-by-state list of maximum claim limits:

Alabama:	$ 500	*District of*	
Alaska:	$1,000	*Columbia:*	$ 750
Arkansas:	$ 300	*Florida:*	$2,500
California:	$ 750	*Georgia:*	$ 300
Colorado:	$ 500	*Hawaii:*	$ 300
Connecticut	$ 750	*Idaho:*	$ 500

Illinois:	$1,000	*New York:*	$1,000
Indiana:	$3,000	*North Carolina:*	$ 500
Iowa:	$1,000	*North Dakota:*	$ 200
Kansas:	$ 300		in Justice of
Kentucky:	$ 500		the Peace Court;
Maine:	$ 800		$500 in County
Maryland:	$ 500		Court
Massachusetts:	$ 400	*Ohio:*	$ 300
Michigan:	$ 300	*Oklahoma:*	$ 600
Minnesota:	$1,000	*Oregon:*	$ 500
	($500 in	*Pennsylvania:*	$1,000
Minneapolis–St. Paul		*Rhode Island:*	$ 300
Missouri:	$ 500	*South Dakota:*	$1,000
Montana:	$1,500	*Texas:*	$ 150
Nebraska:	$ 500	*Utah:*	$ 200
Nevada:	$ 300	*Vermont:*	$ 250
New Hampshire:	$ 500	*Washington:*	$ 300
New Jersey:	$ 500	*Wisconsin:*	$ 500
New Mexico:	$2,000	*Wyoming:*	$ 200

How do you start a small claims case? Visit the office of the clerk of the court where small claims sessions are held. The clerk will give you advice and assistance on how to file your claim. (Lawyers have been getting this sort of help from clerks for decades, so don't be embarrassed to ask questions.) In many small claims courts the clerk actually fills in the necessary information on a complaint form, after asking you a few pertinent questions about who you're suing and why. You will generally have to pay a nominal filing fee, as well as a fee for having your complaint and a summons served on your adversary, the defendant. (These fees vary widely but usually total $10 or so.)

When will your trial be held? Waiting time between filing and actual trial varies widely. Figure on two to four weeks. You will be notified of the date for your trial; sometimes the clerk may be able to tell you when you file your claim.

What evidence should you bring to the trial? Ask the clerk for advice when you file your case. He can often suggest what evidence you should bring. Generally speaking, any witness or piece of evidence that substantiates what you will say in court is worth bringing along. For example, if you're suing your landlord for return of your security deposit, you should bring a copy of your lease, your canceled security-deposit check, and a copy of your letter demanding return of the security deposit. If you suspect the landlord will dispute the condition in which you left the apartment, you might even bring some photos of the apartment (assuming you took them when you left). Of course, witnesses to events can also bolster your case—especially if the witness is not your mother!

Conduct of the trial. Small claims court trials are informal. There are no tricky rules of evidence, so you don't need a lawyer. The judge usually begins by summarizing the case very briefly and asking you to verify whether he has stated your claim correctly. Then you will be sworn in and allowed to tell your side of the story. Don't be nervous. In simple straightforward language, state why you are suing the defendant. Keep things as brief and businesslike as possible; avoid getting personal or argumentative with anyone. The judge may interrupt you from time to time to ask if you have any evidence to back up your testimony—e.g., a paid receipt for repair work to your car.

Then your adversary will be sworn in and allowed to tell his side of the case. Afterward, each of you will probably be allowed to cross-examine the other one (i.e., ask the other person questions). The judge may ask questions of both sides, although this practice varies, depending on how actively involved in the case the judge chooses to be.

The decision. In some instances the judge may announce his decision at the end of your trial, but that's the exception to the rule. Generally, a judge will just say that he "reserves" decision. This technique gives him a chance to consider your case further, perhaps look up some law, and—not incidentally—avoid any outbursts in court from the losing side. You will be notified of the decision, usually by a postcard telling you whether you won and, if so, how much.

Collection. If you win, your adversary will be notified of what he owes you. Your adversary should pay you directly. If he doesn't, contact the small claims clerk again and ask what steps you should pursue in order to collect on the judgment. These steps may include securing a *writ of attachment* or *writ of garnishment,* which are court orders that a sheriff serves on the defendant's bank or employer as a way of tying up his assets and using them to satisfy your judgment.

Appendix A is based largely on data from *Small Claims Court: A National Examination* by John C. Ruhnka, Steven Weller, and John A. Martin (Williamsburg, Va.: National Center for State Courts, 1978), pp. 201–13.

Appendix B

New-Home Warranty Laws

Here are the official names and legal citations for the state laws and cases that establish an implied warranty of habitability on new homes.

Alabama

Cochran v. *Keeton,* a 1971 case found in volume 252 of the Southern Reporter, Second Series, at page 313.

Arkansas

Wawak v. *Stewart,* a 1970 case found in volume 449 of the South Western Reporter, Second Series, at page 922.

California

Pollard v. *Saxe & Yolles Development Company,* a 1974 case found in volume 525 of the Pacific Reporter, Second Series, at page 88.

Colorado

Carpenter v. *Donohoe,* a 1964 case found in volume 388 of the Pacific Reporter, Second Series, at page 399.

Connecticut

Connecticut General Statutes Annotated, sections 47-116 through 47-120, and section 52-563a. Under this law, the implied warranty terminates:

—*in the case of a house that is completed at the time the deed is delivered,* one year after delivery of the deed, or one year after the purchaser takes possession of the house, whichever event occurs first;

—*in the case of a house that is not completed at the time the deed is delivered to the purchaser,* one year after the date of completion, or one year after the purchaser takes possession of the house, whichever event occurs first.

Delaware

Smith v. *Berwin Builders, Inc.,* a 1972 case found in volume 287 of the Atlantic Reporter, Second Series, at page 693.

Florida

Gable v. *Silver,* a 1972 case found in volume 258 of the Southern Reporter, Second Series, at page 11.

Idaho

Bethlahmy v. *Bechtel,* a 1966 case found in volume 415 of the Pacific Reporter, Second Series, at page 698.

Illinois

Conyers v. *Molloy,* a 1977 case found in volume 364 of the North Eastern Reporter, Second Series, at page 986.

Indiana

Theis v. *Heuer,* a 1972 case found in volume 280 of the North Eastern Reporter, Second Series, at page 300.

Kentucky

Crawley v. *Terhune,* a 1969 case found in volume 437 of the South Western Reporter, Second Series, at page 743.

Louisiana

Busenlener v. *Peck,* a 1975 case found in volume 316 of the Southern Reporter, Second Series, at page 27.

Maryland

Maryland Annotated Code, sections 10-201 through 10-205. The time limitations set on the warranty are identical to those imposed by the Connecticut statute (see above).

Michigan

Weeks v. *Slavick Builders, Inc.,* a 1970 case found in volume 180 of the North Western Reporter, Second Series, at page 503.

Minnesota

Minnesota Statutes Annotated, chapter 327A. Under this law, the builder warrants that:

—during the one-year period after the original purchaser takes occupancy of or title to the house, the house shall be free from defects caused by faulty workmanship and defective materials;

—during the two-year period after the original purchaser takes occupancy of or title to the house, the house shall be free from defects caused by faulty installation of plumbing, electrical, heating, and cooling systems; and

—during the ten-year period after the original purchaser takes occupancy of or title to the house, the house shall be free from major construction defects.

Mississippi

Oliver v. *City Builders, Inc.,* a 1974 case found in volume 303 of the Southern Reporter. Second Series, at page 466.

Missouri

Smith v. *Old Warson Development Company,* a 1972 case found in volume 479 of the South Western Reporter, Second Series, at page 795.

Nebraska

Henggeler v. *Jindra,* a 1974 case found in volume 214 of the North Western Reporter, Second Series, at page 925.

New Hampshire

Norton v. *Burleaud,* a 1975 case found in volume 342 of the Atlantic Reporter, Second Series, at page 629.

New Jersey

"The New Home Warranty and Builders' Registration Act" can be found in New Jersey Statutes Annotated, sections 46:3B-1 through 46:3B-12. The time limitations set on the warranty are identical to those imposed by the Minnesota statute (see above).

New York

Centrella v. *Holland Construction Corporation,* a 1975 case found in volume 85 of the Miscellaneous Reports, Second Series, at page 537.

North Carolina

Hartley v. *Ballou,* a 1974 case found in volume 209 of the South Eastern Reporter, Second Series, at page 776.

North Dakota

Dobler v. *Malloy,* a 1973 case found in volume 214 of the North Western Reporter, Second Series, at page 510.

Ohio

Vanderschrier v. *Aaron,* a 1957 case found in volume 140 of the North Eastern Reporter, Second Series, at page 819.

Oklahoma

Jones v. *Gatewood,* a 1963 case found in volume 381 of the Pacific Reporter, Second Series, at page 158; and *Jeanguneat* v. *Jacki Hames Construction Company,* a 1978 case found in volume 576 of the Pacific Reporter, Second Series, at page 761.

Oregon

Yepsen v. *Burgess,* a 1974 case found in volume 525 of the Pacific Reporter, Second Series, at page 1019.

Pennsylvania

Elderkin v. *Gaster,* a 1972 case found in volume 288 of the Atlantic Reporter, Second Series, at page 771.

Rhode Island

Padula v. *J.J. Deb-Cin Homes, Inc.,* a 1973 case found in volume 298 of the Atlantic Reporter, Second Series, at page 529.

South Carolina

Rutledge v. *Dodenhoff*, a 1970 case found in volume 175 of the South Eastern Reporter at page 792.

South Dakota

Waggoner v. *Midwestern Development, Inc.*, a 1967 case found in volume 154 of the North Western Reporter, Second Series, at page 803.

Texas

Humber v. *Morton*, a 1968 case found in volume 426 of the South Western Reporter, Second Series, at page 554.

Vermont

Rothberg v. *Olenik*, a 1970 case found in volume 262 of the Atlantic Reporter, Second Series, at page 461.

Washington

Gay v. *Cornwall*, a 1972 case found in volume 494 of the Pacific Reporter, Second Series, at page 1371.

Wyoming

Tavares v. *Horstman*, a 1975 case found in volume 542 of the Pacific Reporter, Second Series, at page 1275.

Appendix C
State Human Rights Commissions

Alaska:
Alaska Human Rights Commission
204 East 5th Avenue, Room 213
Anchorage   99501

Arizona:
Arizona Civil Rights Division
1645 West Jefferson Street
Phoenix   85007

Arkansas:
Arkansas Governor's Committee on Human Resources
011 State Capitol Building
Little Rock   72201

California:
California Fair Employment Practices Commission
30 Vanness Avenue
San Francisco   94102

Colorado:
   Colorado Civil Rights Commission
   1525 Sherman Street
   Denver   80203

Connecticut:
   Connecticut Commission on Human Rights and
      Opportunities
   90 Washington Street
   Hartford   06115

Delaware:
   Delaware Anti-Discrimination Section
   2413 Lancaster Avenue
   Wilmington   19805

District of Columbia:
   District of Columbia Office of Human Rights
   District Building
   14th & E Streets, N.W.
   Washington   20004

Florida:
   Jacksonville Community Relations Commission
   The Courthouse, Room 406
   Jacksonville   32202

   Dade County Fair Housing & Employment Appeals
      Board
   1425 Northwest 10th Avenue
   Miami   33136

   Orlando Human Relations Commission
   440 Boone Avenue
   Orlando   32801

Florida Commission on Human Relations
2571 Exec. Center Circle, East
Tallahassee   32301

Tampa Office of Community Relations
1467 Tampa Park Plaza
Tampa   33602

Georgia:

Georgia Merit System Administration
244 Washington Street, S.W.
Atlanta   30334

Augusta/Richmond Human Relations Commission
Suite 400, 500 Building
Augusta   30902

Hawaii:

Hawaii Department of Labor & Industrial Relations
825 Mililani Street
Honolulu   96813

Idaho:

Idaho Human Rights Commission
Statehouse
Boise   83720

Illinois:

Illinois Fair Employment Practices Commission
179 West Washington Street
Chicago   60602

Indiana:

Bloomington Human Rights Commission
220 East 3rd, Municipal Building
Bloomington   47401

East Chicago Human Rights Commission
4525 Indianapolis Blvd., Room 9
East Chicago 46312

Evansville Human Relations Commission
City-County Administration Building, Room 133
Evansville 47708

Fort Wayne Human Relations Commission
One Main Street, Room 680
Fort Wayne 46802

Gary Human Relations Commission
401 Broadway
Gary 46402

Indiana Civil Rights Commission
311 West Washington Street
Indianapolis 46204

South Bend Human Rights Commission
227 West Jefferson, 12th Floor
South Bend 46601

Iowa:
Des Moines Commission on Human Rights
Armory Building, East 1st & Des Moines Streets
Des Moines 50309

Iowa Civil Rights Commission
418 6th Avenue, Suite 340
Des Moines 50319

Kansas:
> Kansas Commission on Civil Rights
> 535 Kansas Avenue, 5th Floor
> Topeka   66603

Kentucky:
> Lexington/Fayette County Human Rights Commission
> 207 North Upper Street
> Lexington   40507
>
> Kentucky Commission on Human Rights
> 701 West Walnut Street
> Louisville   40203

Maine:
> Maine Human Rights Commission
> Statehouse
> Augusta   04330

Maryland:
> Baltimore Community Relations Commission
> 100 North Eutaw Street
> Baltimore   21201
>
> Maryland Commission on Human Relations
> Metro Plaza, Mondawmin Mall, Suite 300
> Baltimore   21215
>
> Montgomery County Human Relations Commission
> 6400 Democracy Blvd.
> Bethesda   20034
>
> Howard County Human Relations Commission
> 8950 Route 108, Room 214
> Columbia   21045

Massachusetts:
> Massachusetts Commission Against Discrimination
> One Ashburton Place
> Boston   02108

Michigan:
> Michigan Department of Civil Rights
> 125 West Allegan
> 1000 Stoddard Building
> Lansing   48913

Minnesota:
> Minneapolis Department of Civil Rights
> 2649 Park Avenue, South
> Minneapolis   55407

> Minnesota Department of Human Rights
> 240 Bremer Building
> 7th & Robert Street
> St. Paul   55101

> St. Paul Department of Human Rights
> 515 City Hall
> St. Paul   55102

Missouri:
> Missouri Commission on Human Rights
> 314 East High Street
> Jefferson City   65101

> St. Louis Civil Rights Enforcement Agency
> 3rd floor, Civil Courts Building
> St. Louis   63101

Montana:
Montana Commission for Human Rights
404 Power Block
Helena 59601

Nebraska:
Lincoln Commission on Human Rights
129 North 10th Street, Room 318
Lincoln 68508

Nebraska Equal Opportunity Commission
301 Centennial Mall South, 5th Floor
Lincoln 68509

Omaha Human Relations Department
1819 Farnam Street, Suite 502
Omaha 68102

Nevada:
Nevada Commission on Equal Rights of Citizens
1515 East Tropicana, Suite 590
Las Vegas 89158

New Hampshire:
New Hampshire State Commission for Human Rights
66 South Street
Concord 03301

New Jersey:
Newark Human Rights Commission
920 Broad Street
City Hall, Room B-12
Newark 07102

New Jersey Division on Civil Rights
1100 Raymond Blvd.
Newark   07102

New York:
New York City Commission on Human Rights
52 Duane Street
New York   10007

New York State Division of Human Rights
2 World Trade Center
New York   10047

North Carolina:
Asheville/Buncombe Community Relations Council
311 College Street
Asheville   28801

Durham Human Relations Commission
101 City Hall Plaza
Durham   27701

North Carolina Human Relations Council
116 West Jones Street
Raleigh   27603

Wilmington Human Relations Commission
419 Chestnut Street
Wilmington   28401

Ohio:
Ohio Civil Rights Commission
220 South Parsons Avenue
Columbus   43215

Oklahoma:
Oklahoma Human Rights Commission
2101 North Lincoln Blvd.
Oklahoma City   73152

Oregon:
Oregon Bureau of Labor
1400 S.W. 5th Avenue
Portland   97201

Pennsylvania:
Pennsylvania Human Relations Commission
100 North Cameron Street
Harrisburg   17105

Philadelphia Commission on Human Relations
601 City Hall Annex
Philadelphia   19107

Pittsburgh Commission on Human Relations
908 City-County Building
Pittsburgh   15219

Puerto Rico:
Puerto Rico Anti-Discrimination Unit
414 Barbosa Avenue
Hato Rey   00917

Rhode Island:
Providence Human Relations Commission
40 Fountain Street
Providence   02903

Rhode Island Commission for Human Rights
334 Westminster Mall
Providence   02903

South Carolina:
> South Carolina Human Affairs Commission
> 1113 Bellview Road
> Columbia   29212

South Dakota:
> South Dakota Division of Human Rights
> State Capitol
> Pierre   57501
>
> Sioux Falls Human Relations Commission
> City Hall, 244 West 9th Street
> Sioux Falls   57102

Tennessee:
> Tennessee Commission for Human Development
> C3-305 Cordell Hull Building
> Nashville   37219

Texas:
> Austin Human Relations Commission
> 205 West 9th, Room 209
> Austin   78767
>
> Corpus Christi Human Relations Commission
> 311 South Shoreline
> Corpus Christi   78408
>
> Forth Worth Human Relations Commission
> 1000 Throckmorton Street
> Forth Worth   76102

Utah:
> Utah Anti-Discrimination Division
> 350 East 500 South
> Salt Lake City   84111

Vermont:

Vermont Attorney General's Office
109 State Street
Montpelier   05602

Virginia:

Alexandria Human Rights Commission
110 North Royal Street, Suite 501
Alexandria   22313

Fairfax County Human Rights Commission
9401 Lee Highway, Suite 206
Fairfax   22030

Washington:

Seattle Human Rights Department
105 14th Avenue, Suite C
Seattle   98122

Tacoma Human Relations Commission
955 Tacoma Avenue, South
Tacoma   98402

Washington State Human Rights Commission
1601 2nd Avenue Building, 4th Floor
Seattle   98101

West Virginia:

Charleston Human Rights Commission
1218 Quarrier Street
Charleston   25301

West Virginia Human Rights Commission
1036 Quarrier Street
Charleston   25301

Wisconsin:

Madison Equal Opportunity Commission
351 West Wilson Street
Madison   53703

Wisconsin Equal Rights Division
201 East Washington Avenue, Room 178
Madison   53707

Wyoming:

Wyoming Fair Employment Commission
Barrett Building, 4th Floor
Cheyenne   82002

Appendix D

Equal Employment Opportunity Commission

Regional Offices

Atlanta:
Alabama, Florida, Georgia, Kentucky, North Carolina,
Mississippi, South Carolina, Tennessee
75 Piedmont Avenue, N.E., Atlanta, Ga.   30303

Chicago:
Illinois, Indiana, Michigan, Minnesota, Ohio, Wisconsin
230 S. Dearborn St., Rm. 2643, Chicago, Ill.   60604

Dallas:
Arkansas, Louisiana, New Mexico, Oklahoma, Texas
1100 Commerce St., Rm. 7B11, Dallas, Tex.   75202

Kansas City:
Iowa, Kansas, Missouri, Nebraska
601 E. 12th St., Rm. 113, Kansas City, Mo.   64106

New York:
Connecticut, Maine, Massachusetts, New Hampshire,
New Jersey, New York, Puerto Rico, Rhode Island,
Vermont
26 Federal Plaza, Rm. 1615, New York, N.Y.   10007

Philadelphia:
Delaware, District of Columbia, Maryland, Pennsylvania,
Virginia, West Virginia
124 North 4th St., 3rd Floor, Philadelphia, Pa.   19106

San Francisco:
Alaska, Arizona, California, Colorado, Hawaii, Idaho,
Montana, Nevada, North Dakota, Oregon, South Dakota,
Utah, Washington, Wyoming
300 Montgomery St., Suite 740, San Francisco, Ca.   94104

Appendix E

Federal Trade Commission Main and Regional Offices

Main national office:
Federal Trade Commission, Washington, D.C.   20580

Atlanta:
Alabama, Florida, Georgia, Mississippi, North Carolina,
South Carolina, Tennessee, Virginia
1718 Peachtree Street, N.W., Suite 1000,
Atlanta, Ga.   30309

Boston:
Connecticut, Maine, Massachusetts, New Hampshire,
Rhode Island, Vermont
1301 Analex Building, 150 Causeway,
Boston, Mass.   02114

Chicago:
Illinois, Indiana, Iowa, Kentucky, Minnesota, Missouri,
Wisconsin
Suite 1437, 55 East Monroe Street, Chicago, Ill.   60603

Cleveland:
Delaware, Maryland, Michigan, New York (west of
Rochester), Ohio, Pennsylvania, West Virginia
Suite 500, Mall Building, 118 Saint Clair Avenue, N.E.,
Cleveland, Ohio   44114

Dallas:
Arkansas, Louisiana, New Mexico, Oklahoma, Texas
2001 Bryan Street, Suite 2665, Dallas, Tex.   75201

Denver:
Colorado, Kansas, Montana, Nebraska, North Dakota,
South Dakota, Utah, Wyoming
Suite 2900, 1405 Curtis Street, Denver, Colo.   80202

Los Angeles:
Arizona, Southern California
11000 Wilshire Boulevard, Room 13209,
Los Angeles, Ca.   90024

New York:
New Jersey, New York (east of Rochester)
Federal Building, 22nd Floor, 26 Federal Plaza,
New York, N.Y.   10007

San Francisco:
Northern California, Hawaii, Nevada
450 Golden Gate Avenue, Box 36005,
San Francisco, Ca.   94102

Seattle:
Alaska, Idaho, Oregon, Washington
Federal Building, 28th Floor, 915 Second Avenue,
Seattle, Wash.   98174

Appendix F

Federal Agencies Monitoring Violations of the Equal Credit Opportunity Act

The federal agency you complain to depends on the nature of the creditor with whom you are dealing.

—If you are dealing with a retail store, department store, small loan and finance company, gasoline credit card issuer, travel and expense credit card issuer, state-chartered credit union, or governmental lending program, write to:

> Federal Trade Commission
> Equal Credit Opportunity
> Washington, D.C.   20580

Or write to your regional office of the Federal Trade Commission (see addresses in Appendix E).

—If you are dealing with a *nationally chartered* bank (the word "National" or abbreviation "N.A." will appear in the bank's name), write to:

> Comptroller of the Currency
> Consumer Affairs Division
> Washington, D.C.   20219

—If you are dealing with a *state-chartered* bank that is a member of the Federal Reserve System, write to:

> Board of Governors of the Federal Reserve System
> Director, Division of Consumer Affairs
> Washington, D.C.   20551

—If you are dealing with a *state-chartered* bank that is insured by the Federal Deposit Insurance Corporation (FDIC) but is *not* a member of the Federal Reserve System, write to:

> Federal Deposit Insurance Corporation
> Office of Bank Consumer Affairs
> Washington, D.C.   20429

—If you are dealing with a federally chartered or federally insured savings and loan association, write to:

> Federal Home Loan Bank Board
> Equal Credit Opportunity
> Washington, D.C.   20552

—If you are dealing with a federally chartered credit union, write to:

> Federal Credit Union Administration
> Division of Consumer Affairs
> Washington, D.C.   20456

—If you are dealing with any other kind of creditor, write to:

> Department of Justice
> Civil Rights Division
> Equal Credit Opportunity
> Washington, D.C.   20530

Appendix G

Retaliatory Eviction Laws

Here are the official names and legal citations for the state laws and cases that make retaliatory eviction illegal.

Alaska: Alaska Statutes, section 34.03.310

Arizona: Arizona Revised Statutes Annotated, section 33-1381

California: California Civil Code, section 1942.5

Connecticut: Connecticut General Statutes Annotated, sections 47a-20 and 47a-33

Delaware: Delaware Code Annotated, title 25, section 5516

District of Columbia: District of Columbia Code, section 45-1654

Hawaii: Hawaii Revised Statutes, section 521-74

Illinois: Illinois Annotated Statutes, chapter 80, section 71

Kentucky: Kentucky Revised Statutes, section 383.705

Maine: Maine Revised Statutes Annotated, title 14, section 6001

Maryland: Maryland Real Property Code Annotated, sections 8-208.1 and 8-206

Massachusetts: Massachusetts General Laws Annotated, chapter 186, section 18

Michigan: Michigan Compiled Laws Annotated, section 600.5720

Minnesota: Minnesota Statutes Annotated, sections 566.03 and 566.28

Nebraska: Nebraska Revised Statutes, section 76-1439

New Hampshire: New Hampshire Revised Statutes Annotated, sections 540:13-a and 540:13-b

New Jersey: New Jersey Statutes Annotated, sections 2A:42-10.10 and 2A:42-10.12

New Mexico: New Mexico Statutes Annotated, section 70-7-39

New York: New York Unconsolidated Laws, sections 8590 and 8609; and *Church* v. *Allen Meadows Apartments,* a 1972 case found in volume 69 of the Miscellaneous Reports, Second Series, at page 254

Ohio: Ohio Revised Code, section 5321.02

Oregon: Oregon Revised Statutes, section 91.865

Pennsylvania: Pennsylvania Statutes Annotated, title 35, section 1700-1

Rhode Island: Rhode Island General Laws Annotated, sections 34-20-10 and 34-20-11

Tennessee: Tennessee Code Annotated, section 53-5505

Virginia: Virginia Code Annotated, section 55-248.39

Washington: Washington Code Annotated, sections 59.18.240 and 59.18.250

Wisconsin: In 1970 the Supreme Court of the State of Wisconsin declared retaliatory evictions illegal in the case of *Dickhut* v. *Norton,* which is found in volume 173 of the North Western Reporter, Second Series, at page 297. The case holds that a successful defense to retaliatory eviction requires the tenant to prove: (1) a substandard housing condition existed in violation of local housing codes; (2) the tenant reported this condition to the appropriate government agency;(3) the landlord knew about the tenant's report to the agency; and (4) for the sole purpose of retaliation, the landlord sought to terminate the tenancy.

Appendix H

Apartment Access Laws

Here are the official names and legal citations for the state laws that restrict a landlord's access to your apartment.

Alaska: Alaska Statutes, section 34.03.140

Arizona: Arizona Revised Statutes Annotated, section 33-1343

California: California Civil Code, section 1954

Connecticut: Connecticut General Statutes Annotated, section 47a-16

Delaware: Delaware Code Annotated, title 25, section 5513

Florida: Florida Statutes Annotated, section 83.53

Hawaii: Hawaii Revised Statutes, section 521-53

Kansas: Kansas Statutes Annotated, section 58-2557

Kentucky: Kentucky Revised Statutes, section 383.615

Nebraska: Nebraska Revised Statutes, section 76-1423

New Mexico: New Mexico Statutes Annotated, section 70-7-24

New York: New York City Housing Maintenance Code, section D26-10.07

Ohio: Ohio Revised Code, section 5321.05 (B)
Oregon: Oregon Revised Statutes, section 91.785
Tennessee: Tennessee Code Annotated, section 64-2833
Virginia: Virginia Code Annotated, section 55.248.18
Washington: Washington Code Annotated,
    section 59.18.150
Wisconsin: Wisconsin Statutes Annotated,
    section 704.05 (2)

Appendix I State Security Deposit Laws

Here are the official names and legal citations for the state laws that require a landlord to account for and refund your security deposit.

Alaska: Alaska Statutes, section 34.03.070
Arizona: Arizona Revised Statutes Annotated, section 33-1321
California: California Civil Code, section 1950.5
Colorado: Colorado Revised Statutes, sections 38-12-101, 38-12-102, and 38-12-103
Connecticut: Connecticut General Statutes Annotated, sections 47a-21 and 47a-22
Delaware: Delaware Code Annotated, title 25, section 5511
Florida: Florida Statutes Annotated, section 83.49
Georgia: Code of Georgia Annotated, chapter 61-6
Hawaii: Hawaii Revised Statutes, section 521-44
Idaho: Idaho Code, section 6-321
Illinois: Illinois Annotated Statutes, chapter 74, sections 91 and 92

Iowa: Iowa Code Annotated, sections 562.8 through 562.16

Kansas: Kansas Statutes Annotated, section 58-2550

Kentucky: Kentucky Revised Statutes, section 383.580

Louisiana: Louisiana Statutes Annotated, sections 9:3251 through 9:3253

Maine: Maine Revised Statutes Annotated, title 14, sections 6031 through 6037

Maryland: Maryland Annotated Code, section 8-i203

Massachusetts: Massachusetts General Laws Annotated, chapter 186, section 15B

Michigan: Michigan Compiled Laws Annotated, sections 554.601 through 554.616

Minnesota: Minnesota Statutes Annotated, section 504.20

Montana: Montana Revised Code Annotated, sections 42-301 through 42-309

New Jersey: New Jersey Statutes Annotated, sections 46:8-19 through 46:8-24

New Mexico: New Mexico Statutes Annotated, section 70-7-18

New York: New York General Obligations Law, section 7-103

North Carolina: North Carolina General Statutes, sections 42-50 through 42-56

North Dakota: North Dakota Century Code, section 47-16-07.1

Ohio: Ohio Revised Code, section 5321.16

Oklahoma: Oklahoma Statutes Annotated, title 41, section 43

Oregon: Oregon Revised Statutes, section 91.760

Pennsylvania: Pennsylvania Statutes Annotated, title 68, sections 250.511 and 250.512

South Dakota: South Dakota Codified Laws, sections 43-32-6.1 and 43-32-24

Tennessee: Tennessee Code Annotated, section 64-2821

Texas: Texas Civil Statutes Annotated, title 84,
    article 5236e
Washington: Washington Code Annotated, sections
    59.18.260, 59.18.270, and 59.18.280

Chart of Security Deposit Laws

Here is a state-by-state breakdown of the principal provisions in each of the laws listed above.

Chart of state landlord tenant laws relating to Security Deposits first appeared in the article "Security Deposits You Can Bank On" by Andrew O. Shapiro, in the October, 1978 issue of *Apartment Life* magazine; pages 32, 93 and 108.

State	Maximum Security Deposit	Interest Payable to Tenant	Time for Itemized Accounting and Refund After Tenancy Ends	Maximum Penalty
Alaska	2 months' rent	none	14 days	twice amount wrongfully withheld
Arizona	1½ months' rent	none	14 days	triple amount wrongfully withheld
California	unfurnished, 2 months' rent; furnished, 3 months' rent	none	14 days	amount wrongfully withheld plus up to $200
Colorado	no maximum	none	1 month	triple amount wrongfully withheld, plus attorney's fees and court costs
Connecticut	2 months' rent	4%/year, payable annually ($100 fine for noncompliance)	60 days	twice amount wrongfully withheld
Delaware	1 month's rent	none	15 days	twice amount of deposit

State	Maximum	Interest	Deadline	Penalty
Florida	no maximum	up to 5%/year, payable annually	15 days to itemize; 15 more days for tenant to object; 30 more days for refund	amount wrongfully withheld plus attorney's fees and court costs
Georgia	no maximum	none	1 month (tenant may inspect apartment to verify damage claimed by landlord)	triple amount wrongfully withheld plus attorney's fees
Hawaii	1 month's rent	none	14 days	quadruple amount wrongfully withheld
Idaho	no maximum	none	30 days	amount wrongfully withheld
Illinois*	no maximum	5%/year, payable annually	no provision (allow reasonable time; e.g., 30 days)	amount wrongfully withheld plus attorney's fees
Iowa	2 months' rent	none	30 days	amount wrongfully withheld plus up to $200 and attorney's fees

State	Maximum Security Deposit	Interest Payable to Tenant	Time for Itemized Accounting and Refund After Tenancy Ends	Maximum Penalty
Kansas	unfurnished, 1 month's rent; furnished, 1½ months' rent; with a pet, extra ½ month's rent	none	30 days	2½ times amount wrongfully withheld
Kentucky	no maximum	none	no provision (allow reasonable time, e.g., 30 days); tenant may inspect apartment to verify damage claimed	amount wrongfully withheld
Louisiana	no maximum	none	1 month	amount wrongfully withheld or $200 (whichever is greater) plus attorney's fees and court costs
Maine**	2 months' rent	none	30 days	twice amount wrongfully withheld plus attorney's fees and court costs

310

State	Maximum deposit	Interest	Deadline to return	Penalty for violation
Maryland	2 months' rent or $50, whichever is greater	3%/year, payable at end of tenancy	30 days to itemize; 15 more days for refund	triple amount wrongfully withheld plus attorney's fees
Massachusetts	2 months' rent	5%/year, payable annually	30 days	twice amount wrongfully withheld
Michigan	1½ months' rent	none	30 days; tenant has 7 more days to dispute damage claimed by landlord; landlord can't keep amount disputed unless he sues tenant within 45 days after tenancy ends and wins	twice amount wrongfully withheld
Minnesota	no maximum	5%/year, payable at end of tenancy	3 weeks	twice amount wrongfully withheld plus up to $200
Montana	no maximum	none	30 days	twice amount wrongfully withheld plus attorney's fees

State	Maximum Security Deposit	Interest Payable to Tenant	Time for Itemized Accounting and Refund After Tenancy Ends	Maximum Penalty
New Jersey***	1½ months' rent	regular bank interest (less 1% to land-lord) credited toward tenant's rent annually	30 days	twice amount wrongfully with-held plus attorney's fees and court costs
New Mexico	"reasonable deposit" (e.g., 1 or 2 months' rent)	regular bank interest, payable annually on deposits greater than 1 month's rent	30 days	amount wrongfully withheld plus attorney's fees
New York	no maximum	regular bank interest (less 1% to land-lord) if building has 6 or more units; payable annually or when tenancy ends	no provision (allow reasonable time; e.g., 30 days)	amount wrongfully withheld
North Carolina	month-to-month tenant, 1½ months' rent; longer lease, 2 months' rent	none	30 days	amount wrongfully withheld plus attorney's fees
North Dakota	1 month's rent	regular bank interest, payable when tenancy ends	30 days	triple amount wrongfully with-held

State	Maximum	Interest	Time to return	Penalty
Ohio	no maximum	for deposit in excess of $50 or 1 month's rent (whichever is greater) 5%/year on the excess, payable annually	30 days	amount wrongfully withheld plus attorney's fees
Oklahoma	no maximum	none	10 days (tenant must apply for refund first)	amount wrongfully withheld
Oregon	no maximum	none	30 days	twice amount wrongfully withheld
Pennsylvania	2 months' rent in first year of lease; 1 month's rent in subsequent years; no increase after 5 or more years	regular bank interest (less 1% to landlord) payable annually but only after second year of tenancy	30 days	twice amount wrongfully withheld
South Dakota	1 month's rent	none	2 weeks	amount wrongfully withheld
Tennessee	no maximum	none	no provision (allow reasonable time; e.g., 30 days); tenant may inspect apartment to verify damage claimed	amount wrongfully withheld

State	Maximum Security Deposit	Interest Payable to Tenant	Time for Itemized Accounting and Refund After Tenancy Ends	Maximum Penalty
Texas	no maximum	none	30 days	triple amount wrongfully withheld, plus $100 and attorney's fees
Washington	no maximum	none	14 days	amount wrongfully withheld plus attorney's fees

* Applies only to buildings with 25 or more units.

** Does not apply to owner-occupied buildings with five units or less.

*** Does not apply to owner-occupied buildings with two units or less.

Appendix J

State
Vandalism
Laws

Under "State Statute" we provide you with the official legal citation for the state's vandalism law. Under "Age Limits" we provide the maximum age the child can be for the law to apply. In some cases a state also has a lower age limit. The "Maximum Recovery" is the maximum amount of money you can recover if you sue using the law. Finally, in those states in which you cannot recover for personal injuries you can sue only for damage to property.

State Statute	Age Limit	Maximum Recovery	Are Personal Injuries Recoverable?
Alabama: Alabama Code title 6, section 5-380	18	$ 500	no
Alaska: Alaska Statutes, section 34.50.020	18	$ 2,000	no
Arizona: Arizona Revised Statutes Annotated, section 12-661	minor	$ 500	yes
Arkansas: Arkansas Statutes Annotated, section 50-109	18	$ 2,000	no
California: California Civil Code, section 1714.1	minor	$ 2,000	yes
Colorado: Colorado Revised Statutes Annotated, section 13-21-107	minor	$ 1,000	no
Connecticut: Connecticut General Statutes Annotated, section 52-572	minor	$ 1,500	yes
Delaware: Delaware Code Annotated, title 10, section 3922	18	$ 1,000	no
Florida: Florida Statutes Annotated, section 741.24	18	$ 2,500	no
Georgia: Georgia Code Annotated, section 105-113	18	$ 500	no
Hawaii: Hawaii Revised Statutes, section 577-3	unmarried minor	none	yes
Idaho: Idaho Code Annotated, section 6-210	18	$ 1,500	no
Illinois: Illinois Revised Statutes, title 70, section 51	11–19	$ 500	yes

316

State			
Indiana: Indiana Annotated Statues, section 34-4-31-1	none	$ 750	no
Iowa: Iowa Code Annotated, section 613.16	13	$ 2,000	yes
Kansas: Kansas Statutes Annotated, section 38-120	13	$ 1,000	no
Kentucky: Kentucky Revised Statutes Annotated, section 405.025	minor	$10,000	no
Louisiana: Louisiana Civil Code Annotated, article 2318	minor	no limit	yes
Maine: Maine Revised Statutes Annotated, title 19, section 217	7–17	$ 250	yes
Maryland: Maryland Annotated Code, sections 26-71A and 26-76	minor	$ 2,000	yes
Massachusetts: Massachusetts Annotated Laws, chapter 231, section 85G	7–17	$ 500	yes
Michigan: Michigan Compiled Laws Annotated, section 600.2913	minor	$ 1,500	yes
Minnesota: Minnesota Statutes Annotated, section 540.18	18	$ 100	yes
Missouri: Missouri Annotated Statutes, section 537.045	minor	$ 300	no
Montana: Montana Revised Codes Annotated, section 61-112.1	18	$ 1,500	no
Nebraska: Nebraska Revised Statutes, section 43-801	minor	$ 1,000	yes

317

State Statute	Age Limit	Maximum Recovery	Are Personal Injuries Recoverable?
Nevada: Nevada Revised Statutes, section 41.470	minor	$ 3,000	yes
New Jersey: New Jersey Revised Statutes, section 2A:53A-15	16	$ 250	no
New Mexico: New Mexico Statutes Annotated, section 13-14-44	child	$ 1,000	yes
New York: New York General Obligations Law, section 3-112	10–17	$ 500	no
North Carolina: North Carolina General Statutes, section 1-538.1	18	$ 500	no
North Dakota: North Dakota Century Code, section 32-03-39	minor	$ 1,000	no
Ohio: Ohio Revised Code Annotated, sections 3109.09 and 3109.10	18	$ 2,000	no
Oklahoma: Oklahoma Statutes Annotated, title 23, section 10	18	$ 1,500	yes
Oregon: Oregon Revised Statutes, section 30.765	minor	$ 5,000	yes
Pennsylvania: Pennsylvania Statutes Annotated, title 11, sections 2001 to 2005	18	$ 1,000	yes
Rhode Island: Rhode Island General Laws Annotated, section 9-1-3	minor	$ 500	yes
South Carolina: South Carolina Code Annotated, section 10-2595	17	$ 1,000	no

318

State	Age	Amount	
South Dakota: South Dakota Code Annotated, section 25-5-15	18	$ 300	no
Tennessee: Tennessee Code Annotated, sections 37-1001 to 1003	18	$ 5,000	no
Texas: Texas Family Code, sections 33.01 to 33.03	12–18	$ 5,000	no
Vermont: Vermont Statutes Annotated, title 15, section 901	17	$ 250	yes
Virginia: Virginia Code Annotated, sections 8.654.1 and 8.654.2	minor	$ 200	no
Washington: Washington Revised Code Annotated, section 4.24.190	18	$ 3,000	yes
West Virginia: West Virginia Code Annotated, section 55-7A-2	18	$ 300	no
Wisconsin: Wisconsin Statutes Annotated, section 895.035	minor	$ 1,000	yes
Wyoming: Wyoming Statutes Annotated, section 14-5.1-3	10–17	$ 300	no

Index